PREACHING
THE
NEW COMMON
LECTIONARY

PREACHING
THE
NEW COMMON LECTIONARY

YEAR C

Lent, Holy Week, Easter

Commentary by:

Fred B. Craddock
John H. Hayes
Carl R. Holladay
Gene M. Tucker

ABINGDON PRESS
Nashville

Preaching the New Common Lectionary
Year C   Lent, Holy Week, Easter

Copyright © 1985 by Abingdon Press

This book is printed on acid-free paper.

Library of Congress Cataloging in Publication Data

Main entry under title:
   Preaching the new common lectionary. Year C,
   Lent, Holy Week, Easter.

   Includes index.
   1. Bible—Homiletical use. 2. Bible—Liturgical
   lessons, English. I. Craddock, Fred B.
   BS534.5.P735   1985   251   85-11091
                  (pbk.: alk. paper)

ISBN 0-687-33849-2

MANUFACTURED BY THE PARTHENON PRESS AT
NASHVILLE, TENNESSEE, UNITED STATES OF AMERICA

Contents

Easter

Special Day

Introduction

It might be helpful to the reader if we make a few remarks about our understanding of our task and what we have sought to accomplish in this volume. The following comments will touch on four topics.

The Scripture in Preaching

There is no substitute for direct exposure to the biblical text, both for the preacher in preparation and for the listener in worship. The Scriptures are therefore not only studied privately but read aloud as an act of worship in and of itself and not solely as prelude to a sermon. The sermon is an interpretation of Scripture in the sense that the preacher seeks to bring the text forward into the present in order to effect a new hearing of the Word. In this sense the text has its future and its fulfillment in preaching. In fact, the Bible itself is the record of the continual rehearing and reinterpreting of its own traditions in new settings and for new generations of believers. New settings and new circumstances are properly as well as inescapably integral to a hearing of God's Word in and through the text. Whatever else may be said to characterize God's Word, it is always appropriate to the hearers. But the desire to be immediately relevant should not abbreviate study of the text or divorce the sermon from the biblical tradition. Such sermons are orphaned, released without memory into the world. It is the task of the preacher and teacher to see that the principle of fidelity to Scripture is not abandoned in the life and worship of the church. The endeavor to understand a text in its historical, literary, and theological contexts does create, to be sure, a sense of distance between the Bible and the congregation. The preacher may grow impatient during this period of feeling a long way from a sermon. But this time of study can be most fruitful. By holding text and parishioners apart for a while, the preacher can hear each more clearly and exegete each more honestly. Then, when the two intersect in the sermon, neither the text nor the congregation is consumed by the other. Because the Bible is an ancient book, it invites the preacher back into its world in order to understand; because the Bible is the church's Scripture, it moves forward into our world and addresses us here and now.

The Lectionary and Preaching

Ever-increasing numbers of preachers are using a lectionary as a guide for preaching and worship. The intent of lectionaries is to provide for the church over a given period of time (usually three years) large units of Scripture that have been selected because they carry the central message of the Bible and that have been arranged according to the seasons of the Christian year. Lectionaries are not designed to limit one's message or restrict the freedom of the pulpit. On the contrary, churches that use a lectionary usually hear more Scripture in worship than those that do not. And ministers who preach from the lectionary find themselves stretched into areas of the canon into which they would not have gone had they kept to the path of personal preference. Other values of the lectionary are well known: the readings provide a common ground for discussions in ministerial peer groups; family worship can more easily join public worship through shared readings; ministers and worship committees can work with common biblical texts to prepare services that have movement and integrity; and the lectionary encourages more disciplined study and advance preparation. All these and other values are increased if the different churches share a common lectionary. A common lectionary could conceivably generate a community-wide Christian conversation.

This Book and Preaching

This volume is not designed as a substitute for work with the biblical text; on the contrary, its intent is to encourage such work. Neither is it our desire to relieve the preacher of regular visits to concordances, lexicons, and commentaries, but it is our hope that the comments on the texts here will be sufficiently germinal to give direction and purpose to those visits to major reference works. Our commentaries are efforts to be faithful to the text and to begin moving the text toward the pulpit. There are no sermons as such here, nor could there be. No one can preach long distance. Only the one who preaches can do an exegesis of the listeners and mix into sermon preparation enough local soil so as to effect an indigenous hearing of the Word. But we hope we have contributed to that end. The reader will also notice that, while each of us has been aware of the other readings for each service, there has been no attempt to offer a collaborated commentary on all texts or a homogenized interpretation as though there were not four texts but one. We have tried to respect the integrity of each biblical passage and remain within the limits of our own areas of knowledge. It is assumed that the season of the year, the needs of the listeners, the preacher's own abilities, as well as the overall unity of the message of the Scriptures will prompt the preacher to find among the four readings the word for the day. Sometimes the four texts will join arm in arm, sometimes they will debate with one another, sometimes one will lead while the others follow, albeit at times reluctantly.

A final word about our comments. The lections from the Psalter have been treated in the same manner as the other readings even though some Protestant churches often omit the reading of the psalm or replace it with a hymn. We have chosen to regard the psalm as an equal among the texts, primarily for three reasons: (1) there is growing interest in the use of Psalms in public worship and comments on them may help make that use more informed; (2) the Psalms were a major source for worship and preaching in the early church and continue to inspire and inform Christian witness; and (3) comments on the Psalms may make this volume helpful to Roman Catholic preachers who have maintained the long tradition of using the Psalms in Christian services.

This Season and Preaching

This volume treats the readings for Lent, Holy Week, and Easter, the events and seasons central to the Christian year.

11

Of all the seasons of the Christian's pilgrimage, Lent has probably been most abused. It has in certain times and places become a period of excessive introspection, empty abstinence from tidbits of affluence, and the enjoyment of the gloom of self-denial. Correction of such excesses and distortions does not lie, however, in non-observance of Lent, but rather in the recovery of its rich tradition. The image of forty days as a period of engagement with God, of repentance and prayer is deeply imbedded in Scripture. In the early church, Lent became a time of preparation for baptism, and among the baptized, a time for reflection upon one's baptism and renewal of vows. And in all times and places, Lent looks toward God's act in the resurrection. Sober awareness of sin is appropriate, to be sure, but so is profound joy.

Holy Week is a time of reflection upon the suffering and death of Christ. A major theological task of the early disciples was to understand and accept the death of Jesus as an event transcending tragedy. How did Jesus' passion relate to the purpose of God, to Jesus' own ministry, and to his followers' hopes? In the Passover traditions, in the Suffering Servant of Isaiah, and in the Jewish interpretations of sacrifice, the disciples were able not only to interpret Jesus as "our Passover" (I Cor. 5:7-8) but also to understand in a new way their own sufferings. The preacher will find the Old Testament resources not only enriching during this week but also helpful as a guard against any residue of anti-Semitism which may darken unduly the biblical reports of Jesus' death.

Easter is not one day but a season. It is silence; what does one say when running from an empty tomb? It is a shout, "He is risen!" It is a question, Where do we go from here? When Easter morning fades into late afternoon and some disciples begin to say, "I am going fishing," the church prays and waits for Pentecost.

> *Fred B. Craddock* (Gospels)
> *John H. Hayes* (Psalms)
> *Carl R. Holladay* (Epistles and Acts)
> *Gene M. Tucker* (Old Testament)

Ash Wednesday

Joel 2:1-2, 12-17a; Psalm 51:1-12; II Corinthians 5:20b–6:2 (3-10); Matthew 6:1-6, 16-21

The texts for Ash Wednesday initiate the Season of Lent with calls to confession and repentance, prayers for forgiveness, and admonitions to engage in fasting. They also caution people not to display their acts of contrition before others, but only before God. The Old Testament reading from Joel has a call to repentance at its center. The responsorial psalm, one of the penitential psalms, is a confession of sin with the goal of restoration to the joy of salvation. The epistolary reading is likewise a call to be reconciled to God. The Gospel text sounds the warning about doing alms or fasting in order to impress others with one's righteousness.

Joel 2:1-2, 12-17*a*

The Book of Joel is one of the most liturgically oriented of the prophetic books. Some commentators have argued that the book itself provides the script for a prophetic liturgy, and that Joel was a cultic prophet. Whether that is the case or not, it is clear that Joel is familiar with the liturgical practices in the Jerusalem temple, and that he combines his convictions about proper ritual actions with prophetic expectations concerning the Day of the Lord.

Joel is among the latest of the prophetic books, coming from the postexilic period, the time when the Persian Empire exercised control over Judah. The temple of his day would have been the one rebuilt after the Exile. The book frequently alludes to or directly quotes the words of the earlier prophets, indicating that he and his contemporaries had come to treat many of those books as sacred scriptures.

13

The Book of Joel has two distinct parts, 1–2:17 and 2:18–3:21. The first section is in effect the prophet's instructions for the community to convene a service of prayer, to offer complaints and petitions to God. The account of the locust plague and the words about the coming Day of the Lord give the reasons for calling such a service. The second part of the book reports how the Lord responds to genuine repentance, with promises of salvation and words of assurance that the prayers have been heard. The Day of the Lord, feared at the outset, has become the day of the Lord's salvation because the people trusted in their compassionate God.

Our reading, then, concludes the first section of the Book of Joel. In fact, its last verse (2:17) is the pivotal point in the entire book. Virtually everything before that presents a dark and terrifying picture, and all that follows is hopeful and promising. The turning point is the prophet's instructions for a service of prayer and petition, expressing the people's genuine repentance. The preceding prophetic words have prepared the way for that repentance.

Joel 2:1-2 is a prophetic call to sound the alarm for the Day of the Lord is near. The description of that day in terms of darkness and gloom contains an allusion to the earlier words of Amos 5:18. One cannot miss the eschatological overtones, which eventually prepare the way for the language of the final day of battle, as in Rev. 16:16. The intervening verses not assigned for reading (2:3-11) describe the approach of the enemy, either a metaphorical account of the plague of locusts of Joel 1 or an army. In any event, in 2:10-11 it becomes clear that the enemy is working the will of God, as the Lord's army.

Verses 12-14 present two calls to repentance, the first expressed by the Lord himself, and the second by the prophet. The repentance is to be both external and internal. It is to be acted out in terms of fasting, weeping, and mourning, but it is to be more: "Rend your hearts and not your garments" (2:13). Rending one's heart and returning to the Lord refer to the transformation of the will in the deepest sense. Verses 13*b*-14 give the reasons for believing that the repentance will have effect, and those reasons lie in the nature of God. God is so abounding in steadfast love that he is even capable of repenting. There are few more powerful words in scripture than these.

The remainder of the passage consists of the call to a public service of prayer. It begins, as did chapter 2, with a call to sound the trumpet. What had been a warning note now becomes a call to worship. All are to participate, young and old, male and female. Everything leads up to the single petition, "Spare thy people, O Lord" (2:17). The passage, then, stresses the corporate dimensions of worship. It is not just individuals but the people as a whole who repent. That is perhaps an important note for the preacher to sound as Lent begins.

That petition is the appropriate one for Ash Wednesday. It is a prayer that acknowledges human sinfulness and need, and rests the case entirely upon the gracious will of God. That the bad news of the Day of the Lord becomes an announcement of salvation does not mean that Joel's congregation has manipulated God by saying the right words and performing the right ritual actions. It means that confession and repentance acknowledge the free and gracious will of God. The God of the last days is the God who repents when the people pray.

Psalm 51:1-12

Of the seven penitential psalms (6, 32, 38, 51, 102, 130, 143), Psalm 51 is by far the one most characterized by personal intensity and depth of feeling. It is the penitential psalm par excellence, the *Miserere* of the Psalter.

Since the words of this psalm are so well-known and ingrained into the Ash Wednesday ritual, we shall here focus on some of the conceptual frameworks that lie behind the surface words of the text.

First of all, verses 1-2 assume that sin/iniquity has a staining, polluting, contaminating quality about it. Sin can be seen as dirt that taints and discolors the human and the human personality. All of us are aware of the general sense of shame, inferiority, and feeling of being wrongly different that so often comes our way. Sometimes we speak of feeling filthy, or we feel that way even though we do not talk about it. In priestly theology in the Old Testament, it was assumed that human sin as well as life's impurities dirtied or polluted the temple (Lev. 15:31). Sin sacrifices and the blood ritual associated with them purged the temple and the altar from the pollution that became attached to them. "Washing" and "cleansing" are thus appropriate images to associate with sin/dirt/filth.

Verses 3-4 manifest the assumption that sin is fundamentally a theological matter. Sin violates God, is an affront to the Deity. In addition to their moral and ethical dimensions, sins are acts against God, disruptions in the human-creator relationship.

Verse 5 assumes that sin is a universal, human condition that pervades the whole of life. Conception and birth are here related to sin. Perhaps behind this view lies the fact that in the Old Testament sexual intercourse rendered the man and woman unclean (filthy, dirty) for a day (Lev. 15:18) and a woman was unclean for days after giving birth, forty days if the child was a male, eighty days if it was a female (Lev. 12:1-5). The view that life was tainted by sin was shared by most of the ancient world. A three-thousand year-old Sumerian proverb written centuries before Psalm 51, for example, declares:

> Never has a sinless child been born to its mother,
> a sinless youth has not existed from of old.

Even if these texts affirm no more than the utter guilt, the total misalignment of life, they are sharp testimony to the pervasiveness of sin.

The plea for help in verses 6-12 makes its requests in a torrent of practically synonymous appeals. Two aspects are noticeable. (1) On the one hand, there is the plea that the stain, the pollution, the sense of being marked be removed. "Purge," "wash," "hide," "blot out"—these are words from the realm of ritual bathing, of cultic cleansing, of material substance, of dirt removal. One might say that these give expression to the hope for surface cleansing, for the type of salvation that makes possible facing life again unmarked.

16

(We must remember that in much of Christendom we have given up those earthy, materialistic acts that signify change and newness; we have thrown out ritualization with its substance, stuff, and feeling and substituted cognition with its conceptualization, sanitation, and synthesized sentiments.) (2) On the other hand, there is the recognition that matters must be changed, altered, reformed, reshaped, and even re-created from the center out. The secret heart, the bones, the spirit, all these must be reshaped. A cleansing of the old and the creation of the new are the sources of joy and gladness, and both are needed.

II Corinthians 5:20*b*–6:2 (3-10)

Even though the short form of today's epistle reading sounds the central themes of Ash Wednesday, the longer form may be profitably explored.

There is a clear shift at 6:3. In the first part of the lection (5:20*b*–6:2), we have a direct appeal being made to the readers (and to us). We are urged, "Be reconciled to God" (5:20) and cautioned "not to accept the grace of God in vain" (6:1). A note of urgency concludes the appeal: "Now is the acceptable time; . . . now is the day." We are thus reminded: "Do not delay. Wait no longer. The time is now."

Here we are being confronted with the eschatological urgency of the gospel. Through the gospel comes God's appeal. As we listen to the minister and messenger of reconciliation tell the story of God's love and Christ's death, we hear God calling us directly. It is a summons related by God's ambassador, but it comes from God. This is why we cannot blithely ignore it. As the quotation from Isaiah 49:8 suggests, God has lent an open ear to us and come to our rescue (6:2). Since God has acted decisively, so must we.

At this point, the emphasis shifts. The remainder of the passage deals with Paul's apostolic ministry. The tone is apologetic, and we get the clear sense that he is defending his ministry, both form and content. This is consistent with the epistle as a whole, much of which is Paul's defense against various charges. But what he insists on here is that neither he, his colleagues, nor their form of ministry have stood as obstacles to the gospel. This of course suggests that in the mind of some they had. Perhaps his manner of life had appeared too boorish. Perhaps his manner of speaking had not sounded "apostolic" enough. In any case, his apostolic credentials appear to have been called into question, and verses 3-10 provide us an insight as to the kind of credentials Paul thought worthwhile.

His remarks here pertain primarily to apostolic ministry. In verse 3, he speaks of "our ministry." But even though he is talking about "servants of God" in a restricted sense (verse 4), his remarks have a wider import. In fact, they provide us with useful reflections about what, in Paul's mind, really counts when it comes to certifying or authenticating service done in the name of God. On Ash Wednesday, at the beginning of Lent, as we consider the themes of penance and death, we do well to reflect on what actually qualifies any of us to live as "servants of God" for the sake of the gospel.

We should notice the way in which Paul commends himself, or authenticates his ministry of service. As we look more closely at verses 4b-10, what otherwise appears to be a long and cluttered list of vicissitudes and virtues turns out to have a certain pattern. In fact, we can organize and summarize his remarks under three headings.

1. Authentication through hardship (verses 4b-5). Under the heading "great endurance," Paul includes a series of nine hardships, which can be arranged in three groups of three. Some of these have clear reference to experiences in his own life that we find mentioned elsewhere, others are quite general. Commentaries will supply the details on the precise significance of each. The general point we can make is this: for Paul, the place to begin talking about meaningful service in the name of God is with hardship and difficulty. The discussion must begin "from below" for Paul, not with experiences "from above" or with a list of triumphs. Being an authentic servant of God, before it means anything else, means knowing and experiencing the difficulties of human existence. We should note that here he speaks not of authentication *after* endurance, but *through* endurance.

2. Authentication through moral character (verses 6-7). We tend to describe the next set of qualities as "virtues," and

surely they are in one sense. But they are more than this. Eight items are listed, the last of which is "the power of God," which in a way summarizes all of them. Elsewhere, these are spoken of as "gifts of the Spirit" (Gal. 5:22-23). Again, commentaries can supply detailed treatment of each one. But the general point we should note is that service in the name of God is also authenticated by our active participation in the very nature and character of God as we experience it through God's own Spirit. We become servants of God when the effects of God's power are visible within the contours of our own life and service.

3. Authentication through paradox (verses 8-10). There is some question whether "paradox" is an apt description of this final set of remarks. They are unlike the first two groups because in each case they join opposites. Perhaps they are better called "antitheses." They are not arranged in a uniform pattern. For example, verse 8*a* is in chiastic form: honor (a) and dishonor (b) are set over against ill repute (b) and good repute (a). The form of the final list is "as . . . and yet." What is striking about this section is that genuine servanthood is seen as a dual existence. It is neither wholly vicious nor wholly virtuous. It is rather life in which opposites converge within us. But more than that it is the capacity to affirm while being denied. In each case, Paul's own apostolic identity is severely called into question. He is regarded as an impostor, unknown, dying. What he sees himself to be is being radically denied. In face of such denial, his is a stance of radical affirmation. What emerges then, as a criterion for authentic servanthood, is the capacity for radical affirmation in the face of radical denial.

In the context of Ash Wednesday, this longer form of the traditional epistolary lection, enables us to reflect soberly on the meaning of service in the name of God—the form it takes and the way to tell if it's real or fake.

Matthew 6:1-6, 16-21

The liturgical year revolves around two foci, Christmas and Easter, and of the two, Easter is the older and longer season. It is older in that the first witness of the church was to the resurrection, and it is longer in that it consists of forty days (except Sundays) from Ash Wednesday to Easter and fifty days from Easter to Pentecost. Ash Wednesday is, as its name suggests ("sackcloth and ashes"), a day of repentance and sorrow for sin, the proper beginning of faith's journey toward Easter. It is important to keep in mind, however, that Lent is not a period of unrelieved penitence. Sundays are not included in the forty days, and Sundays historically have never been fast days since every Sunday is a celebration of the resurrection of Christ. According to our calendars we move through Lent to Easter, but according to our faith, all our days, even Lenten ones, flow out of Easter.

In the ancient church Lent was a period of preparing candidates for baptism and preparing the faithful for the renewal of baptismal vows. For both groups the instruction in our Gospel for today was and is most crucial: "when you give alms," "when you pray," "when you fast."

It is important for the preacher first of all to attend to the structure of this lection which, while apparently in two parts (verses 1-6, 16-21), does not conform to a twofold division. After an introductory and general warning about the practice of piety (6:1), the Evangelist focuses upon three acts: alms (verses 2-4), prayer (verses 5-6), and fasting (verses 16-18). That these units belong together in formalized instruction is evident in the repeated patterns of speech and identical phrasing. The introduction of the subject of prayer (verses 5-6), however, provides Matthew the occasion to enlarge the instruction (verses 7-15), which our lection omits because it clearly has a different structure and moves in another direction. For example, the contrast is not with "the hypocrites" (verses 2, 5, 16) but with "the Gentiles" (verse 7). Matthew also places here the Lord's Prayer which Luke locates elsewhere (11:2-4). The preacher might do well to decide against trying to include verses 19-21 in today's sermon. This unit not only differs from 6:1-6, 16-18 in form, but also in subject. It might be more comfortably joined to the instruction on materialism which follows (verses 22-34).

There can be no doubt that in Matthew's church the three acts of piety here named were valued and were to be observed: *when* you give alms, pray, and fast. All three were worthy of special attention and praise in the Jewish synagogue and were continued by Christians. The giving of alms for the poor was a priority in the early church and to it Paul gave a great deal of time and effort (Gal. 2:10; Rom. 15:25-31; II Cor. 8–9; Acts 11:27-30). In the matter of prayer, the practice of the church (Acts 1:14; 6:4; 10:9; 13:3) was grounded in both the example (Mark 1:35; 14:32-40; Luke 3:21; 6:12; 9:29) and the instruction (Matt. 6:5-15; Luke 11:1-4) of Jesus. Fasting also was not confined to Matthew's church but apparently was a widespread Christian practice (Mark 2:18-20; Acts 13:3).

However, just as surely as Matthew affirmed the value of these acts of piety, so he understood that any of them could degenerate into hypocritical displays. It would be a mistake to view the text as presenting a contrast between Jewish and Christian practices; the contrast is between piety which offers alms, prayers, and fasts to God and piety which goes in search of applauding audiences. None of us is exempt from the forms of seduction that rob acts of devotion of their meaning and worth. But the answer does not lie in the cessation of these acts, reducing our faith to feelings in the heart. Neither does it lie in waiting until our motivation is totally pure before acting. Our reasons and promptings are always mixed. Rather the answer is in living all of life, including alms, prayer, and fasting, before God. And awareness of the presence of God will produce in us the humble and contrite heart, even when we are doing and giving the best we have, the best we are.

First Sunday of Lent

Deuteronomy 26:1-11; Psalm 91:9-16; Romans 10:8b-13; Luke 4:1-13

Since Lent commemorates the forty days of Jesus' temptation and fasting in the wilderness, the Lucan account of that period comes to the fore. The Gospel lection stresses that the response of Jesus to the temptations was faith in God and the confession of that faith. These are the themes that the other readings for the day carry forward. Deuteronomy 26:1-11 presents the instructions for the celebration of the festival of the first fruits, including the recital of a confession of faith. The responsorial psalm is a meditation on God's care for those who trust in the Lord, and the epistolary text is a classical Pauline statement that justification follows belief and salvation follows confession.

Deuteronomy 26:1-11

The journey of the church from Ash Wednesday to Easter includes a review of the history of ancient Israel by means of the Old Testament readings. Today's text, with its summary of the saving events from the patriarchs to the entrance into the Promised Land, is the appropriate beginning. On subsequent Sundays the lections call attention to the covenant with Abraham, the call of Moses, the first Passover in the land in the time of Joshua, and then Deutero-Isaiah's proclamation of release from captivity and a new way through the wilderness.

As is the case throughout the Book of Deuteronomy, except for the verses at the beginning and end, this passage is presented as part of the speech of Moses just before his death. The circumstances are the last stop in the wilderness before the people enter the land of Canaan. The instructions envisage and actually presuppose the circumstances of the people of Israel centuries after the time of Moses. While there are doubtless genuinely ancient traditions behind our text, the Book of Deuteronomy originated in the seventh century B.C.

Deuteronomy 26 comes at the end of a long series of laws, ordinances, and instructions of various kinds, all of them intended to be valid for the members of the community throughout all time. Chapter 25 is a collection of such instructions having to do mainly with responsibilities to others in the society. The unit that immediately follows our text (Deut. 26:12-16) concerns tithes. Chapter 27 begins the instructions for a covenant ceremony to be carried out once the Israelites enter the land.

The style of the Book of Deuteronomy is quite distinctive. Although it is identified as a law book, and it contains numerous legal sentences and instructions, the form and style on the whole are more hortatory and parenetic than legal. That is, a great many of the individual sections and paragraphs of the book are like short sermons on the law or on the events of the history of salvation. The style is the second person of direct address, urging the hearers to obedience and faithfulness. Often an old law known from tradition is cited, then explained, frequently even reinterpreted for a new situation, and then laid upon the hearts of the listeners. It seems clear that the speakers and writers who actually developed the Book of Deuteronomy stood in a situation centuries removed from the saving events and the revelation of the law. In that respect their situation parallels that of contemporary preachers and their congregations.

Deuteronomy 26:1-11, however, is not in the form of a sermon but is structured as an ordinance, the instructions for the feast or ceremony of the first fruits. The faithful Israelite is given the liturgical actions to perform and the words to say. The instructions open with the indication that the ceremony is to begin "when you come into the land which the Lord your God gives you for an inheritance, and have taken possession of it, and live in it" (verse 1). The liturgy actually reaches from the farmer's field to the sanctuary. The Israelite is to take some of the first fruits, put them in a basket, and take them "to the place which the Lord your God will choose, to make his name to dwell there," that is, Jerusalem. There is some conflict in the instructions at this point. Whereas in verse 4 the priest takes the basket and places it before the altar, in verse 10 the worshiper is told to set it down "before the Lord your God." It is possible that this slight discrepancy reflects stages in the oral or literary development of the instructions.

Words are at the heart of the ritual. Notice that they are uttered not by the priest but by each individual worshiper. There are two speeches. Although they are words addressed to God they are not in the form of prayers. The first (verse 3b), a declaration made to the priest but addressed to the Lord, is a simple statement that the participant is here in the land promised to the patriarchs. Its point is the one emphasized throughout the passage, namely, that the land is God's gift. The second (verses 5-10a) is one of the central passages in Deuteronomy, a confession of faith frequently identified as the little historical credo.

The credo is a summary of the central themes of the Pentateuch: the promise to the patriarchs (the "wandering Aramean" was Jacob), the Exodus from Egypt (here spelled out in some detail), and the entrance into the land ("a land flowing with milk and honey"). Note above that all the events are the work of the Lord on behalf of the people. The acquisition of the land in particular should not be described as "conquest," as if Israel could have taken something not granted by God. These are the historic events central to the entire nation's confession. However, the words of the individual there at the altar with a gift for the Lord do not end at that point. Rather, the concluding line turns from confession to a personal prayer of thanksgiving. The Lord has done all that, "now I bring the first of the fruit of the ground, which thou, O Lord, hast given me" (verse 10a).

Given the fact that the ritual occasion is a thanksgiving service for a harvest, the contents of the confession are remarkable. One might have expected praise and thanksgiving for the God of creation who makes the land fertile, and thus cares for the people. The focus of attention is, however,

24

upon the actions of God in history, and especially the actions that brought the people into a particular territory and gave it to them.

The Deuteronomic preachers have a great deal to teach us, both about style and contents. In terms of style, they constantly keep the hearers and their immediate situations in view. They appeal to the heart, they plead, they work to evoke a response of faithfulness. In terms of contents, their themes concern, as here, the action of God and the response of human beings. A favorite term in the book is "remember," as in "do this in remembrance of me." Those who remember what God has done to bring them into a blessed land will respond with deeds and words of thanksgiving.

The Season of Lent is a time for such remembrance and response.

Psalm 91:9-16

The use of this psalm in the writing of the temptations of Jesus by both Matthew (4:6) and Luke (4:10-11), who probably wrote independently of each other, indicates that the early church in the very beginning employed this text when talking about the nature and shape of Jesus' ministry. Psalm 91 oozes with religious assurance, with divine promises and pledges. It expresses elements of faith ready-made for over-confidence and pious extravagances.

In some respects, the psalm is an enigma for scholars. In what context did it originate? Who is being spoken to and about in the psalm? A breakdown of the psalm may help answer these questions. Verses 1-8 seem to me to be a brief sermonette addressed to a "you" but spoken in reasonably general terms. The thrust of these verses is to assure the worshiper of divine care and preservation in the face of a forthcoming situation of grave danger. In verses 9-13, the address to the worshiper becomes a little more personal, a little more directly assuring. Reading these verses, one gets the feeling of a particular "thou," an actual human person being spoken to. Verses 14-16 shifts from human-human speech to divine-human speech. In God's address, the "thou" has become a "he," the person earlier spoken to has become the person spoken about.

One way of interpreting this psalm is to see it as originally utilized in a worship service in which the king was the central figure (see Pss. 20–21). The king was perhaps facing the dangers of a forthcoming war. (If not about a king going to war, then perhaps the context was a situation in which an ordinary person was confronting a major but dangerous undertaking—a long journey, a dangerous job, military service. At any rate, the psalm was to launch one forth with confidence and chutzpah.)

The verses for this lection contain the positive words addressed to the worshiper, perhaps by the priest (verses 9-13), but also by God himself, the words probably delivered as divine address by the priest (verses 14-16). The basis of confidence is expounded in verse 9 (compare verses 1-2), namely the worshiper's willingness to seek refuge with and take recourse in God. The consequences of such protection are stated negatively and then positively. Negatively, the person will not fall victim to any evil or scourge (two general terms, the first perhaps denoting evil in the sense of moral wrong and the latter signifying amoral ill fortune). Positively, the worshiper is assured that God's angels (or messengers; the Hebrew and Greek words mean both) will be guards for the person watching over even such small matters as the foot stumbling against a stone. Playing off the imagery of the foot, the writer declares that the worshiper can tread on snakes and trample beasts underfoot.

The divine speech that finishes off the psalm utilizes language that is both calming and consoling. There is no longer reference to snakes, thousands dying on every hand, pestilence in the night, and "things that go 'bump' in the night." There is, however, the repetition of the causal relationship as in verses 1-2 and 9: "Because he cleaves to me in love." These final verses are dominated by a focus on the divine: In God's speech, the first person pronoun or suffix occurs twelve times in Hebrew. The divine I hovers over the sentiments of the psalm and is the source of the promises of protection.

Romans 10:8*b*-13

It makes a smoother introduction to begin this epistolary lection with the words, "The word is near you" (verse 8*b*), but we should look at the larger context. It should be noted that Paul here is contrasting "legal righteousness" (verse 5, NEB) with "righteousness that comes by faith" (verse 6, NEB). The background to his exposition is provided by Deuteronomy 30:11-14, which emphasizes the nearness and accessibility of God's covenant with Israel. What God requires through the covenant is not remote. It is neither in the heaven nor beyond the sea, as if Israel had to go find it. Rather, "the word is very near you; it is in your mouth and in your heart, so that you can do it" (Deut. 30:14). In establishing a covenant with Israel, Yahweh had graciously reached out in their direction, drawn near to them, had indeed come to be within them—on their lips and in their hearts (cf. Jer. 31:31-34).

Drawing on these words from Deuteronomy, Paul reads them in light of the Christ-event. Just as Israel was reassured that the covenant was not remote and far away, so Paul insists that Christ is to be sought neither in the heavens nor in the abyss of Hades. It is not as if we must go in search of Christ to find him. He may be physically absent, but he is nevertheless fully present—here. And how is this so? Through the "word of faith which we preach" (verse 8). It is through this proclaimed word, the gospel, that the "word is near you, on your lips and in your heart" (verse 8). Here Paul is insisting that Christ as mediated to us through the preached Word is as near, as much within us, as was the covenant Yahweh made with Israel.

It is difficult to think of anything nearer or more existentially present than the very words on our lips or the convictions of our hearts. What is said and what is believed define who we are. Here, what is said is the Christian confession—"Jesus is Lord" (I Cor. 12:3; II Cor. 4:5; Phil. 2:11; Col. 2:6)—and what is believed is the Easter faith: God raised Christ from the dead (Rom. 4:24; I Pet. 1:21). It is on the basis of this conviction and this confession that we are justified, or saved.

27

It follows rather naturally that salvation should be universally available. After all, every human being has convictions in the heart that are uttered with the lips. Consequently, Paul cites Isaiah 28:16 to show that everyone who believes will find their faith coming to fruition. They will not be put to shame. They will not be disappointed. This applies to everyone—Jew and Gentile alike. Since there is only one Lord, that is Jesus Christ (Acts 10:36; Phil. 2:9-11), there can be no two ways of salvation. Everyone is justified on the same grounds and in the same way—through faith. We should recognize that the Lord's bounty is extensive enough to accommodate everyone who is willing to yield in faith. Thus, "every one who calls upon the name of the Lord will be saved" (verse 13; cf. Joel 2:32).

We should note the repeated insistence that everyone has access to God in faith. If we see ourselves as the elect of God, it is only too easy to conclude that we have a monopoly on God's riches. But God draws near through the preached Word to everyone, and those who respond by calling on the name of the Lord for help and hope will not be disappointed —they will be saved.

From this midrashic exposition of Deuteronomy 30:11-14, and its use of other Old Testament passages, we can make the following observations:

First, salvation is not so much a matter of our drawing near to Christ, as if to seek him out and find him at the end of a long search. It is rather that Christ has drawn near to us through the gospel. This means that the presence of God as mediated through Christ has become both universalized and localized. It is no longer necessary for us to go find Christ in a sacred place (cf. John 4), for now the Word of God has become portable. Christ becomes present whenever and wherever the gospel is preached. Salvation is to be found here and now—within us—because God has drawn near.

Second, salvation belongs to the faithful—all the faithful, not to a select group who regard themselves as the most faithful, or the only faithful. The basis on which all of humanity comes to know God is now common to us all. We can be assured that our faith, if it is genuine, will not come to nought. We can also be assured that God's riches are bountiful enough to go around. We may believe that God is exclusively ours, or that we relate to God in a uniquely close relationship, but the fact is that everyone who calls out to God for help, even as we do, can and will be heard.

Luke 4:1-13

The forty days of Lent (except Sundays) bring immediately to mind the forty days of Jesus' struggle and testing in the wilderness, a story which had its antecedents in Moses' forty days without food on the mountain (Exod. 34:28; Deut. 9:9), Elijah's forty days in flight to the mountain of God (I Kings 19:4-8), and, of course, the forty years of Israel's struggle in the wilderness. In fact, this last reference to the wilderness trials of Israel, especially as recited in Deuteronomy, is clearly the immediate background for the Gospel lesson today. Not only does Deuteronomy provide the Old Testament reading, but the Epistle draws upon Deuteronomy 30, and in Luke 4:1-13 Jesus quotes from Deuteronomy three times.

Since the temptation of Jesus is recorded in all three Synoptics, the preacher would do well to spend some time getting into focus the story as Luke tells it. Evidently Luke owes little to Mark's brief account (1:12-13) but holds much in common with Matthew (4:1-11). However, even there noticeable differences appear. Matthew, following Mark, joins the temptation directly to the baptism. Paul, in describing Israel's wilderness experience, moves directly from "baptism" in the Red Sea to temptations and tests of loyalty (I Cor. 10:1-10). Luke, however, places the genealogy of Jesus between the baptism and the temptation accounts. This pattern may have been suggested by the fact that Moses' call and ministry are separated by a genealogy in Exodus 6:14-25. The break is not disruptive, however, since the baptism, the genealogy, and the temptation all affirm Jesus as Son of God (3:22; 3:38; 4:3, 9). In Luke, Jesus not eating "in those days" (verse 2) is not formalized into a forty-day fast as in Matthew (4:2). In Luke, the devil's showing Jesus all the kingdoms of the world is stated temporally ("in a moment of time," verse 5), whereas the reference is spatial in Matthew ("to a very high mountain," 4:8). Luke's second and third temptations are reversed from Matthew's order. Because the temple was given so much importance in Luke's story of Jesus and the early church (Luke 2:41-52; 24:53; Acts 2:46; 3:1; 22:17), the temple temptation may have been made the story's climax. Finally, it is worth noting that Luke, although quite comfortable with angels, has none here, as Mark and Matthew do (Mark 1:13; Matt. 4:11). Instead, the devil simply leaves until an opportune time arrives for renewing the struggle, a time which did present itself through Judas (22:3).

Now that we have Luke's telling of it more clearly before us, what emphases present themselves for consideration?

First, it should be said that Luke's Jesus, though less dramatically than Mark's, opposes and is opposed by strong forces of evil. In whatever images or concepts the power of evil may be presented, it is the testimony of experience as well as Scripture that there is in the world opposition to love, health, wholeness, and peace. It does not go away by closing the eyes and smiling. In fact, it is those called of God and committed to the way of God in the world who experience most forcefully the struggle with evil. If Jesus wrestled, why should any of his followers think that believing makes them exempt from the fray?

Second, notice Luke's accent on the Holy Spirit. Jesus was born of the Spirit (1:35); he received the Spirit at baptism (3:22); he was full of the Holy Spirit (4:1); he was led by the Spirit (4:1); and following his temptations, Jesus went into Galilee to minister in the power of the Spirit (4:18). This Spirit was not Jesus' alone but was promised to and is experienced by the church (Luke 24:49; Acts 1:8; 2:1-4, 38). Resisting evil and ministering to human need are not left to will power and psychic strategies; the effective presence of God is offered and available.

Third, Jesus is the victor in the time of testing by joining to the presence of the Spirit the appropriate use of Scripture (4:4, 8, 12). Scripture can be used inappropriately, to oppose obedience to God and to undermine the purposes of God, as the devil demonstrates by quoting Psalm 91:11-12. But the fact that even the grossest errors may be blessed by some misused biblical text should not cause the people of God to shun the use of Scripture to enlighten, inform, and discipline faith. It is important for Luke and Luke's church that the story of Jesus, from birth, through death and resurrection, to the proclamation of good news to the nations, is "according to the Scriptures" (24:27, 44-49). The church armed with the Spirit and with the Scriptures will not be overcome by evil but will overcome evil with good.

Second Sunday of Lent

Genesis 15:1-12, 17-18; Psalm 127; Philippians 3:17–4:1; Luke 13:31-35 or Luke 9:28-36

The readings for the Second Sunday of Lent stress promise and expectation. The account of the covenant with Abraham in Genesis 15 presents God's promise of a child to the childless, and Abraham responds with faithful trust. The second part of the responsorial psalm (127:3-5) picks up that promise directly with its affirmation that sons are a blessing from the Lord, while the first part of the psalm (verses 1-2) can be heard as a comment on that other theme of the Old Testament lesson, faith. The epistolary reading calls attention to the cross and reminds the church that it awaits its Savior. The words of Jesus to Herod in Luke 13:31-35 spark anticipation of the events commemorated during Holy Week.

Genesis 15:1-12, 17-18

The literary and theological context of Genesis 15 is the story of the patriarchs (Gen. 12–50), in which the dominant motifs are the promises God gives the ancestors and the covenants God makes with them. Covenants are, in effect, promissory oaths, in which one party swears to do something in the future for the other party. Our text is but one of the accounts of the covenant with Abraham. At the heart of this covenant is God's promise to Abraham to be with the patriarch, to give him a son, and through that son descendants as numerous as the stars in the sky. Those descendants will in turn inherit the land in which Abraham is only a resident alien. A close parallel to this covenant occurs in Genesis 17, and the contents of the covenantal promise was presented with the initial call of Abraham in Genesis 12:1-3. Similar if not identical promises and covenants will define the stories of the other patriarchs, Isaac and Jacob.

The identification of Genesis 15 with one or more of the Pentateuchal sources has long been a matter of dispute. In addition to the parallels to other material in the Abraham story, evidence for a complex history of transmission is seen in the duplicates, repetitions, and slight inconsistencies within the chapter itself. Some commentators see here the beginning of the Elohistic source, and others see mainly the work of the Yahwist. If E material is present it is only in bits and pieces, and hardly in the form of a complete story. It is likely that the tensions within the account reflect the history of its oral transmission rather than the combination of literary sources. In any case, the chapter comes from the older literary strata of the Pentateuch.

Consider the structure and contents of the passage. It is a narrative, an account of the Lord's encounter with Abraham for the purpose of establishing a covenant. It is not at all clear how much of the activity is understood to have occurred within a "vision" (verse 1), as a dream while Abraham slept (verse 12), or as a divine audition (verses 1, 4) like those of the prophets. Only two characters appear, the Lord and Abraham, and much of the story recounts the dialogue between them. There are two rather distinct units, verses 1-6 and 7-18.

The first section of the dialogue (verses 1-6) deals with the promise of descendants to Abraham. The Lord speaks first with a word of assurance (verse 1), and Abraham responds with an expression of his fear and concern about his childlessness (verses 2-3). The Lord's next speech (verses 4-5) is a specific promise concerning the patriarch's descendants. Abraham's response is belief, which the Lord "reckoned . . . to him as righteousness" (verse 6).

The next series of dialogues (verses 7-21) concerns the covenant itself, its contents and the ritual for concluding it. The Lord speaks (verse 7) identifying himself in terms of past actions (bringing Abraham out of Ur) and future promises (the gift of the land). As in his response to the initial encounter, Abraham raises a question that suggests uncertainty if not doubt (verse 8). The Lord then instructs the patriarch to bring certain animals (verse 9), Abraham does so, cuts them up and lays them out in a specific ritual pattern, and then falls into a deep sleep (verses 10-12). In the dark a "smoking fire pot and a flaming torch passed between these pieces," and the Lord concluded the covenant with Abraham, promising to his descendants the land from "the river of Egypt to the great river, the river Euphrates" (verses 17-18).

A number of points require some explanation. The structure of verses 1-6 is similar to the oracle of salvation, found in prophetic literature and probably rooted in cultic practice. Verses 3-4 presuppose an ancient practice whereby a slave could be the heir of one who had no natural children. The animals of verses 9-10 are not sacrifices, but part of a covenant ritual. Covenants are like oaths in that they are conditional self-curses. The practice of cutting up the animals and passing between their halves is a symbolic representation of the covenant curse, calling down upon the participants such a fate if they do not abide by the stipulations. Such practice is probably behind the idiom "to cut a covenant." The "smoking fire pot" (better, "oven") and "flaming torch" that passed between the pieces is a representation of the presence of the Lord.

Under the general theme of promises for the future, the main motifs that call for homiletical reflection seem to correspond to the two parts of the passage. Verses 7-18 stress the covenant, its establishment through solemn—even fearful—ritual, and its contents, the promise to Abraham of descendants who will later possess the land. As in virtually all divine-human covenants in the Old Testament, the initiative is God's. The promise comes without precondition, but it does call for response. Note also what is concrete and what is not. God's future has a concrete and specific place in view, and a particular people. But Abraham himself has only the hope, and the signs of its eventual fulfillment in the form of ritual and, later on, the first of his descendants.

The issue of the first section (verses 1-6), as stated in its concluding verse, is faith. A problem—fear, anxiety, doubt?—is assumed at the very outset, else there would be no need for reassurance. Moreover, Abraham at first challenges God, finding the promise difficult to accept, for he is childless (verse 2). When the Lord responds with the specific promise of descendants as numerous as the stars, "he believed the Lord; and he reckoned it to him as righteousness" (verse 6). "Belief" here does not refer to a single act or experience, but to a continuous response. Nor does it mean agreement to certain ideas or propositions. Rather, this "belief" or faith is trust and commitment to the God of the covenant, the acceptance of the promise. To have that faith "reckoned" as "righteousness" should be understood in the context of the covenant relationship. "Righteousness," frequently linked in prophetic literature to "justice," concerns being in accord with the covenant stipulations and expectations. There is no indication of what in particular Abraham did that God took to be faith. The account at that point reports no words at all. Could that be it? Could faith be found in the silent acceptance of the divine promise? On the other hand, both before (verse 2) and after (verse 8) being accounted faithful, Abraham is heard to express to God his doubts and questions.

Psalm 127

Two themes, the building of a house and children as a blessing, dominate this psalm and thus parallel some of the interests of Genesis 15.

In the heading to the composition, the psalm is associated with Solomon. Such an association reflects the attempt of late Hebrew exegetes to connect the Psalms with various personages and events. Two features probably led to connecting the psalm with Solomon: (1) the reference to the building of a house was taken as a reference to the temple constructed by Solomon, and (2) the word for "beloved," in verse 2, is the same as the name given Solomon by the prophet Nathan in II Samuel 12:25.

Verses 1-2 proclaim the futility of labor unless it has Yahweh's blessing. Building a house, watching a city, early to work, late to bed, working hard for bread—none are of consequence unless God is somehow part of the picture. (The

35

last line of verse 2 is difficult to interpret; it seems to mean that it is God who is the source of rest at night, not the diligence of our labor nor our commitment to our effort.) Although stated negatively, this text has many similarities to Jesus' affirmation that the flowers of the field and the birds of the air possess something that labor and effort cannot give; that is, one should hang loose in life and trust the beneficence of the Creator and the creation.

Verses 3-5 affirm the benefit of progeny, especially males. Again, the source of the blessing is seen as Yahweh. The author, like people in all generations, recognizes that there is always an uncertainty about childbearing. Taking thought and taking action do not an offspring insure. Sons are here seen as a source of authority in the gate. A person with a retinue of sons possessed clout in public places. Social protection, personal welfare, social security, survival assurance, continuity of the name, inheritance insurance, comradeship in life, all of these were involved in male progeny. In ancient society, much would be lost without them.

Philippians 3:17–4:1

It may seem presumptuous to us for Paul to charge his readers to imitate himself and others whose way of life conforms to his own. But it was accepted practice for Greek and Roman moralists to urge their readers to follow a certain course of action and then offer them examples of the behavior they wished to promote. It was quite acceptable for a teacher to offer himself as a model for his students, for parents to offer themselves as models for their children, or for the elderly to serve as examples for the young.

Today's epistolary lection conforms to this well-accepted form of moral instruction. First, we have the exhortation or appeal (verse 17), and it is specifically a call to imitation. Then, we have a negative depiction of a way of life to be avoided—an earthly mind-set (verses 18-19), followed by a positive portrait of the way of life Paul himself exemplified—heavenly citizenship (verses 20-21). Finally, there is an endearing call to steadfastness (4:1)

As to the call for imitation, this is a note frequently

sounded in Pauline paraenesis (I Cor. 4:16; 11:1; I Thess. 1:6; II Thess. 3:7-9; also Gal. 4:12). Even further, we find repeated instances in early Christian teaching where the faithful serve as "role models" (I Thess. 1:7; 2:14; II Thess. 3:9; I Tim. 4:12; Tit. 2:7; Heb. 6:12; 13:7). In some cases, the object of imitation is God (Eph. 5:1) or Christ (I Cor. 11:1; I Pet. 2:21; perhaps Phil. 2:5-11).

Viewed one way, imitation as a form of ethical praxis appears hollow and thoughtless. After all, what is there to be gained by rote behavioral simulation? Does this not remove the center and motivation for moral renewal from ourselves to someone else? And yet as little as we admire mindless copying of mannerisms and life-style, we all recognize the intrinsic worth of an exemplary life. Martin Luther King, Jr., regarded Gandhi's life and teaching as exemplary, yet his appropriation of Gandhi's philosophy of non-violence and radical love for peace was by no means rote. Imitation as a form of exhortation simply recognizes a fundamental human truth—the capacity for a human life to shape, form, influence other human lives. This no one can deny.

Having issued the call for imitation, Paul sketches the negative side. Those who have brought him to tears are the "enemies of the cross of Christ" (verse 18). We can tell very little about who they actually were because his description of them employs fairly stock phrases used to pillory opponents. They are bent on destruction (cf. II Cor. 11:15; II Pet. 2:1). They have no capacity for restraint or moderation, since they give in to their own appetites, probably for food but possibly for sex (Rom. 16:18; II Tim. 3:4). They are self-indulgent. The "shame" in which they glory may be a euphemism for circumcision. The language is supplied by Hosea 4:7. In a word, they have an earthly mind-set (Col. 3:2).

In sharp contrast to this is the outlook defined by the transcendent reality of the risen Lord (verses 20-21). The life to which Paul has committed himself is impelled by a view of the city of God of which he is a heavenly citizen (cf. Eph. 2:6; Col. 3:1; Heb. 11:10; 12:22; 13:14; Rev. 21:2). This is what engenders hope in the coming Savior (I Cor. 1:7; I Tim. 6:14; II Tim. 1:10; Tit. 2:11, 13; 3:6: II Pet. 1:11). Nor is this merely a hope that awaits an arrival of a visitor from heaven, but one that transforms the earthly into the heavenly. The resurrection hope entails a radical change in the form of human existence—from "our lowly body" to a resplendent form that is like "his glorious body" (verse 21; cf. I Cor. 15:43, 49, 53; Rom. 8:29; 12:2; II Cor. 3:18; I John 3:2). How is all of this achieved? Through the resurrection power (cf. I Cor. 15:27; Eph. 1:19-22).

With these two options clearly sketched, we stand at the fork in the road, and Paul's final appeal is to "stand firm . . . in the Lord" (4:1; cf. I Cor. 16:13). It is couched in tender language reminiscent of the letter as a whole (1:4; 2:2, 17; 4:10). It is, after all, "in the Lord" where our lives are lifted to heavenly heights as we share in the resurrection hope. It is from this position that we are able to transcend "earthly things" (verse 19).

Numerous themes appropriate to Lent are sounded in this passage. First, the theme of imitation obviously provides one way of thinking about Lent, whether it is Christ's own suffering that serves as the focal example or that of the faithful people of God. In either case, this can become a time for conforming our own ways and wills to a form of life whose enduring feature is the capacity to appropriate the cross of Christ rather than become its enemy through radical self-indulgence.

Second, the "earthly" life-style is seen as one which gives in to our own desires without any capacity for restraint or self-denial. Even though the portrait here is stereotypical, it etches the outlines of a style of life avidly pursued by many, even many of us.

Third, heavenly citizenship is that which transforms us even as we live "below," and eventually enables us to move from an ordinary to a resplendent existence.

Luke 13:31-35

Luke 13:31-35 is especially appropriate for the Lenten Season in that this text looks toward Jerusalem and the passion of Jesus. And if Lent be understood as a pilgrimage to Good Friday and Easter, this passage is doubly appropriate since it falls within Luke's lengthy "journey narrative" (9:51–19:27). This large section begins with the declaration, "he set his face to go to Jerusalem" (9:51), and that controlling image of Jesus had been repeated as recently as 13:22: "He went on his way . . . journeying toward Jerusalem." Luke is fond of the journey format not only for presenting Jesus' ministry in the Gospel and Paul's in Acts, but also for characterizing the Christians as pilgrims, those of "the Way" (Acts 9:2; 19:9, 23; 22:4; 24:14, 22). When the travel narrative is understood as Luke's way of giving a frame to a number of sayings and events in Jesus' life, then the extremely difficult task of reconstructing a chronology for the journey to Jerusalem ceases to be of primary importance.

Luke 13:31-35 consists of two distinct sub-units: verses 31-33 and verses 34-35. The latter part is found in Matthew 23:37-39 but with one noticeable difference in what otherwise is an almost word-for-word parallel. The former part, verses 31-33, is in Luke alone.

Perhaps most striking here is the favorable picture of the Pharisees, especially for those of us who had been given the impression that the Pharisees were always and everywhere the villains in the story of Jesus. Herod Antipas, son of Herod the Great, was tetrarch of Galilee (Luke 3:1) during Jesus' ministry. He had beheaded John the Baptist and now was perplexed about Jesus, especially since there was a rumor that Jesus was John raised from the dead (Luke 9:7-9). Apparently Herod now wishes to cure his perplexity by killing Jesus also (13:32). Jesus is neither intimidated nor deterred in his ministry for he lives and works under the divine necessity: "I must go on my way" (verse 33). This means that even though death for Jesus is near ("the third day" is surely intended here to refer to what is impending and not to the exact time frame), he will continue to exorcize demons and heal the sick, he will bring his ministry to its consummation (verse 32), and he will die in Jerusalem (verse 33). This reaffirms the divine imperative with which this entire section began (9:51). That the Pharisees, in an act of friendship, would warn Jesus about Herod should not surprise the reader of Luke. While Mark 3:6 states that Pharisees and Herodians joined in the design to kill Jesus, Luke's parallel to that omits the Herodians and offers the more moderate description of the Pharisees discussing "what they might do to Jesus" (6:11). In Luke many Pharisees seem open to Jesus (7:36; 11:37; 14:1) even though they do differ strongly with him on certain interpretations of the law. A Pharisee, Gamaliel, was a moderating voice in the Jewish council when dealing with the followers of Jesus (Acts 5:34), and some of the early Christians were, according to Luke, Pharisees (15:5), including, by his own admission, Paul (23:6). But even so, Luke wants us to understand that neither friends (Pharisees) nor foe (Herod) alter Jesus' sure obedience to the will of God.

Very likely it is the attention on Jerusalem which prompts Luke to place here the lament over that city (verses 34-35). Jerusalem is central in Luke's narrative, not only about Jesus but also about the early church. Luke mentions Jerusalem ninety times; the remainder of the new Testament, only forty-nine. But the fact that verse 33 ends with the word "Jerusalem" is hardly sufficient reason for Luke to locate here a passage that seems so clearly out of place. "How often would I have gathered your children" (verse 34) implies a Judean ministry which has yet to occur. Matthew places the saying near the close of Jesus' ministry in Jerusalem (23:37-39), a natural setting for it. Hence, when Jesus says in Matthew, "you will not see me *again*, until" (verse 39, italics added), the reference is to the final crisis. In Luke, however, Jesus is on his way to the city, and therefore, when he says, "you will not see me until," the reference is to his arrival at Jerusalem when the people shout, "Blessed is the King who comes in the name of the Lord" (19:38), almost the exact words of 13:35.

By locating this apostrophe to Jerusalem earlier, Luke is saying there is yet time to repent, yet time to receive the Christ, yet time to avoid the final catastrophe. With repentance comes forgiveness, an offer to the world, beginning with Jerusalem (24:47).

Luke 9:28-36

Luke 9:28-36 is offered as an alternate lesson for today, with no suggestion that it be tied to 13:31-35. Interestingly enough, a connection could easily be made since in Luke's account of the Transfiguration, Jesus, Moses, and Elijah are talking of Jesus' coming departure (exodus) in Jerusalem (verse 31), the very theme of 13:31-35. However, Luke 9:28-36 is offered here (the parallels in Matthew and Mark appear as alternate lections the other two years) to honor a long-standing tradition in some churches to consider the Transfiguration on the Second Sunday of Lent. If such a text seems unusual for the Lenten Season, consider two facts: (1) none of the Sundays of Lent are fast days but preserve the Easter joy even in repentance; and (2) the Gospels themselves set their Transfiguration stories in the context of passion predictions and the turn toward Jerusalem. In fact, the immediately preceding verses (9:23-27) deal with discipleship and cross bearing, themes certainly fitting for Lent.

As recently as the Last Sunday After Epiphany the Transfiguration text was the Gospel lesson, as it always is on that Sunday. The preacher may not wish to return so soon to Luke 9:28-36, but if so, it would seem wise to focus on the elements of the story appropriate for Lent. Four comments may be suggestive:

1. Luke places the event "about eight days" after the preceding sayings (verse 28), departing from Mark 9:2 which follows closely the Moses story of Exodus 24:16. Since "eight days" was a way of referring to Sunday, perhaps Luke is conveying the message and mood of resurrection.

2. Unlike Matthew 17:1-8 and Mark 9:2-8, Luke inserts the content of the conversation among Jesus, Moses, and Elijah (verse 31) and the response of the disciples (verse 32). The discussion of Jesus' approaching death was for Jesus, not the disciples, therefore sleep kept them from hearing. They did see the glory and that was enough. In fact, it was too much; they did not understand. However, some experiences, though not comprehended, still leave their lasting marks on us.

3. What the disciples do hear is addressed to them (verse 35). While Jesus' death had its confirmation in the law (Moses) and the prophets (Elijah), Jesus alone is the Son of God and is to be obeyed.

4. While Matthew 17:9-13 and Mark 9:9-13 conclude the story with conversation between Jesus and the disciples, including a command not to tell anyone until after the resurrection, Luke simply offers a closing comment on their silence "in those days" (verse 36). Perhaps like Luke's Mary, they pondered these things in their hearts. When words of witness finally break such silence, they command attention and are worth hearing.

Third Sunday of Lent

Exodus 3:1-15; Psalm 103:1-13; I Corinthians 10:1-13; Luke 13:1-9

Our readings for today are linked to one another in various ways. The Old Testament, Psalm, and Epistle refer to Moses, but in different ways. Exodus 3:1-15 reports the call of Moses. The responsorial psalm gives thanks to the God who saves, including establishing justice for the oppressed and making known his ways to Moses. In the epistolary text Paul employs the history of Israel, especially the tradition of Moses and the rebellious people of Israel in the wilderness, as a warning to the church concerning idolatry and immorality. Theologically, the Gospel and epistolary readings converge on the theme of sin and punishment. In that respect there is an important reversal of our usual expectations. The New Testament readings call attention to the law, while the Old Testament texts proclaim the good news of God's intentions to save.

Exodus 3:1-15

Because this text stands at the heart of the tradition concerning Moses and the Exodus of the Israelites from Egypt, and because of the intrinsic importance of its contents, it has been the object of considerable interest in the history of interpretation. Attention often has focused upon the meaning of the divine name revealed to Moses, but numerous other aspects of the text have been studied in Judaism and the church. Clearly the passage deserves the attention it has received.

The account of the call of Moses, which is not completed until Exodus 4:17, is a coherent account of events. Still, modern biblical criticism recognized in it evidence of the composite nature of the report, either the combination of

43

literary sources or multiple oral traditions. This evidence includes the different divine names, God and Yahweh ("Lord" in most translations), the duplication of contents (verses 7-8 parallel verses 9-12), the different names for the sacred mountain ("Horeb" in some texts, including this one, and "Sinai" in others), and the manner of divine revelation (through an angel or direct address). It appears most likely that we have here the combination of the two older Pentateuchal sources, J (the Yahwist) and E (the Elohist). As we shall see, the recognition of sources turns out to be important in understanding a central feature of the report.

The account of the call of Moses presents us with at least three theological issues that could be the basis for homiletical reflection:

1. Throughout we are invited to consider the encounter of a particular human being with the divine presence. The encounter happens in a particular place, located in the wilderness, on or near "the mountain of God" (verse 1). Moses did not choose the place, nor did he decide that it was a holy site; rather, as elsewhere in the Old Testament, the sacredness is disclosed to him. Furthermore, he did not set out to find it. Finding himself there has the sense of meeting his destiny.

The encounter itself is awesome, even frightening. The burning bush attracts Moses' attention, but then God speaks, warning him to remove his shoes. To approach God—radically Other yet personal—is both attractive and dangerous. We are told explicitly that Moses hid his face, fearing to see God (verse 6). No one, the Old Testament knows, can see God and live (cf. Isaiah 6).

2. The passage, as the account of the call of Moses, invites our reflection upon vocation. The major narrative tension for the story as a whole (Exod. 3:1–4:17) concerns whether or not Moses will accept his call to lead the people of Israel out of Egypt, and, if so, on what terms. Most readers of the text are struck by Moses' resistance to the call. As soon as God says that he will send Moses to Pharaoh to bring the people out, Moses demurs: "Who am I that I should go to Pharaoh?" (verse 11). God responds with reassurance, and then Moses insists upon knowing God's name (verse 13). The dialogue

continues well beyond our reading for the day, with Moses presenting other objections (Exod. 4:1, 10). Finally, armed with reassurance, the name of God, signs and wonders to perform, and the help of his brother Aaron, Moses obeys.

It is tempting to analyze the personality of Moses, or even speculate about physical limitations that might have hindered his ability as a public speaker. However, this vocation report has a great deal in common with others in the Old Testament. In virtually all of those reports—Gideon in Judges 6, Isaiah in Isaiah 6, Jeremiah in Jeremiah 1—the one who is called resists, finding himself unworthy. (The single exception is Ezekiel 1–3). Consequently, we may conclude that a sense of unworthiness or inadequacy is part of being called to do the divine will. After all, one stands in the presence of the God of the world and of history. The resistance to the call, then, is related to the experience of the Holy. One need not be especially timid, shy, or cowardly to express reluctance.

3. Then there is the revelation of the divine name. It comes in response to Moses' second objection: If the people ask me the name of the God of the fathers, what shall I say to them? (verse 13). The divine response is, to say the least, enigmatic: "I AM WHO I AM" (verse 14). The response is a popular, and not necessarily accurate, etymology for the name of Israel's God, Yahweh. The expression is the first person singular imperfect form of the Hebrew verb "to be," and could be translated with a future tense, "I will be what I will be" (RSV footnote). "Yahweh" could be a third person singular imperfect of the same verb. It is not possible to determine whether or not the divine name itself actually originated from this verb, as a confession of faith in the God "who is," or "who will be," or even "who causes to be." This text does identify Yahweh with being or becoming. However, it would be a mistake to make this text the heart of one's theology, for this is virtually the only Old Testament text that reflects on God as Being.

This account of the divine name, which comes from the Elohist, has a parallel in Exodus 6:2-9, which stems from the Priestly Writer. These two sources share the view that the name Yahweh was unknown until the time of Moses, so their accounts of the events before that time carefully avoid use of that name. The Yahwist, on the other hand, obviously believed that God was known by that proper name even to the first human beings. These are not so much two different theologies as different doctrines of revelation and history. In P especially and also in E on this point, God revealed himself more and more specifically by stages in history.

Equally important as the identification of God by name is the identification by activity in history. The God who appears to Moses is "the God of your father, the God of Abraham, the God of Isaac, and the God of Jacob" (verse 6; cf. verse 15), who now appears to initiate the fulfillment of the promise to them. This is the God who has heard the cries of Israel and will bring them out of oppression in Egypt into a good land (verses 7-10).

If Yahweh is "Being" that also means that history is this God's sphere of activity. The name is revealed so that salvation from slavery is possible, and also so that the future descendants of the patriarchs will know how to address their praise and petitions (verse 15). The account is, from beginning to end, good news.

Psalm 103:1-13

This psalm has been selected to accompany the account of the call of Moses because of verse 7 and to accompany the reading from Luke because both the psalm and the Gospel reading wrestle with the problem of correlating human actions and divine reactions.

This psalm is essentially a psalm of thanksgiving but it is thanksgiving expressed in hymnic form. The psalm contains no direct address to the Deity, thus it is not a prayer of thanksgiving. In fact, the composition begins as a self addressing the self (verse 1). In the final stanza, the range of vision is greatly expanded, arching out to include the angels, the heavenly hosts, and all the works of creation.

The verses selected for the lection are fundamentally theological affirmations; their content is composed of descriptive statements about God. If we include verse 6 with verses 1-5, and this is a possible although not an obvious division, then the first six verses speak of seven deeds of the Deity:

forgives iniquity
  heals diseases
    redeems from the Pit
      crowns with steadfast love and mercy
     satisfies with good as long as one lives
   renews youthful vigor like that of an eagle
works vindication and justice for all oppressed.

All of these actions are expressed through participial forms of the verbs. One might take such formulations, like participles in English, as describing states of being. Thus the actions denoted are taken as descriptions characteristic of the Deity.

Verses 8-13 contain a second series, this time containing six items that describe the character of Yahweh, particularly with regard to the divine reaction to human error, wrongdoing, and rebellion. Verse 14 should be considered in conjunction with these verses since it offers anthropological insight and rationale for divine behavior, offering reasons anchored in human existence for God's grace and mercy.

Throughout this section, descriptions of God's treatment of the sinner and explanations of divine behavior are interlaced. Each verse makes independent but interrelated points. (1) God's nature is oriented to mercy and grace; he is not easily upset and when he is, there is mercy abounding (verse 8). (2) God does not perpetually torment or nag incessantly since his anger does not abide forever. The text does not deny that God has anger and that he does react in wrath; however, the divine is willing to let bygones be bygones (verse 9). (3) God does not operate on a tit-for-tat basis. The punishment is not made to fit the crime. God is free to reduce the penalty, to soften the shock of human actions (verse 10). (4) Divine mercy is compared to the greatness of the heights of the heaven above the earth (verse 11). (5) The vertical dimension used in verse 11 is replaced by a horizontal dimension in describing the removal of transgressions. East and west, or literally the rising and setting (of the sun), is a way of stressing the radical separation (verse 12). (6) The parent-child relationship and parental pity form an analogy by which to understand divine love. It should be noted that such pity is granted to those fearing (= obeying the will of) God (verse 13; note verses 17-18). The human condition helps incline God to mercy: God knows the weakness of the human condition; people's dusty origin and their dusty destiny.

I Corinthians 10:1-13

This passage should be read in the overall context of I Corinthians 8–10, the section in which Paul discusses the question of eating meat that had been sacrificed to idols. The underlying issue was that some of the Corinthians wanted unqualified freedom to act without being under restraint by the wishes or needs of their fellow members. At root, their attitude knew little or no restraint.

In response to this, Paul first offers his own apostolic behavior as a positive example of self-restraint (chapter 9, esp. verse 25). He then turns to Israel as a negative example (10:1-13). Instead of restraint they had been indulgent, giving in to their own desires and following their own will. In addition, they had become self-confident and arrogant. Israel epitomized what some in the Corinthian church were becoming—indulgent, self-willed, overconfident.

Paul's remarks exhibit a fairly clear structure. First, he elaborates on the biblical theme of Israel's Exodus (10:1-5). Then, he draws several lessons from this midrashic exposition (10:6-13).

We may consider these in turn. He begins by noting that Israel's passage through the Red Sea was a baptism into Moses. After they entered the wilderness they ate and drank supernatural provisions. Clearly here an Old Testament theme has been Christianized, that is, read and interpreted in light of Christian experience. In Israel's experience Paul saw a kind of baptismal initiation and a form of eucharistic eating. Indeed, the rock from which they drank is said to be Christ.

Apparently, some of the Corinthians had concluded that their baptism and participation in the Eucharist insured their position before God. One scholar has referred to their "robust sacramentalism." They had received the sacraments and thereby felt confident. As a way of cautioning against such false confidence, Paul stresses that even though all of Israel had shared the same saving experience of the Exodus and had received the same spiritual nourishment, they still remained vulnerable. Note the way in which "all" is played off against "most"—*all* were under the cloud, *all* passed through the sea, *all* were baptized, *all* ate the same supernatural food, *all* ate the same supernatural drink. They all experienced the common deliverance and received the same nourishment. Yet, with *most* of them, God was displeased! Even though they all experienced divine deliverance and were sustained by divine nourishment, the majority of them buckled.

In the remarks that follow, Paul warns against four vices: (1) idolatry (verse 7), (2) immorality (verse 8), (3) tempting God (verse 9), and (4) grumbling (verse 10). In at least two cases, these are vices of indulgence that result from being unable to practice restraint. After reminding us that Israel's experience serves as a warning to us (verse 11), he warns against false confidence (verse 12). Yet the passage ends on a note of reassurance. We are reminded that the temptations we face everyone faces. But besides the universality of temptation there is the fidelity of God. Just as Israel was provided a way of escape, so can we be confident that God will not tempt us beyond what we are able to bear.

This passage has several features which relate to Lenten observance.

First, the baptismal metaphor in verse 2 reminds us that historically the Season of Lent served as a period for preparing candidates for baptism. It serves as a sober reminder that our initiation into the faith can in no way insure us against the vices of indulgence. In fact, it may lead to false confidence. Similarly, we may assume that our partaking of the eucharist somehow makes us immune to the evils of selfishness and fleshly desires. Paul here is calling us to reflect soberly on our baptism and participation in the Lord's Supper and not to develop a false sense of security.

Second, since Lent serves as a time for penitence and prayer, we are prompted to think both of the temptations to which we are all subject and of the confident hope that God strengthens us to stand firm. In one sense the passage is a warning, but before it ends it becomes a passage of solid reassurance, inviting us to trust in a God who is faithful. Even if Israel was unfaithful, God was not.

Third, the overarching theme of Paul's "lessons" in verses 6-10 is not to desire evil. The common denominator of the vices he mentions is that they all grow out of inordinate desire, which itself is the basis of evil. It is this sense of craving, setting our hearts on that which we want, indeed on that which we feel compelled to possess, that the sober reflection of Lent helps us curb.

Luke 13:1-9

One could hardly find a Gospel lection more appropriately Lenten or more characteristically Lukan than our text for today. The entire passage is an urgent call to repentance, a turning from sin and a reformation of action and attitude. The theme of repentance occurs more in Luke than in other New Testament writers. In fact, the Gospel for Luke is the proclamation of repentance and forgiveness of sins (24:47). Also typically Lukan is the parable of the fig tree (verses 6-9) with its accent on the appeal for mercy which stays the hand of judgment. The reader is reminded of the grace which spared wicked Nineveh even though that city was also under the judgment of God (Jonah is a favorite of Luke). Furthermore, the design of 13:1-9 is common to Luke: a parable that is interpreted at the beginning rather than at the end (10:29; 12:15; 15:1-2; 18:1, 9). And finally, Luke again includes in the travel narrative (9:51–19:27) materials selected thematically rather than chronologically or geographically, all pointing to the approaching crisis in Jerusalem.

This passage consists of two statements by Jesus (verses 1-5) which serve as an introduction to and commentary on a parable about a barren fig tree (verses 6-9). In form the two sayings are exactly parallel, each ending with the pronouncement, "but unless you repent you will all likewise perish." But the differences in the two sayings combine to make them inclusive in their application. The first has to do with Galileans, the second with Jerusalemites. Jesus is speaking to all. The first has to do with tragedy caused by a human being, the second with tragedy caused by natural calamity. Jesus is including all the violence and suffering that strikes without reason or meaning.

The question, Why this to these particular people? is as old as the human race. The Book of Job, Psalm 37, and Psalm 73 ask the question. The disciples asked Jesus, "Rabbi, who sinned, this man or his parents, that he was born blind?" (John 9:2). The question assumed that there was direct correlation between sin and suffering. To those disciples (John 9:3) and in today's lection Jesus denied that direct correlation. But still the idea persists: illness, poverty, disease, loneliness, and death are the punishment for sins known or unknown. For Christians, the fatal blow to the idea that suffering and death are the lot of the guilty came at Golgotha. The One without sin suffered and died on the cross; some present took that as proof he was not the Son of God (Matt. 27:39-43), but Jesus' disciples are forever freed from the ancient notion that prosperity and good health are evidence of divine favor while poverty and suffering are clear signs of divine wrath. Even so, the idea persists. Thornton Wilder's novel, *The Bridge of San Luis Rey* (Harper & Row, 1967), is the account of a priest's effort to prove that the reason a bridge collapsed with certain persons on it was to be found in the moral flaws in the lives of those persons. Needless to say, the priest's efforts, and all such efforts, fail. Jesus rejects such attempts at calculation, not simply because they are futile, but because they direct attention from the primary issue: the obligation of every person to live in penitence and trust before God without linking one's loyalty to God to life's sorrows or joys. *All* are to repent or perish.

Luke's parable of the barren fig tree may be a recasting of the story of the cursing of the barren fig tree (Mark 11:12-14; Matt. 21:18-19), or perhaps Mark and Matthew recast the parable. In either case, Luke's story leaves open the possibility of fruitfulness, and at least a temporary triumph of mercy over judgment. The delay of God's judgment because of the intercession of a prophet or Moses is not uncommon in the Old Testament. In Christian circles, one explanation for the delay of the Day of the Lord was that God, for the sake of mercy, was giving more people a chance to avoid the terror of that day (II Pet. 3:8-9). Luke's message here is similar: there is still time for Israel to repent and to bear fruit as evidence of that repentance. In other words, God's mercy is still talking to God's judgment, and on that conversation hangs our salvation.

Fourth Sunday of Lent

Joshua 5:9-12; Psalm 34:1-8; II Corinthians 5:16-21; Luke 15:1-3, 11-32

All the readings converge on the theme of God's actions to save the lost or sinful. The key phrase in the Old Testament reading affirms that the Lord has "rolled away the reproach of Egypt" (Josh. 5:9). The psalm is a song of thanksgiving for deliverance from fears and trouble. Its call to "taste and see that the Lord is good" (Ps. 34:8) becomes a comment on the first reading's report of the first meal in the land of Canaan. The Epistle proclaims the good news in cosmic terms: "In Christ God was reconciling the world to himself" (II Cor. 5:19). In the Gospel lection Jesus proclaims forgiveness through the parable of the prodigal son.

Joshua 5:9-12

The events reported in our reading occur when there is a lull in the narrative as a whole, and at the point of a key transition. The people of Israel have entered the land, miraculously crossing the Jordan under the leadership of Joshua as they had crossed the sea under the leadership of Moses. But they have not yet begun the battles for possession of the land. The transition has great significance, for it marks the move from life in the wilderness to life in the land promised to the ancestors.

The immediate context of the reading is the account of three events between the entrance and the battles. All are, in different ways, ritual events of preparation. The first (5:2-9) reports a ceremony of circumcision at Gilgal, the second (5:10-12) is the account of the Passover in the land of Canaan, and the third (5:13-15) is the story of Joshua's encounter with the captain of Yahweh's army. The reading for the day then encompasses the last verse of the first incident and all of the second.

Doubtless ancient traditions stand behind this material, which must reflect ritual practices from the premonarchical period in Gilgal, certainly an important cultic center in Israel's early days. However, the text has passed through the hands of the Deuteronomistic editors who were responsible for the history that begins in the Book of Deuteronomy and is concluded in Second Kings, working as late as the period of the Exile (ca. 560 B.C.).

Joshua 5:9 concludes the report of the circumcision of all the males who had been born during the wandering in the wilderness; all the generation of the Exodus had died (5:4). The account comes at this point because circumcision is a prerequisite for participation in the Passover (Exod. 12:43-49). While there are other reports of adult circumcision (Gen. 34), and it is likely that it was originally a puberty rite, in Israel it was done in infancy. Moreover, although the practice was not limited to Israel, it came to be a physical sign and symbol of membership in the covenant community (Gen. 17).

The account of the circumcision ritual is concluded with a pronouncement from the Lord to Joshua and an etiology of the name of the place. The etymology is not linguistically accurate, but is based on similarity of sounds. It is called "Gilgal"—that is, "rolling"—because there the Lord "rolled away" the reproach of the Egyptians. Unfortunately, the text does not tell us what it means by "the reproach of Egypt." Is it assumed—incorrectly—that the Egyptians did not practice circumcision? Does it concern the separation from the religiously unclean practices of the foreigners? Does it refer to the shame and humiliation of slavery? There seems to be no way to know. It is clear, however, that now the Lord has declared the people to be "right," either ritually or otherwise, in a way that had not before been the case.

The celebration reported in 5:10-12, which in historic times was a single occasion, originally had been two, Passover and Unleavened Bread. Passover, a one-day festival, must have begun as a part of pastoral practice, marking the movement from winter to summer pasture. Unleavened Bread, on the other hand, was a seven-day celebration of the spring harvest, in which Israel would not have participated before arriving in Canaan. As Exodus 12 indicates, Passover was a family festival, celebrated in the home, although here it seems to have been a corporate affair held outside.

Significantly, the festival marks both the change of Israel's diet and the transition from wilderness to holy land. The "unleavened cakes and parched grain" were "of the produce of the land" (verse 11). On that very day the manna ceased and the people "ate of the fruit of the land." God substitutes one miracle for another, equally marvelous. This note might serve to remind us that the series of events that follow in the Book of Joshua do not amount to "conquest," for the Lord gives the land to the people. Moreover, the appropriate response to such gifts, says the Book of Deuteronomy, is that "you shall eat and be full, and you shall bless the Lord your God for the good land he has given you" (Deut. 8:10). Such rituals of thanksgiving and identification should always mark imporant transitions, for individuals and for communities.

Psalm 34:1-8

One of the acrostic psalms, along with 9/10, 25, 37, 111, 112, 119, and 145, this composition moves through the alphabet from "A to Z."

Although a thanksgiving psalm, this psalm does not address the Deity. Although most thanksgiving psalms are made up of human speech to a human audience, the majority contain at least some direct speech to the Deity.

The nature of the distress from which the person was saved is lacking in specificity. Verses 4 and 6, which describe the plight upon which the worshiper can now look back, speak only of "fears" and "troubles"—generalities that allowed the psalm to be utilized over and over again regardless of the circumstances.

The opening call to worship has the worshiper confess individually (verses 1-2*a*) and then call upon a community (friends, associates, family) to join in a service of praise.

II Corinthians 5:16-21

So popular is this famous Pauline text that it is used more than once in the lectionary. Part of this passage is the standard epistolary reading for Ash Wednesday (II Cor. 5:20*b*–6:2 [3–10]), and the reader may wish to consult our remarks for this day on pages 17-18 in this volume, or those for Year A or B. Also, in our remarks on the epistolary readings for Propers 6 and 7 for Year B, which treat II Cor. 5:6-10, 14-17, and 5:18–6:2 respectively, we have treated certain aspects of this text that will not be repeated here. For introductory remarks to Second Corinthians, which provides the epistolary readings for Propers 4–9 After Pentecost in Year B, consult Proper 4 for Year B.

Apart from the fact that Paul calls for a complete reorientation of our outlook on life and the world, which transcends the "human point of view," or looking at life or Christ "according to the flesh" (*kata sarka*, verse 16), today's text is a classic statement of Paul's theology of the "new creation." To understand this fully, we must remember that Paul saw the Christ-event as the event that triggered a new creation. It was as if the events of Genesis 1–2 were reenacted. As he says in II Corinthians 4:6, the God who had spoken so dramatically in bringing the created order into being by saying, "Let light shine out of darkness," has once again broken through the chaos of human darkness. This time the light of life and order now shines through "the face of Christ."

We should try to grasp the implication of Paul's theology of new creation. He calls us to see the Christ-event as a new beginning, when the universe is quite literally remade, reordered, reconstituted. This is what is meant when the Christ-event is referred to as the "turn of the ages." It becomes the moment when "all things," including time, history, and all that goes to make up life and the world as we know it, are created over again. That he saw the Christ-event as having this hinge quality is seen in his opening words, "From now on . . . " (verse 16). A new age has dawned. Time has shifted its course. A new order has begun.

But new creation has not merely occurred "out there."

Christ not only served as the triggering device for the reordering of all things, he also becomes the means through which we participate in the reordering. This is what is signified by the pregnant Pauline notion of being "in Christ." It has a local connotation—we are incorporated into the risen Christ, but it is not merely a union of our person with his. It involves my stepping into this process of new creation begun with Christ, becoming a participant in this newly created order, where the old is gone, and the new has come. To be "in Christ" means that the new creation God effected in Christ is reenacted within us. So, "if any one is *in Christ,* he [or she] is a new creation" (verse 17, italics added). The reordering of the cosmos that began in Christ now begins in us.

It is in this context that we should understand Paul's various remarks (as well as other New Testament remarks) about "newness." Clearly, being part of the new creation entails personal transformation, or "newness of life" (Rom. 6:4). No longer is it a matter of outward rite but inward transformation (Gal. 6:15). What's more, it is the beginning of a process of renewal that continues as our "minds," that is our thoughts, attitudes, and overall outlook begin to be made over (Rom. 12:2). On a broad scale, what emerges is a "new humanity" (Eph. 2:15). Even our ways of conceiving the future and life in the future are oriented toward the new (Rev. 21:5).

We should also notice that "all this is from God" (verse 18). Accustomed as we are to thinking that personal transformation results from our own capacity to improve ourselves and our world, Paul issues this stern reminder that the new creation is not our own doing. God tipped the first domino. God is the Prime Mover. The initiative lay with, and lies with, God (cf. I Cor. 1:30).

But what form does this "new order" take? One in which alienation gives way to reconciliation. The essence of the new creation is the work of God in bringing humanity, indeed all things, back into covenant relationship with God. The distinguishing mark of the new creation is reconciliation—bringing together. If the old order saw the collapse of God's relationship with humanity, the new saw its restoration.

Where God and humanity were once at a standoff, through Christ we now stand together with God, even becoming God's co-workers (II Cor. 6:1). The new creation may be regarded as the fulfillment of the prophetic hope that depicts Yahweh as "doing a new thing" (Isa. 43:18-19).

None of this was, or is, possible apart from Christ (cf. Col. 1:19-20), and through Christ we are now able to become the "righteousness of God" (verse 21; cf. Rom. 1:17; 3:5, 21-26; 10:3; Phil. 3:9; also Matt. 6:33). Such a relationship becomes a state of blessedness (Rom. 4:8).

If we come to share in God's reconciling work through Christ, it is a natural corollary that we ourselves become ministers of reconciliation, extending God's reconciling love throughout the world. The new creation that God began in Christ, that was reenacted within us, is now continued through the world, through time and history—and continues until the ultimate and complete renewal of all things.

Luke 15:1-3, 11-32

Even a surface reading of the lections for today reveals their common theme, reconciliation, presented as covenant in Joshua, a theological statement in Paul, and a parable in Luke. Luke's parable of the loving father, more commonly referred to as the parable of the prodigal son, is set in a large section of teaching dominated by many of the parables found only in Luke. Most of these parables: the unjust steward, the rich man and Lazarus, the widow and the judge, and the Pharisee and the publican, are characterized by more narrative quality and more human interest than the briefer parables about seed, leaven, nets, and weeds. Especially is this true of the story before us.

As we observed last week, Luke typically offers a word of interpretation at the beginning rather than at the end of a parable. In 15:1-3 the brief interpretation is in the form of a setting for the story. The setting consists of three statements: Jesus attracts tax collectors and sinners (verse 1); Pharisees and scribes criticize his receiving and eating with such persons (verse 2); Jesus responds to his critics with a parable (verse 3). Actually, Luke offers this setting as an introduction to a trilogy of parables: the lost sheep (verses 4-7), the lost coin (verses 8-10), and the loving father (verses 11-32). The first two are very similar in length, form, content, and concluding comment about joy over the return of the penitent. However, the comment hardly fits a sheep and a coin, both of which are found, not by a return, but by the diligent search of caring owners. The return of the penitent as a theme more properly anticipates the third parable. In fact, the setting (verses 1-3) and the parable in verses 11-32 fit so naturally that the opinion to the effect that Luke inserted the other two parables seems most plausible. Certainly the lectionary has violated nothing in the omission of verses 4-10 for today's Gospel lesson.

The judgment of a few scholars that the parable in verses 11-32 was originally two parables, the younger son (verses 11-24) and the older son (verses 25-32), misses both the point of this parable and a literary feature common to many parables. The focus of this story is the father: "There was a man who had two sons." Calling this story the parable of the prodigal son moves the focal point off center. And the apparent conclusion in verse 24, found again in verse 32, does not mark out two stories, for repetition of lines is common in parables (note, for example, Matt. 25:14-30).

Without question this story was offensive to its first hearers, and the preacher should not assume that time has removed that offense. The edge of Jesus' message will remain sharp and effective if at least three radicalities in the story are not blurred. The first lies in the contrast between Jesus' behavior and that of his critics (verses 1-3). Tax collectors and sinners are not simply friendly folk who have been misunderstood. Publicans had taken jobs with the foreign government occupying Israel and made good money collecting taxes from their own people. Sinners were persons so designated because their offenses had gotten them thrown out of the synagogues. That Jesus ate with them was the clear evidence of his acceptance of them. The Pharisees, guardians of law and high standards of behavior, sensed the erosive force in not distinguishing between good people and bad people. "Birds of a feather flock together." After all, does not forgiving look very much like condoning? To cartoon Jesus' critics as villains is not only unfair; it weakens the story.

Second, notice the radical difference between the younger son's decline to the status of a Gentile, a nobody (Lev. 11:7; Isa. 65:4; 66:17), and the extravagant welcome home. It is that party which is so offensive. The older brother has a point: of course, let the penitent come home. Both Judaism and Christianity provide for the return of sinners, but to bread and water, not fatted calf; to sackcloth, not a new robe; to ashes, not jewelry; to kneeling, not dancing; to tears, not merriment. Who in the church today would have attended that party?

Finally, and perhaps most radically, the father must be presented as one who had two sons, loved two sons, went out to both (verses 20, 28), and was generous to both. The embrace of publicans and sinners does not mean a rejection of the Pharisees; the reception of sinners is not a rejection of saints. Our is a "both/and," not an "either/or" God.

Fifth Sunday of Lent

Isaiah 43:16-21; Psalm 126; Philippians 3:8-14; John 12:1-8

As the Season of Lent takes us closer to the commemoration of the death and resurrection of Jesus, the assigned texts sound different notes. The Old Testament reading and the psalm proclaim, look forward to, and pray for God's salvation of the people. The mood is joyful. The New Testament lections are not so unambiguous. The epistolary text has Paul announcing the surpassing worth of knowing Jesus Christ, affirming his faith in the resurrection, and—not without a note of warning—calling for his readers to press on with him and hold true. In the Gospel lesson we see Martha's love for her Lord, and also recognize foreshadowings of Judas' treachery and the death of Jesus.

Isaiah 43:16-21

Texts from Isaiah 40–55 provide more Old Testament readings for the lectionary than any other body of literature of comparable length. They are especially prominent during Holy Week and the Sundays just preceding, and for good reason. In addition to including the Servant Songs, the work of Second Isaiah is filled with proclamation of salvation and celebrations of the Lord's redemptive work. Christian readers have always seen the similarity of this prophet's message to the New Testament's good news.

The central message of this prophetic poet, who was active in Babylon shortly before the fall of that empire to Cyrus in 539 B.C., is that the captive exiles will be set free and the Lord will lead them home to Jerusalem. As we hear the soaring and joyful words of Second Isaiah, we must remind ourselves that they were uttered to a community not yet set

61

free, and one far from hopeful. The fact that he so often argues the case for a God both willing and able to redeem his people suggests that the opposite view was held by many of his contemporaries.

Isaiah 43:16-21 is a self-contained and coherent unit of prophetic poetry, although in the final form of the book verses 14-15 have been attached to its beginning. In terms of literary genre, the passage is a proclamation of salvation, a type well-known in Second Isaiah, and perfectly suited to his central message. The form of poetic speech is like that of Second Isaiah's prophetic predecessors in that it begins with the messenger formula ("Thus says the Lord," verse 16) and then quotes the words of God concerning a future that he will bring about. Such proclamations appear to be addressed to a people complaining or lamenting about their past or present situations, either directly to God or in an argument with the prophet. There is therefore an argumentative tone to the speech, an attempt to convince the audience that the news is good.

There is a movement in the passage from past events through the (assumed) present situation to the immediate future and on to a more distant goal. Formally, the unit consists of two distinct parts, the prophetic introduction in verses 16-17 and the speech of Yahweh in verses 18-21.

In the introduction the messenger formula is elaborated by means of relative clauses that define the Lord in terms of past actions: "who makes a way in the sea, . . . who brings forth chariot and horse . . . " (verses 16-17). The style is not unlike that of hymns of praise or doxologies. The contents refer to the heart of ancient Israel's confession of faith, the fundamental salvation event of the Exodus from Egypt. This is traditional confessional language that enables Israel to affirm not only who God is, but also who they are. For Second Isaiah, the old saving events, especially those of the Exodus, are types of the new ones to come.

The divine speech includes injunctions (verse 18), proclamations concerning the future (verses 19-21*a*), and a statement of purpose (verse 21*b*). There seems to be an abrupt shift from the recollection of the past to injunctions to forget "the former things . . . the things of old." This could be hyperbole: Even the great saving events of the past will pale into insignificance in comparison with the "new thing" the Lord will do. Or the "former things" could refer to the past troubles and complaints of the people.

In any case, the center of the divine speech is the proclamation of the "new thing" that the Lord will do, first stated generally and then more and more concretely. (The rhetorical question in verse 19 suggests the sense of dialogue with an audience.) The actual "new thing" itself is, as it were, offstage. It is the release of Israel from Babylon and their return to Jerusalem. Attention here is focused upon the miraculous transformation of the desert through which the people will travel. The imagery echoes the stories of the Exodus and the wandering in the wilderness. As Yahweh had brought them through the Red Sea, so he will bring them through the desert. As Yahweh had fed them with manna and provided water from the rock, so he will make rivers in the desert, give them drink, and even turn the wild beasts into a choir to praise the Lord.

Second Isaiah's announcements and proclamations of salvation seldom give the reasons for God's intervention. When they do it is either that Israel has paid for its sins (40:2), that the reason lies in the Lord's grace and love for a chosen people (54:8), or in order for them to be God's witnesses among the nations (42:6; 43:12). The concluding line of this passage seems consistent with that last understanding. The new saving event on behalf of the people, God says, "I formed for myself," is "that they might declare my praise" (verse 21). Thus, the new event will open up into more, for God's salvation will be made known to others in the form of songs of praise.

The scope of Second Isaiah's vision is both cosmic and eschatological. The cosmic dimensions are visible in the allusions to creation ("I formed you") and the transformation of the desert with its "wild beasts." The eschatological vision encompasses all of history under the saving will of the God who acted, acts, and will act. The future is open, open to the declaration of God's praise.

Psalm 126

Like the text from Isaiah 43, this psalm has a forward-looking orientation that befits the Lenten Season. In addition, it looks backward at the past as a means of giving confidence about the future.

As part of the collection of pilgrim psalms (Pss. 120–134), Psalm 126 would have been sung as the pilgrims moved toward Jerusalem for festival celebrations. In going on pilgrimage, the people assembled at the main town in their district. They spent the night outside in the open, to avoid any contamination or contact with uncleanness. (For example, persons became unclean if they were in the house where another person died.) Under the leadership of a pilgrim director (see Ps. 42:4), the people set out for Jerusalem in the early morning. The trip might take several days. As the people made their way to the Holy City, they sang and recited the material in Psalms 120–134.

Several things about this psalm can be applied to the Lenten Season and the Lenten pilgrimage.

1. A pilgrimage is a movement away from ordinary, everyday life to the more sacred, the more holy. For the ancient Hebrew, pilgrimage took one to the sacred city of Jerusalem and to the most sacred spot in Judaism, the temple in the sacred city. As the pilgrims moved toward Jerusalem, they were moving toward the sacred center to observe the festivals that gave meaning and direction to life. Lent, too, is a pilgrimage, a movement to the most significant, the central celebration of the Christian year.

2. The psalm, like Lent, looks backward and forward. Backward to the last festival, "when the Lord restored the fortunes of Zion" (verse 1) and forward to the new time (verse 4). Thus the psalm blends together thanksgiving for the past and requests for the future.

3. The polarity of human sentiments are found in the psalm—weeping and rejoicing. Lent is a season of weeping, but weeping in anticipation of the joy and singing to come.

4. The psalm assumes that the upcoming celebration, the holy events of the festival, will be life-changing, life-refreshing, like the transformation that comes in the desert

when rain falls (verse 4). The sense of expectation in the psalm should be the expectation of the Lenten Season.

Philippians 3:8-14

With its stress on "giving up" what is regarded as gain, and "leaving behind" a past way of life and point of view, this text clearly echoes Lenten themes. It addresses us directly as an autobiographical text depicting Paul's own experience. It is both a confession and a diary. Here we are able to see inside the mind and heart of one for whom the suffering of Christ had become life-shaping. In every respect this epistolary lection is a suitable Lenten text.

First, a word about its context. It occurs within a polemical setting, as seen by the opening words (Phil. 3:1-3). As the chapter draws to a close, Paul singles out the "enemies of the cross of Christ" (3:18-19). It is difficult to tell much about the opponents against whom these remarks are directed. From the sound of things, they are Jewish Christians who perhaps insist on keeping the laws of the Torah, especially the law of circumcision. When Paul contrasts human righteousness based on law with God's righteousness that comes in response to faith (verse 9), we hear echoes of themes played out much more fully in Romans and Galatians.

The one thing that is clear is Paul's insistence of having suffered loss. On this note today's lection begins. What is in view are the privileges implied by his pedigree sketched in the verses 5-6. If we establish our identity and find our security in such things as family background, social and religious status, and legal rectitude, Paul insists that we are trying to establish our confidence "in the flesh." In this context, he is doubtless referring to the rights and privileges he enjoyed as a circumcised Jew. In many ways, he gained much by virtue of who he was. Yet for all the advantages his position offered him, they finally became of no consequence. At one time they were gain; now he counted them as loss.

His scale of values shifted through his encounter with Christ. The superlative value now became "the surpassing worth of knowing Christ Jesus my Lord" (verse 8). We see unfolded here a spiritual consciousness turned inside out by the Christ-event. The aim of his intellectual quest is now Christ. The object of his pursuit is Christ. The existential locus in which he defines who he is and knows where he is is Christ. He reaches out to seize Christ just as a sprinter reaches forward to seize the tape. Yet he knows all the while that he seeks to possess Christ only because Christ has already possessed him (verse 12).

It may seem odd that our text still presents Paul as one who is driven to possess a goal. Was not his religious crisis caused by the mistaken notion that he could finally attain perfection through the law? Surely he should have learned the futility of religious compulsion.

But our text suggests that his pursuit of Christ differed from his pursuit of the law. For one thing, he now realizes that the righteousness in which he is involved is not his but God's (verse 9). It is not "my own"; it comes from God. It is no longer his human pursuit of God but God's pursuit of him in which he is involved. In addition, the way to the righteousness he formerly pursued was "based on law" (verse 9). It involved "legal rectitude" (verse 9, NEB). The way to the new righteousness is through faith: "the righteousness which comes from faith in Christ, given by God in response to faith" (verse 9, NEB). At the heart of his new quest was absolute trust in Christ. Even though such faith was not as reliable or predictable as law in terms of measuring progress, it was far more compelling.

We should note especially the futurity of Paul's expressed hope. What unfolds is an unrealized vision of faith. He repeatedly stresses that his quest is partial and incomplete (verses 12-13). This may be because his opponents were already claiming eschatological perfection, or even moral perfection (cf. I Cor. 4:8-9; II Tim. 2:18). Perhaps theirs was a Gnostic outlook that saw their resurrection with Christ, and thus their perfection, as already realized. In any case, the clear thrust of Paul's remarks is that his knowledge of Christ, his empowerment through the resurrection of Christ, and his participation in the resurrection of the dead still lay in the future. Indeed, that which impels him is the "prize of the upward call of God in Christ Jesus" (verse 14; cf. Heb. 3:1).

As we read these words closely, we see the nature of Paul's

exchange: it was an exchange of that which he actually possessed for that which he might finally possess, the past for the future, past certainty for future hope. And this is what is especially instructive: as we experience loss, it is usually loss of the known, of that which we own and have, whether it is our past or our possessions. As we lay all this aside for the superlative worth of Christ, it is a cardinal act of faith for what we gain is a vision that is not ever fully ours until Christ makes us fully his own in the resurrection.

John 12:1-8

The pilgrimage toward Easter has taken us almost to Passion/Palm Sunday. The Fourth Gospel prepares us for that occasion by placing immediately before Jesus' entry into Jerusalem the story of Jesus being anointed for burial.

In order properly to hear John 12:1-8 it is essential that the story here not be blended into the similar accounts in the Synoptics (Mark 14:1-9; Matt. 26:6-13; Luke 7:36-39). It is likely that all four have a common source, but they come to us bearing the clear intentions of the different writers.

The anointing of Jesus is more vividly a part of the passion narrative in this Gospel than in Matthew or Mark (In Luke, the anointing is earlier, in Galilee, and with a different message.) John makes this clear in several ways.

First, its literary context is between the raising of Lazarus (11:1-44), the event which precipitated the decision to kill Jesus (11:45-57), and the entry into Jerusalem (12:9-19), the occasion on which Jesus announced that the hour of his death had come (12:20-36).

Second, the place of the anointing is Bethany where Jesus had raised Lazarus from the dead. According to the Evangelist, Jesus knew that calling Lazarus out of the tomb meant that the Son of God would have to enter the tomb so that life would be given not to Lazarus alone but to the world. In the language of this Gospel, the Son of God would be glorified as a result of the event in Bethany (11:4; 12:23, 32-33). It is important to keep in mind that in John, Jesus' entry into Jerusalem was from Bethany, not Galilee; the crowds were already in the city and were not followers from

Galilee, and the excitement had been generated by the reports of raising Lazarus and the resultant plots on Jesus' life (11:55-57; 12:9-19). Bethany, the city of Lazarus' life, figures now in the death of Jesus.

The third signal that the anointing is a passion story is its location at Passover time (11:55; 12:1). Passover is, for this Evangelist, death time: the cleansing of the temple with its prophecy of Jesus' death is a Passover story (2:13-22); the feeding of the five thousand with its message of Jesus' life-giving death (6:52-58) is a Passover story (6:4); and, of course, Jesus died as the Passover lamb (19:31-37).

The fourth indicator that the anointing points to Jesus' death is at the banquet table itself. Not only is Lazarus there, the one whose life sets in motion the forces against Jesus, but also Judas (verse 4). This dark intruder upon this scene of life and joy in the home of a grateful family casts across the table the shadow of approaching death for Jesus.

And finally there is the statement of Jesus himself to the effect that what Mary did was for "the day of my burial" (verse 7). Not that it was Mary's intention to anoint Jesus for burial; here was an act of hospitality, love, and gratitude to Jesus. However, for many biblical writers, and for this Evangelist in particular, words and deeds have meaning beyond the intentions of those who speak and act. When Caiaphas said, "It is expedient for you that one man should die for the people" (11:50), he spoke politically, not realizing the greater truth of his words. When the Pharisees said, "Look, the world has gone after him" (12:19), they were unaware of the irony in a remark which anticipated Jesus' own words shortly thereafter: "And I, when I am lifted up from the earth, will draw all men to myself" (12:32). We speak and act in ways we think most appropriate for the occasion. We may never know, however, what lives are influenced, what differences are made because God takes a word spoken, a gift given, a hand extended, an effort expended, and gives it a life and a power far beyond the intention and expectation which prompted it. As Mark said of this act in Bethany, "Wherever the gospel is preached in the whole world, what she has done will be told in memory of her" (14:9).

Passion/Palm Sunday

Luke 19:28-40; Psalm 118:19-29; Isaiah 50:4-9a; Psalm 31:9-16;
Philippians 2:5-11; Luke 22:14–23:56 or Luke 23:1-49

In various communions the Sixth Sunday of Lent may be celebrated either as Palm Sunday, Passion Sunday, or both. In those traditions which celebrate both, the Palm Sunday lections provide the readings for the beginning processional or for an earlier "said" service of worship. The Palm Sunday Gospel text is the Lucan account of the triumphal entry into Jerusalem. The responsorial psalm, a liturgy for entrance into the temple precincts, is the same in all three years of the lectionary cycle. The Old Testament and espistolary readings, the same for either Palm or Passion Sunday, call attention to both the suffering and the triumph of God's servant. The Passion Sunday response is a painfully appropriate lament psalm of an individual. The Passion Sunday Gospel lection in its long form takes us from the Last Supper to the death of Jesus.

Luke 19:28-40

In sharp contrast to the observance of the Sunday before Easter as Passion Sunday, the celebration of this day as Palm Sunday focuses on Jesus' entry into Jerusalem as an occasion of triumph and praise. In fact, some feel the mood of victory and joy is premature, stealing its message from Easter yet to come, and hence not an appropriate way to worship prior to Good Friday and Easter. In favor of such an observance, however, is the Gospels' own record of the event as the beginning of the final days of Jesus. Traditionally, Palm Sunday services draw from all the Gospels: John contributes the palm branches (12:13), Matthew the prophecy in

69

Zechariah 9:9 (21:5), and Mark, along with Matthew and John, contributes the shouting throng (11:8-10). Luke, while following Mark 11:1-10 rather closely, tells the story his own way, providing the reader with a slightly different understanding of the occasion.

In general, it would be fair to say that Luke's account of Jesus' entry into Jerusalem is more subdued, less crowded and less noisy, than those of the other Evangelists. Notice several features of Luke's story.

First, verse 28 not only ties this event to what precedes but reminds the reader that this episode is a part of the larger narrative begun at 9:51, Jesus' journey to Jerusalem. And the account of Jesus' arrival in Jerusalem is followed by Jesus' weeping over the city and prophecy of its destruction (19:41-44). Such a context prevents the story before us from becoming autonomous, having a life of its own.

Second, Luke's record makes no mention of hosannas or branches cut from trees. Since those belonged commonly to nationalistic demonstrations and parades, perhaps Luke wants this event to carry no such implication. Jesus is called "King," to be sure (verse 38), but Luke makes it clear very soon that the term is in no sense political or military (23:2-5).

Third, and very important, the entry into Jerusalem is very much a disciple event rather than a burst of enthusiasm on the part of a large crowd surrounding Jesus, as in Matthew 21:8-10 and Mark 11:8-10. Notice: the disciples set Jesus on the colt (verse 35); the disciples spread their garments on the road (verse 36); the disciples rejoice and praise God (verse 37). That the ovation is not by a general multitude in the city for the festival (Matt. 21:9) or gathered as a result of reports about the raising of Lazarus (John 12:12) is an important detail. Christ is praised and hailed as king by his followers, says Luke, and not by the general public. And this is not the group, says Luke, which later called for Jesus' crucifixion. To be sure, Jesus' followers did not understand him or the nature of his messiahship, but neither are they persons who sing praise and scream death within the same week. Such a portrait of a fickle crowd must be drawn from accounts other than Luke's.

Fourth, the expressions of praise in Luke make no

reference to David or to Davidic images of the Messiah. "King" is used (verse 38), but as stated above, Luke does not permit that word to carry political force. Actually, the praise on this occasion (verse 38) echoes the praise in the announcement to the shepherds of the birth of Jesus (2:10, 13-14).

But even the rather modest parade offered by Luke evokes an objection by some Pharisees (verse 39). We are not told whether their objection was due to disagreement, envy, fear of political repercussions, or some other motive, and therefore honesty demands that the preacher not read into the story information unavailable to us. Nor does Jesus identify the problem the scene generates for the Pharisees; he simply states in a vivid image the clear and certain appropriateness of his disciples' praise. "If these were silent, the very stones would cry out" (verse 40) is a statement conveying one or more of several messages: Some things simply must be said; the disciples are expressing ultimate truth; truth cannot be silenced; God will provide a witness though every mouth be stopped; opposition to Christian witness cannot succeed. With all these interpretations of the expressions Luke would agree.

And so Jesus comes to *the* city: the city where God dwells (Ps. 84:1); the city where all go to worship (Ps. 122); the city where all nations shall gather (Isa. 2:1-5). Here Jesus will die, but in this city his disciples will tarry, because from Jerusalem the gospel will be carried to the nations (Luke 24:47; Acts 1:4-8).

Psalm 118:19-29

Portions of this psalm are used as the psalm reading for Easter (see pages 145-46). The entire psalm was probably composed initially for use in a thanksgiving service when the Jerusalemite king returned from a victory in battle and participated in a service of thanksgiving in the temple.

The selection and association of this psalm and these verses for Palm Sunday, which occurred just before Passover, are based on several considerations. (1) It contains the words said to have been sung as Jesus rode into Jerusalem (verse 26). (2) The psalm was used in the Passover celebrations of Jesus' day. Psalms 113–118, the so-called Egyptian Hallel, were sung by the Levites in the temple as the Passover lambs were slaughtered in the afternoon before the Passover meal. The same psalms were again sung in the homes as part of the Passover Seder or service in conjunction with eating the Passover meal. (3) The psalm celebrates the victorious entry of a royal figure which may be seen as paralleling Jesus' entry into the city. (4) The theme of the psalm, which moves from depicting the ruler as oppressed, attacked, and humiliated to being triumphant, victorious, and celebrated, parallels the fundamental shape of New Testament Christology.

Verses 14-24 are analyzed in the treatment of the psalm in the Easter lection and will not be discussed here. Verse 25 is a congregational or priestly prayer appealing to God for divine favor (see Matt. 21:9). The next verses constitute some of the most difficult textual problems in the Old Testament. Verse 27*b* defies a fully intelligible translation. Compare the RSV ("Bind the festal procession with branches . . .") with the NEB ("the ordered line of pilgrims . . ."). The following is one suggested interpretation. The priests or a choir blesses the one who has entered the sanctuary (verse 26). A theological affirmation or confession is made in 27*a*. (The opening portion reads "Yahweh is El.") The second half of the verse seems to refer to the animals, brought for the sacrifice and celebration, being tied to the altar. The sacrificial meal with its attendant celebration would have climaxed the festive occasion. Verse 28 is the prayer of the ruler and verse 29 is an admonition or call to thanksgiving addressed to the community.

If one applies Psalm 118 to Jesus' entry into Jerusalem, it must be remembered that for the original supplicant, the valley of anguish lay in the past, on the fields of war; for Jesus the valley lay ahead, within the walls of Jerusalem.

Isaiah 50:4-9*a*

The Servant Songs of Second Isaiah take us from Passion Sunday to Good Friday. This is the third of the songs; the first

(Isa. 42:1-9) and second (Isa. 49:1-7) are read on Monday and Tuesday of Holy Week. This one is repeated on Wednesday, and the fourth (Isa. 52:13–53:12), the song of the suffering servant, is the Old Testament reading for Good Friday. Read in the context of Christian worship on these occasions, the texts help interpret for us the life and death of Jesus, just as they did for the earliest church.

The text, of course, did not arise in the church, but in ancient Israel. Although there has been some debate on the point, it is generally accepted that the Servant Songs come from the same figure responsible for their literary context, Isaiah 40–55. That dates this as well as the other poems to a time immediately before the end of the Babylonian Exile in 538 B.C. Second Isaiah, who almost certainly was one of the exiles, announced the good news of release and return to Jerusalem. The prophet's understanding of suffering as part of the servant's role came in important ways from the experience of Israel in Exile.

Who was Second Isaiah's servant of the Lord? No convincing consensus has emerged on the question, and answers vary to a great extent, depending upon which of the songs one emphasizes. If Isaiah 50:4-9 is viewed alone, then an individual rather than a corporate interpretation suggests itself. The text is in the first person singular, as if the prophet were speaking, and the images are personal and physical. Notice the references to the parts of the body: "tongue" and "ear" (verses 4-5), "back," "cheeks," "beard," and "face" (verses 6-7). But a specific individual role is indicated by the references to hearing and speaking, that of the prophet. This is not to conclude that the servant was necessarily a particular prophet—either Second Isaiah himself, one of his contemporaries, or a prophet from the past such as Jeremiah. It indicates, however, that among the roles of the servant was that of the prophet, namely, the hearing and communicating of the word of God.

There are two main parts to the song, verses 4-6 and 7-9. In both of them an individual speaks, at first reflecting the language of the individual lament psalm, such as the responsorial psalm for this text (Psalm 31:9-16). Verses 4-5 allude to the prophetic vocation and reception of revelation.

There are close parallels to some of the so-called confessions of Jeremiah, which also reflect the individual lament psalms. Both the servant and Jeremiah have suffered because of faithfulness to their callings (Jer. 20:7-16). The second part of the song becomes an affirmation of confidence that borrows language and ideas from the Israelite law court.

Several expressions in the poem call for some explanation. The Hebrew word translated "those who are taught" (verse 4) is rare and is best understood as "disciples" (see Isa. 8:16), indicating faithfulness to the teacher and to what is taught. The imagery of verse 6 suggests violent and hostile opposition to the servant, endured without complaint or reaction. Pulling out the beard was a particularly humiliating treatment (II Sam. 10:4; Neh. 13:25). In verse 8 the speaker issues a formal summons of an adversary to a lawsuit, in which he expects the Lord to be a trustworthy judge who will not find him guilty.

The passage has a distinctly autobiographical tone and content. It moves from allusions to the vocation of the servant as a disciple (verse 4), through his faithful execution of his duty (verse 5), gives an account of his patient endurance of suffering (verse 6), and then affirms his confidence that God will in the end vindicate him (verses 7-8). The Lord God is with him to help, making him resolute (verse 7) and enabling him to contend against his adversaries. His confidence is not in his own strength, but in the Lord who helps.

Psalm 31:9-16

The misery and suffering that flow through Psalm 31 make it a fitting piece for Passiontide. Although only verses 9-16 are set aside for this lection, one needs to see the complex structure of the whole in order to place these verses in perspective. The following is an outline of the components in the composition: opening address and appeal (1-2), statement of confidence (3-6), anticipatory thanksgiving (7-8), description of the distress and trouble (9-13), plea for help interspersed with statements of confidence (14-18), statement of confidence (19-20), blessing of God (verse 21), thanksgiving (verse 22), and admonition to a human audience (23-24). Only verses 21 and 23-24 are addressed to a human audience; the remainder of the psalm is prayer addressed to God. Thus the psalm is similar to other laments in that laments are fundamentally human speech addressed to the Divine. The optimism and confidence manifest throughout this psalm indicate that the worshiper had faith in receiving a favorable response to his plea from the Divine or that a favorable divine response had already been received (though note the reference to having been heard in verse 22).

The similarity between verse 5a—"Into thy hand I commit my spirit"—and Jesus' cry from the cross (Luke 23:46) has helped anchor this psalm to the passion of Jesus. The psalm and its contents also have many linguistic parallels to the Book of Jeremiah (in which the prophet frequently laments his condition) and the book of Lamentations, both of which come out of conditions of suffering and duress.

The lection includes the worshiper's description of distress, the person's tale of trouble (verses 9-13), and part of the plea for help (verses 14-16). If the terms of the lament are taken literally, then the worshiper is suffering from physical illness and social ostracism. Bodily illness and approaching death (verses 9-10) and harsh treatment by neighbors and friends make the worshiper feel like someone who is already dead and forgotten (verses 11-12). Social opponents and gossip mongers suggest that enmity and persecution are everywhere (verses 13, 15). If the expressions of personal distress and anguish are merely metaphorical, they, at least, must have been intended to congeal and shape the worshipers' sense of alienation.

Physical torment, in verses 9-10, is depicted in terms of the erosion and failure of the body. Over against the nouns denoting physical factors—eye, soul, body, strength, bones—are those denoting psychic factors—distress, grief, sorrow, sighing, misery. Along with such nouns march a string of verbs, all negative in their connotation—wasted, spent, fails, waste away. The person experiences the body (and thus life and years) as degenerating. What should be a source of joy and happiness has become a spring of pain and misery.

The sense of physical suffering is conjoined with the feeling of social alienation in verses 11-13. Note the terms referring to "those out there" who have ostracized the person—adversaries, neighbors, acquaintances, faces in the street, enemies, and persecutors. All are said to hold the person in scorn, ridicule, or dread. Adversaries, one would expect them to treat you badly. Neighbors and acquaintances, one would hope for sympathy but your sickness may make you a burden and a drag. Even those unacquainted with the sufferer—as adversaries and friends would be—even the bypassers on the street are horrified. On every hand, there is terror. Such a depiction of human life may sound a bit paranoid, and may be. The minister ought to struggle with how sermons can be preached that take seriously a person's feeling of being overwhelmed by opponents, misunderstood and neglected by family, shunned by the healthy and the well-off. Perhaps the Psalms allowed worshipers in ancient Israel the occasion to get it off their chests even if the depiction produced a picture with image and reality distorted. Perhaps, at the same time, such expressions aided people to live in a world where altruism is the exception, not the expected.

The plea for help that begins in verse 14 contains many elements of confidence, many statements that are God and life affirming. (The lection omits the negative wishes of verses 17-18 with their desire to see opponents Sheol-bound and put to shame. Such expressions of vengeance demonstrate that even the worshiper was not altruistic!) The plea affirms the worshiper's willingness to place the ultimate destiny of life in the Deity's hands and thus reiterates the theme "into thy hands I commit my spirit."

Philippians 2:5-11

Since this is the well-established epistolary lection for the Sixth Sunday of Lent, whether observed as Passion or Palm Sunday, the reader may wish to consult our remarks in Years A and B. Also, semicontinuous readings from Philippians occur in Propers 20–23 of Year A, and Philippians 2:1-13 is the epistolary text for Proper 21.

On the eve of Holy Week, the part of the passage that seizes us is verse 8: "[He] became obedient unto death, even death on a cross." This surely sets the tone for the intense observance of Christ's Passion that is to follow. Already we hear themes that will be played and replayed as we approach Good Friday and Easter.

In dealing with today's lections, we face an embarrassment of riches. The Gospel texts themselves are quite lengthy and will be difficult to appropriate within the service in any case. The problem is compounded by the choice of Philippians 2:5-11 as the epistolary lection, since it is without doubt one of the most influential texts in Christian history and literally packed with pregnant phrases and homiletical possibilities.

Should it become the basis for the homily, we should recognize that even in its compact form it rehearses the Christ drama from preexistence to heavenly exaltation. It begins the story of Christ with Christ "in the form of God" and concludes with Christ exalted to God's right hand.

Scholars have long noted its rhythmical structure and for this reason, among others, it is believed to be an early Christian hymn unfolding the drama of Christ's descent to earth and ascent to heaven. It has been suggested that the hymn unfolds in six stanzas, each unfolding a different stage in the Christ drama. The following arrangement uses the text of the Jerusalem Bible:

Stanza I—The Preexistent Christ

(6) His state was divine,
    yet he did not cling
    to his equality with God

Stanza II—Christ Becoming a Human Slave

(7) but emptied himself
    to assume the condition of a slave,
    and became as men are;

Stanza III—Christ's Humiliating Death

    and being as all men are,
(8) he was humbler yet,
    even to accepting death,
    death on a cross.

Stanza IV—God's Exaltation of Christ

(9) But God raised him high
    and gave him the name
    which is above all other names

Stanza V—Universal Recognition of Christ

(10) so that *all beings*
     in the heavens, on earth and in the underworld,
     should bend the knee at the name of Jesus

Stanza VI—Universal Confession of Christ as Lord

(11) and that every tongue should acclaim
     Jesus Christ as Lord,
     to the glory of God the Father.

There is some dispute about whether the hymn should be arranged in six stanzas, as above, or in four stanzas. In either case, there is a clear break at verse 9, and at the very least we can conceive of two parts, the one (verses 6-8) relating Christ's descent from heaven, the other (verses 9-11) relating his ascent to heaven.

Stanza I—"Was in the form of God" attributes to him a divine status that was his from the beginning (John 1:1-16; 17:5; Col. 1:15-20; Heb. 1:3). That "he did not cling to his equality with God" (JB) is a highly controversial phrase that probably implies a level of status fully comparable to that of God.

Stanza II—Becoming human required Christ's self-emptying, or literally making himself nothing (cf. II Cor. 8:9). Specifically, it meant entering human form as a servant (Gal. 4:1; Col. 3:22-23; cf. Matt. 20:28). The language doubtless recalls the Servant Songs of Isaiah (52:13–53:12; 42:1). His identity with humanity was complete (Rom. 8:3; Gal. 4:4; Heb. 2:17).

Stanza III—Here we have depicted yet another step downward. Entering human existence was one form of humiliation. It was an even deeper level of humiliation to be subjected to crucifixion. That he "accepted" death may recall Gethsemane (Matt. 26:39-46). In any case, his acceptance constituted full obedience (Rom. 5:19; Heb. 5:8; 12:2).

Stanza IV—At the very nadir of humiliation—the cross— God turned the tables of history and exalted Christ by raising him from the dead. Even though he was humbled, he became exalted (Matt. 23:12, John 10:17; Eph. 1:20-23). Here resurrection and exalted are seen as one "exaltation." In his exalted status, he received the name "Lord" (Acts 2:21; 3:16), a title far surpassing that of any other heavenly being, including the angels (Eph. 1:21; Heb. 1:4; I Pet. 3:22).

Stanza V—In his exalted position, Christ is recognized as Lord by the whole cosmos, here conceived as having three tiers—heaven, earth, and underworld (cf. Isa. 45:23; Rom. 14:11; Rev. 5:3, 13).

Stanza VI—In this final stanza recognition gives way to confession. Finally, all the hosts of heaven acknowledge the basic Christian confession: Jesus Christ is Lord (Rom. 1:4; 10:9; I Cor. 12:3; Col. 2:6).

In this early Christian hymn, we are confronted with the dual focus of the Christ-story—humiliation and death along with exaltation and life. As such, it is a text that propels us toward Easter but also through Good Friday. It embodies the essential paradox of Christian faith—exaltation through humiliation.

Luke 22:14–23:56 *or* Luke 23:1-49

The New Common Lectionary honors the two traditions for observing the Sunday before Easter as Passion Sunday and as Palm Sunday. The Gospel lections have been selected in an effort to be appropriate to those two traditions and the comments given for this (Passion) and the next (Palm) services have the two emphases in mind.

For the observance of Passion Sunday, the preacher has a choice between the longer narrative (Luke 22:14–23:56) or a segment of that narrative (23:1-49). Even this briefer selection may seem prohibitively long for a sermon, not to mention the entire narrative. Of course, the preacher is free to focus upon only a portion of the story or to base the message primarily on the Epistle or Old Testament lections. However, since passion and resurrection form the center of the Christian proclamation, and since about one-third of the Gospel records concerns the events and teachings of the final days of Jesus' life, the minister is encouraged to use as fully as possible the passion narrative, even if the sermon contains little more than the recitation of the Evangelist's story.

Luke 22:14–23:56 opens with the Last Supper and concludes with the burial of Jesus. Since the narrative is Luke's, it is important that the preacher not presume to tell "what happened" by a general blending of all four Gospels but let the church hear and understand the story as Luke tells it. While the passion narrative is remarkably the same in all the Gospels, indicating how early this material became a sacred tradition, still each Evangelist made certain emphases appropriate to the overall purpose and understanding of the event of Jesus Christ. The following is a broad outline of the lection with notes pointing out Lukan accents:

The Last Supper—22:14-20. While Matthew and Mark introduce early the subject of betrayal, Luke delays it, so primary attention is on the Passover and the institution of the Lord's Supper. The preacher needs to decide whether verses 19*b*-20 are part of the text. Without it, the order of cup and then bread recalls I Corinthians 10:16.

Farewell Instruction—22:21-38. The announcement of approaching death and what the followers are to do at that time and afterward provides a dramatic and sobering context for Jesus' words. Notice Luke places here the dispute about greatness, found earlier in Matthew (20:25-28) and Mark (10:42-45). Luke shows his customary respect for Peter's leadership, even in Jesus' prophecy of denial. The enigmatic saying about swords dramatizes the critical nature of the times but does not condone violence (verse 51).

At the Mount of Olives—22:39-46. In this familiar place (verses 39-46) called Gethsemane by Matthew and Mark, Jesus prays alone, not with Peter, James, and John. Even with heaven's help, the agony is extreme.

Jesus Taken Captive—22:47-53. The question of use of the sword is asked and Jesus answers with a word and with healing.

The Hearings and Trials—22:54–23:16. Jesus is taken that night to the home of the high priest, and in the morning to the council. (Notice much of this section is devoted to Peter's denial. Luke adds a moving line in verse 61.) On several matters Luke is very emphatic: the council determined Jesus' death; Pilate never believed the threefold charge against Jesus (23:2); neither did Herod Antipas find Jesus deserving of death (only Luke includes Herod); at the hands of the Jews Jesus was beaten and mocked (22:63-65), but not by Pilate's soldiers (as in Matt. 27:27-31; Mark 15:16-20).

The Sentencing—23:17-25. After Pilate's efforts to release Jesus failed, he delivered Jesus "up to their will" (verse 25), not "to be crucified."

The Road to Golgotha—23:26-32. Characteristically, women are present and Luke's Jesus ministers to them.

The Crucifixion—23:33-43. Lukan themes of forgiveness and ministering to the penitent sinner are present to the last.

The Death—23:44-49. At his death Jesus is again declared innocent by Rome (verse 47). Luke's church and state have no quarrel, and Israel's crime against Jesus was in ignorance (verse 34; Acts 3:17).

The Burial—23:50-56. The women of Galilee wait to prepare the body because it is the sabbath. From birth to death, Jesus' story is always, says Luke, according to the Scriptures.

Were the preacher to choose to use the shorter passage (23:1-49), the same procedure could be followed but with more detailed attention to events from the appearance before Pilate until the death on the cross. Of special importance in this section is Luke's repeated insistence to Theophilus, his reader (1:1-4), that the government is not anti-church nor is the church anti-government. We do not know if Luke is reflecting the condition of his time or trying to create a better church-state climate.

Monday in Holy Week

Isaiah 42:1-9; Psalm 36:5-10; Hebrews 9:11-15; John 12:1-11

The mood of the texts for this day is one of hope and celebration, already beginning to look beyond the death of Jesus. There are particularly strong connections between the Old Testament text and the reading from Hebrews, for both expect a covenant that will bring salvation to all peoples. The psalm is a song of praise to God for his steadfast love. The tone and message of the Gospel lection are mixed, from a celebration with Martha and Mary, to grumbling by Judas, to a foreshadowing of the death of Jesus, to a foreshadowing of his resurrection.

Isaiah 42:1-9

This reading includes the first of the Servant Songs, and more. There are two originally independent units, the song itself in verses 1-4 and a distinct prophetic speech in verses 5-9. Both stem from Second Isaiah shortly before the end of the Exile in 538 B.C. This literary juxtaposition of the two units addresses one of the perennial problems in the interpretation of the Servant Songs, namely, the identity of the servant. While the answer to that question is unclear within the song, the following verses interpret the servant as the people of Israel (verses 6-7). At the same time, the poetic description of the servant's call and role becomes an interpretation of the experience of Israel in and beyond the Babylonian Exile.

The Servant Song, 42:1-4, has the form of a public proclamation in which the speaker is the Lord, introducing the servant to an unspecified audience. The proclamation has the force of ordination, indicating first that God has chosen this particular one, and second, giving the purpose for which he has been chosen. Thus the form as well as the contents make it explicit that the servant's role is an extension of—one could say metaphorically, incarnation of—the divine intention. What the servant does and how he accomplishes it have the divine blessing and will accomplish God's purposes.

The only reason given for the election of this servant is God's love: "in whom my soul delights" (verse 1). The Hebrew word for "soul" here refers simply to the self, so NEB accurately translates, "in whom I delight." The ordination with the Spirit of God parallels the understanding of the selection of kings and other leaders as well as the empowerment of prophets.

The central term in the song is "justice" (verses 1, 3, 4). The understanding of "justice" in ancient Israel must begin with the law court, but not end there. It refers to the establishment of the right, including what we would call procedural justice (due process), as well as what we would call distributive justice—the equitable distribution of rights, resources, and responsibilities. To establish justice was to maintain balance and to correct deviations from fairness, sometimes in the form of retribution. Not only prophets but also the legal traditions were particularly concerned about the protection of the rights—the justice due—the weak and the poor. Underlying procedural and distributive justice for Israel was the substance of this justice, known and maintained in the covenant. Justice among human beings was based upon the conviction that the God of Israel was just and intended for his justice to be reflected in the world.

Another key term for understanding the role of the servant is "law" (verse 4), the traditional translation of the Hebrew *torah*. The concept was deeply ingrained in Israel's view of its relationship to its God. In one sense it is the instruction in covenant responsibilities given by the priests. Thus the NEB reads here "teaching." Eventually it came to mean the whole body of divine revelation, embodied in the first five books of the Bible.

Especially important here are the extent and manner of the promulgation of justice and law, which promulgation was the servant's role. Its extent is to be universal: "to the nations" (verse 1), "in the earth" (verse 4). Justice and law, which were to characterize the relationships between Israel and her God and among Israelites, are now proclaimed to all. As remarkable as the extent is the manner by which this will be accomplished. The text presents this point only indirectly. Not by force of arms or by power, but by gentleness, concern (verses 2-3), and persistence to the completion of the task (verse 4).

Verses 5-9 are not simply an interpretation of the servant as the people of Israel, but a summary of the message of the prophet. Following the introductory messenger formula ("Thus says God, the Lord") is a divine speech to Israel. God identifies himself as creator of the earth and all life in it (verse 5), not to be compared with images (verse 8). Next God affirms the election and, implicitly, the redemption of Israel (verse 6a), and then proclaims the purpose for which he chose and redeemed Israel, namely, to be "a covenant to the people, a light to the nations," and to set the prisoners free (verses 6b-7). Israel's role thus parallels that of the servant: to mediate God's justice to the world.

With such powerful theological texts as this, it is easy to become carried away with the general and the abstract. That would be to miss the point. Both in its ancient Israelite and its early Christian contexts, the force of the text is its specific and concrete focus. God chooses particular human beings or particular peoples to carry out his will. While the text has an unmistakable eschatological direction, it also has in view the establishment of God's will for justice in the midst of concrete human realities and conditions, including all forms of blindness and prisons of all kinds. Moreover, God's purposes are not fulfilled until all the redeemed see themselves as "a covenant to the people, a light to the nations."

Psalm 36:5-10

The first two sections of this lament differ radically from each other. The first, verses 1-4, describes the wicked in human to human speech. (Verse 1 has probably suffered from textual corruption; the opening line makes little sense in Hebrew.) The character and activity of the wicked are described in several ways: life is lived as if it were self-explanatory without reference to the Deity (verse 1*b*); self-deceit and self-flattery have convinced the wicked of their self-security (verse 2); their words (and actions) are the source of mischief and deceit, threats, denunciations, and accusations, probably because they wish to force their world to march to their tune (verse 3); and even in the private confines of the house while waiting for sleep to come, evil machination and plotting are present setting the course for next day's behavior (verse 4).

Over against this first section stands the second, verses 5-9, which comprises the bulk of the present lection, verses 5-10. The tone, the content, and addresses have all shifted. Verses 5-9 are hymnic praise, addressed directly to the Diety, spoken in worship perhaps by the one making the requests and pleas in verse 11 (but note the "we" in verse 9).

The hymn praises God for steadfast love and righteousness—divine fidelity or faithfulness and equity we might say. Unlike the wicked, God is consistent and equitable and loving.

Verses 5 and 6 compare the divine attributes to natural phenomena. The heavens and the clouds, the mountains of God (or "lofty mountains" if we take the word God as the means of expressing a superlative), and the great deep are ways of saying that they reach everywhere. The great deep lay underneath the earth and the base of the mountains extended into the deep (see Jon. 2:5-6). The same inclusiveness is denoted in the expression "man and beast thou savest."

The security of refuge and the abundance of sacrificial celebrations is extolled in verses 7-9. In this psalm they may be employed metaphorically but their imagery is that of the temple service. (Jesus' cleansing of the temple, by the way, was on Monday of Holy Week, according to Mark 11:15-19.)

The plea or request in verse 10 asks that God's steadfast love continue but hedges that continuity by referring to "those who know thee" and the "upright of heart." There is, in other words, a conditionality with regard to God's love.

Hebrews 9:11-15

The central image through which Hebrews interprets the work of Christ is that of high priest (2:17; 3:1; 4:14; 5:5, 10; 6:20; 7:26; 8:1; 10:21). But it was not as if he were a high priest who simply outperformed the Levitical high priests, doing his work better, or longer, or more efficiently. It was that he had been raised from the dead, and "passed through the heavens" (4:14) to receive an exalted position with God (7:26).

This is the overarching image unfolded in Hebrews: the risen Christ, exalted to the heavens, marching triumphantly into God's Holy Place, the heavenly sanctuary. There he performs the priestly rites. Lest we think that this is an ordinary sanctuary, we are reminded that Christ carries out his high priestly service in a "greater and more perfect tent (not made with hands)" (verse 11; cf. 8:2; 9:24). What happens in this heavenly service far surpasses anything that ever occurred "below," in the earthly tabernacle.

What was different? The sacrifices offered below were animals. The Levitical priests dealt with "the blood of goats and bulls and with the ashes of a heifer" (verse 13; 9:19; 10:1-4; cf. Num. 19:2-10). Such animal sacrifices were offered as purification rites. In this way, the worshiper obtained ritual purity or "purification of the flesh" (verse 13). Hebrews sees such sacrifices as inherently deficient. The very fact that they had to be offered repeatedly showed that they were inadequate (10:1-4). But they were most seriously deficient because they failed to deal adequately with the conscience of the one who made the offering. Purification of the flesh is one thing, purification of the conscience quite another.

What was needed was a way for the human conscience to be genuinely and truly forgiven, in other words, "eternal redemption" (verse 12). And this is what was achieved by the sacrifice of Christ, "who through the eternal Spirit offered himself without blemish to God" (verse 14). Unlike the animal sacrifices offered by the Levitical priests, this was a *human* sacrifice. It was a sacrifice "without blemish" (I Pet. 1:19). Not only was it an unblemished life, but a sacrifice willingly made by Christ himself: He "offered himself" (verse 14; 9:25; John 10:18). In a word, it was a self-sacrifice.

But why does the sacrifice of Christ resolve the problem of human sin any better than animal sacrifices? It may be human instead of animal, unblemished instead of blemished, willingly made instead of forced, but it addresses the heart instead of the flesh because it is made not only on behalf of us but instead of us (cf. Rom. 3:24-25; 5:9; I John 1:7). Our text also reminds us that Christ offered himself "through the eternal Spirit" (verse 14). The human will can only be brought into the service of the living God as it is prompted by the Spirit of God. Through Christ's self-offering we see the ultimate conquest of the human will as it lives in response to the call of God. It is at this level that our consciences can become purified "from dead works to serve the living God" (verse 14).

Because Christ is officiating in the heavenly sanctuary, having become our high priest through the sacrifice of himself, he now serves as "mediator of a new covenant" (verse 15; 8:6-10; 10:29; 12:24; 13:20; also I Tim. 2:5; Gal. 3:19). It is new not only because it invites us into a lasting relationship with God, but also because it makes our entry into the heavenly sanctuary possible. It is also new in the sense that Jeremiah foresees the future covenant between Yahweh and Israel (31:31-34; cf. Heb. 8:6-12). It envisions a time when the law of God is written on the heart, when sins are finally and fully forgiven.

As a text for Holy Week, today's epistolary lection confronts us squarely with the Christ who willingly offered himself for the sins of humanity. As we reflect on this self-sacrifice that was made in the service of the living God, we are urged to consider the nature of our own service and how it is made possible through the sacrifice of Christ. Our text also speaks of promise, reassuring us that "those who are called [will] receive the promised eternal inheritance" (verse 15).

John 12:1-11

The Gospel of John provides the lections for Monday, Tuesday, and Wednesday of Holy Week. Therefore, those who have services these three days may not choose to preach from John 12:1-8 on the Fifth Sunday of Lent, knowing that this text will reappear within a matter of days. The reader is referred to the commentary on those verses for use here.

However, it is important to note that for today the lection includes verses 9-11. Attention to this portion will be especially important if one is treating John 12–13 as an extended narrative during these three days. Verses 9-11 provide four observations vital for this Evangelist's story of Jesus:

1. The crowd that gathers here and is present for Jesus' entry into Jerusalem (12:12-19) is from Judea, not Galilee as in the Synoptics.

2. The crowd has gathered because of the report that Jesus raised Lazarus.

3. The decision to destroy Jesus is precipitated by the raising of Lazarus (12:10-11; 11:45-57). The Synoptics, which do not have the Lazarus story, link the plot against Jesus to the cleansing of the temple and the multitude's favorable response to Jesus (Mark 11:15-19; Matt. 21:12-17; Luke 19:45-48). In John, the irony is clear: it is for giving life that Jesus is to be put to death.

4. Lazarus, whose being alive was persuasive witness to the power of Jesus, is included in the death plot. In this Gospel, and in the experience of many, those who receive Jesus' blessing must bear the brunt of the world's wrath. (See also 5:1-14; 9:1-34.)

Tuesday in Holy Week

Isaiah 49:1-7; Psalm 71:1-12; I Corinthians 1:18-31; John 12:20-36

The readings for today take us a step closer to the commemoration of the crucifixion of Jesus, enabling us to reflect seriously upon the last days of his life and upon God's intentions through his life and death. The Old Testament lection, the second Servant Song of Second Isaiah, in this liturgical context is seen to parallel the experience of Jesus: empowered by God, challenged by others, yet expressing confidence in God. The psalm is a prayer for help as well as an expression of confidence, picking up the Old Testament references to selection before birth and to the mouth of the one who responds to God's call. The passage from First Corinthians is an interpretation of the cross as human foolishness but divine wisdom, human weakness but divine strength. The Gospel lesson anticipates the cross as God's glorification of Jesus and includes calls for faith in the one to be crucified.

Isaiah 49:1-7

The reading consists of the second Servant Song (49:1-6) plus one additional verse (49:7) that actually begins a new and distinct unit. In the Book of Isaiah as a whole and Deutero-Isaiah in particular, this passage begins a distinct section of material. Most of the speeches in Isaiah 40–48 are addressed quite explicitly to the Israelites in Babylonian Exile, while those in chapters 49–55 seem directed more to Jerusalem and the Israelites there. In any case, the passage comes from the unnamed prophet in Babylon ca. 539 B.C., immediately before the end of the Exile.

Like the third Servant Song (Isa. 50:4-9) and unlike the first and fourth (Isa. 42:1-9; 52:13–53:12), this one is presented as a speech by the servant himself. The address to the "coast-lands" and the "peoples from afar"—better, "peoples far away" (NEB)—is international in scope, already hinting at the message of the poem. Although it is the servant who speaks, in two instances he is heard to quote the words of Yahweh. The substance of the address concerns the servant's call, his response to it, and his mission.

The elements of the poem are easily recognizable on the basis of the shifts in speaker, from the servant's own addresses to his quotations of the Lord. After calling for attention (verse 1*a*), he gives an account of his vocation (verses 1*b*-3). Then the servant reports his frustration and sense of failure, which was overcome by his confidence that his life and work were grounded in the Lord (verse 4). Then an elaborate messenger formula (verse 5) introduces a divine speech in which the Lord spells out the servant's mission.

The question of the identity of the servant as the nation would appear to be solved in verse 3 ("my servant, Israel"), until one reads in verse 6 that the servant has a mission *to* Israel. This has led some who favor a collective interpretation to see the servant as a group within Israel, or even an ideal Israel.

The servant's vocation certainly is identified here with the prophetic role in ancient Israel, and the language is especially dependant upon Jeremiah. Like that prophet (Jer. 1:5), the servant was called "from the womb," that is, God designated him even before he was born, choosing him by naming him (cf. Isa. 43:1). His "mouth" in particular was prepared for the task ahead. Like Jeremiah, he had doubts and frustrations (verse 4; cf. Jer. 20:7-11). As in the prophet's accounts of their calls, the servant goes on to report the specific task for which he was called.

It is not immediately obvious how the account of the servant's task is related to the prophetic vocation. The duties are two: (1) The Lord expects the servant to bring Israel back to him (verses 5*a*, 6*a*). This return is quite specific and concrete, referring to the return of the exiles from Babylon and the restoration of the people on their land, and especially in the Holy City, Jerusalem. (2) The servant, as the call to the nations hinted at the beginning, is to be "a light to the nations" in order that God's salvation may "reach to the end of the earth" (verse 6b). Thus the restoration of Israel is no end in itself, but a step on the way toward the inclusion of all peoples in the reign of God. The completion of that task is prophetic in so far as it entails the proclamation of the word of God. That word, as the prophets have believed all along, has the power to change the future. It is one of the ways that God intervenes in human affairs.

Psalm 71:1-12

Psalm 71, a lament and supplication in time of trouble, is characterized by a high level of trust and confidence. The trouble appears to have been old age as verses 9 and 18 suggest. The pleas in these two verses—not to be forsaken— speak of "the time of old age" and "old age and gray hairs." Thus we can imagine this psalm initially being used by the elderly who still hoped to be revived and reinvigorated in spite of old age (see verse 20) and who had confidence that there was still a future and still a time of life ahead (note the vows regarding the future in verses 14-16, 22-24).

This psalm may have originally been written for use by Judean kings rather than for just average people. The fact that the psalm speaks of God having taken the person from the womb of the mother could imply that the person occupied some position of prominence (see Jer. 1:5). The average person probably would not have made such a claim.

The placement of Psalm 71 to precede 72 may not be purely accidental. Psalm 72 is one of only two psalms (see Ps. 127) associated with Solomon who became king in his father's old age (see I Kings 1), when David, like the "psalmist" in Psalm 71 was facing death and the end of life. Thus the two psalms could be seen as speaking of David (Ps. 71) and Solomon (Ps. 72).

The passage selected for this lection contains an opening address to the Deity (verse 1), an appeal pleading for help (verses 2-4), a statement of the worshiper's confidence in God (verses 5-8), a description of the distress (verses 9-11), and a second appeal (verse 12).

We can examine the salient features of this psalm in terms of (1) the nature of the distress, (2) the worshiper's statements of confidence, and (3) the nature of the help requested from God.

1. The troubles undergone by the worshiper are related primarily to the opposition of enemies. The gallery of opponents is described as "the wicked," "the unjust and cruel man," and "enemies" who seek the worshiper's life. (Reference is made to accusers in verse 13.) The bitterest opponents appear to be those enemies who consider the person forsaken by God and thus without help and support (verses 10-11). One might assume that the person had some malady or problem which was taken as the sign that God had forsaken or was no longer supporting the one praying.

2. This psalm is permeated by a strong sense of trust and confidence. As the person looks back to the past, there is the affirmation that God has been his/her trust from youth. God is even seen as the one who like a midwife took him/her from the mother's womb (verse 6). Looking to the future, the psalmist prays that the trust in and association with God which was begun as a child will continue into the days of old age and gray hairs (verses 9, 18). A common theme throughout the psalm is that of God as refuge. The worshiper can confess that God is a refuge and at the same time pray that God will be a refuge (compare verses 1 and 7 with verse 3). The concept of a refuge is further explicated with reference to God as a strong fortress and a rock—all expressive of both stability and protection.

An interesting feature of the psalm's statements of confidence is the reference to the special role the person has for making known or proclaiming God not only to the contemporaries of the day but also to generations yet to come (verses 7-8, 18). This would suggest that this psalm was not originally composed for use by an ordinary Israelite but was probably written for use by the king who had a special responsibility for proclaiming the nation's God.

3. The petitions and appeals made to God for help primarily focus on the requests that God not forsake the worshiper (verses 9-10) or let the person be put to shame (verse 1). Shame plays both a positive and a negative function

in the psalm. The worshiper asks to be preserved from shame (verse 1) and at the same time prays that the accusers be put to shame and consumed (verse 13). Shame, of course, would have involved being put into a humiliating situation and at the same time being made to accept the identity that the situation imposed.

This psalm can be exegeted and preached in the context of Holy Week, since it expresses many of the factors that we think of in terms of Jesus' suffering: the opposition of enemies who doubt that God is his supporter, the trust and confidence of the worshiper, and the sense of possessing a message that must be proclaimed and made known to generations yet to come.

I Corinthians 1:18-31

At the heart of the Christian gospel is the paradox of the cross. As a symbol, the cross expresses the sum and substance of Paul's gospel: Christ and him crucified (I Cor. 2:2). To think of the cross is to think of suffering, as the passion narratives of the Gospels attest. It can scarcely be thought of apart from weakness and impotence. How odd it is, then, that God should choose this, the most fragile of symbols, to express the divine will!

As Paul insists in today's epistolary lection, when viewed rationally the cross is a stumbling block, something on which the mind trips. Both Jews and Greeks (Paul's way of saying everyone) saw the doctrine of the cross as quite incredible if not bordering on the absurd. And so it is when measured in the scale of human judgment. If we want proof of divinity, we normally expect some show of force—thunder, lightning, waters dividing, heavens opening, and such like. The last thing we expect is for God to be manifested in a moment of sheer helplessness and abandon. And yet God has chosen to be revealed in this riddle we call the cross.

But Paul has little use for human wisdom as the standard for measuring God's ways. In this, he stands squarely in the Old Testament tradition which often ridicules the presumed wisdom of human beings (Isa. 19:11-12; 33:18; 44:25; Job 12:17). Moreover, he insists that the human point of view is the short view, limited as it is "to this passing age" (verse 20, NEB).

Even more important, perhaps, is to notice the limits of human wisdom. It can take us only so far. It can bring us to the edge, perhaps allow us to peer over, but in Paul's view, it cannot reveal God to us. This can only happen when God calls us. To put it simply, "The world failed to find [God] by its wisdom" (verse 21, NEB). It led the quest, but the quest was unfulfilled. Alas, it was a matter of God's choosing us, not of our finding God.

For Paul, this was a crucial difference, for had human wisdom succeeded in finding God, it could have been justifiably proud. It could openly say, "Eureka! I have found it!" The natural result would have been arrogance, or human pride (verse 29).

As it is, however, God has chosen to confound the wisest of the wise and in doing so undercut human boasting. God has worked the divine will according to the divine way, and in doing so has succeeded in demonstrating both divine power and wisdom. This way is wiser because it keeps humans human. In no way can we lay claim to God's saving power because we have solved the riddle of the cross. It is also more powerful because it gives God room to work.

We do well to admit that divine folly is wiser than human wisdom, and divine weakness is stronger than human strength (verse 25). If we need further proof of this, we only have to look as close as our own calling and consider "what sort of people [we] are" (verse 26, NEB). If we paint honest self-portraits, like the Corinthians we actually have very little to commend us. Neither our wisdom, our position, nor our pedigree takes us very far. With very little to offer, then, we are summoned by God, and through this divine calling we become transformed from nothing into something. What we are, we are by God's act, not our own (verse 30). The initiative lay with God in calling us, and the change that occurred in us was wrought by God's power. Ours was divine generation not human reproduction.

The cross will always be a symbol that divides. For some, it can only be seen as "sheer folly" (verse 18, NEB). Others will be able to see in it "the power of God" (verse 19, NEB). The latter will always be in the minority, for it requires special perception to conceive of a God who works this way—demonstrating wisdom in folly, strength in weakness.

To be able to see only power through power and wisdom through wisdom is for Paul a sure sign of ruin. Those whose world is put together this way are "those who are perishing" (verse 18). By contrast, if we wish to experience the power of God, we must begin at the place where all boasting is excluded—at the intersection of human weakness and ignorance—the cross of Christ.

John 12:20-36

Today's Gospel lection continues, from yesterday, John's story of the crisis precipitated by the raising of Lazarus. Omitted, of course, is the unit on Jesus' entry into Jerusalem (12:12-19) since that event was observed in the worship service of last Sunday. In preparation for 12:20-36 one would do well to reread 12:1-19.

The raising of Lazarus had created a furor and the galvanizing of religious opposition to Jesus. Fearing Roman interference in order to maintain law and order, Caiaphas determined that "one man should die for the people, and that the whole nation should not perish" (11:50). The Evangelist comments: "He did not say this of his own accord, but being high priest that year he prophesied that Jesus should die for the nation, and not for the nation only, but to gather into one the children of God who are scattered abroad" (11:51-52). And again, "The Pharisees then said to one another, 'You see that you can do nothing; look, the world has gone after him'" (12:19). Even unbelievers unwittingly speak the truth.

These two prophecies, spoken by opponents who did not know the truth of their own words, prompt the story of the coming of Greeks to see Jesus, which in turn prompts Jesus to say, "The hour has come for the Son of man to be glorified" (12:23). "To be glorified" is Johannine language for the death and return of the Son to God. For the world (symbolized in the Greeks) to come to Jesus, it is necessary for him to die so that in his unlimited and continuing presence he will be available to all believers in all places in all generations. That abiding presence of Christ is a major theme of the farewell discourses of chapters 14–16.

Before we proceed with Jesus' comments on his coming death, a word about the Greeks is in order here. It is evident that the writer's interest is not historical, because the Greeks appear, their request generates a series of statements from Jesus, and they do not return to the narrative. Were one to ask the historical questions, it would be reasonable to suppose these are Greeks who had been attracted to the faith and expectations of Judaism. Their coming to Jesus through Philip and Andrew, disciples with Greek names, may simply be a case of going to those friends of Jesus whose names would indicate they were familiar with Greek culture and language. This text may also witness to an apostolic mission to Gentiles by Philip and Andrew. However, it is clearly more in line with the content of this passage to pursue theological rather than historical concerns.

Jesus offers a threefold commentary on his pronouncement that the hour of his glorification has come: (1) he observes that there is a law of nature that death is a precondition of life (verse 24); (2) he observes that there is a law of discipleship to the effect that death is a precondition of life (verses 25-26); and (3) Jesus raises the question as to whether the divine Son is exempt from these two laws (verse 27). Without the Synoptics' Gethsemane experience of "if it be possible, let this cup pass" (Mark 14:32-42 and parallels), Jesus responds to his own question: "Make me an exception? Never!" (verses 27-28). Although Jesus says his soul is troubled (verse 27), John's Christ does not agonize or wrestle with the will of God. Even though heaven's voice confirms Jesus' decision to offer up his life, Jesus does not need that confirmation; the voice is for the people standing by (verses 28-30). See 11:41-42 for a similar case. Not all hear the voice, of course (verse 29); in the Scriptures and in our experience, the same events that are to some God's self-disclosure are to others natural occurrences.

The section concludes with a statement of victory and an offer of life. Jesus' death is a victory over the ruler of this world (verse 31), for by his being lifted up (a double meaning is intended: lifted up on the cross and lifted up to God) Jesus will reclaim the world for God. The offer of life (verses 35-36) is an invitation to all who will hear: there is yet time to walk in the light and live as children of light. In Jesus' time, in the time of the Fourth Gospel, and in our own time, the grace of God has stayed the final judgment: "The light is with you for a little longer" (verse 35).

Wednesday in Holy Week

Isaiah 50:4-9a; Psalm 70; Hebrews 12:1-3; John 13:21-30

The readings for this occasion are somber reminders of persecution and suffering. The Old Testament lesson is the third of the Servant Songs of Second Isaiah, in which the servant reports how he suffered humiliation at the hand of enemies because of his faithfulness to his vocation. The responsorial psalm is an individual lament, asking for deliverance from enemies. The reading from Hebrews provides relief from the somber mood as it looks beyond the suffering and death of Jesus to his exaltation. In the Gospel reading Jesus discloses that Judas will betray him.

Isaiah 50:4-9*a*

This is the same reading assigned for Passion/Palm Sunday, and has been discussed at that point in this volume.

Psalm 70

For all practical purposes, Psalm 70 is identical with Psalm 40:13-17. In the latter psalm, this material forms one of the pleas in the psalm (see also Ps. 40:11) for deliverance and salvation in a time of trouble. The content of Psalm 70 would suggest that the psalm was composed for use by persons who were under attack and threatened by opponents, perhaps false accusers bringing charges of wrongdoing (as was the case with Jesus at his trial) or, on the basis of Psalm 40, perhaps national enemies attacking the Judean king.

Psalm 70:1-3 provides a good example of what has been called the double wish of the lament psalms, because the request to be saved is balanced by a request for the destruction of one's enemies or opponents. Frequently, the calamity that is requested to befall one's enemy is very similar to the condition that the one praying faced. Thus numerous psalms reflect something of that attitude, so widely felt, namely, that those who plan evil should have a corresponding evil beset them. Christians often shy away in horror from the prayers in the psalms which request a destruction or a calamity to fall on one's enemies. Such sentiments seem contrary to the teaching and life of Jesus. We must, however, understand that the Psalms sought to give full and appropriate outlets for people to express their true feelings and sentiments. It may be that only by verbalizing such sentiments and expressions can they be overcome or transcended. Expressions of one's truest and deepest feelings may be necessary before that person can release them and replace them with better feelings. In many ways, some of the Psalms probably allowed persons to vent their anger and hostility to such a degree of animosity and with such a degree of revenge that the mere recital of such cursing wishes relieved the anxiety and pent-up emotions of the worshiper (for example, Ps. 109).

The opening verse of Psalm 70, with its plea for God to hasten and to deliver, is followed by two verses asking that the enemies be put to shame and turned back; that is, make their plans go awry, so they will end up being shamed. If the prayer was originally offered by the king, then the adversaries could be foreign powers or nations who were threatening hostile military action.

Verse 4 is an intercessory prayer, although the worshiper is included in the group being prayed for. The intercessor requests that all those who seek God and love his salvation rejoice and proclaim forever that God is great. This is obviously a prayer asking that the king and his subjects be victorious over the enemy or that they be spared a possible impending conflict.

In the final verse, the worshiper reverts to an appeal on his/her own behalf. The fact that the one praying is described as poor and needy does not mean that the person was destitute and poverty-stricken. Such expressions are metaphorical statements characterizing the person in the most sharply drawn and the humblest terms in order to evoke God's aid.

The association of this psalm with Holy Week can be made in two ways: (1) like Jesus, the psalmist was challenged by enemies who sought his death and destruction; and (2) like Jesus, the psalmist prayed and made intercessory requests on behalf of others.

Hebrews 12:1-3

Every one of us, athlete or not, knows how difficult and painful it is to hold out to the very end until the task before us is finished. It may be making a dress, wallpapering a room, ploughing a field, writing a book, or finishing a report—the temptation is always the same. We grow weary at the end and find it difficult to maintain the same level of quality, commitment, and enthusiasm with which we began. Almost inevitably, the job is more than we bargained for. Had we known how hard it would be, how long it would take, how many fresh starts would be required, we would never have begun. In retrospect, we were naïve. But we have now gone too far to stop or turn back. How can we hold out?

Today's epistolary text addresses this fundamental human tendency "to lose heart and grow faint" (verse 3, NEB; cf. Gal. 6:9; Deut. 20:3). At issue, however, is no everyday project but the life of faith on which we have embarked. For the author of Hebrews this is most appropriately envisioned as a race, a rather common metaphor for the life of faith in the New Testament, especially for Paul (cf. I Cor. 9:24-26; Gal. 5:7; Phil 2:16; 3:12-14; II Tim. 4:7-8; cf. also Gal. 2:2; Phil. 1:27-28). The other athletic metaphor commonly used is the fight, such as a boxing or wrestling match (cf. I Tim. 6:2; Jude 3).

To think of the Christian life as running the race introduces several images. We lay aside the warm-up suit and anything else that will slow us down. We look around at the crowds whose eyes are staring at us (we think). But we are especially mindful of the other athletes, perhaps old-timers in the stands or those who've just finished their heats in earlier races, for we know they know as others cannot know. Yet this "cloud of witnesses" reassures us because we know others have run and won. So can we. Then there is the final lap, the final turn, the stretch. Here is where cramps can set in, someone can stop in front of us, or where we simply run out of steam. We call up Olympic images of other runners whose fondest dreams evaporated in this final struggle with weakness, fatigue, and opposition.

When all of these images begin either to merge or vanish, it becomes clear that the real test is one of endurance and patience. The one who can hold out—with patience—finally wins.

At first, it may seem remarkable how much the New Testament urges us to endure. The seed sown in good soil, Jesus reminds us, are those who "hold it fast" in their heart and "bring forth fruit with patience" (Luke 8:15). Or, in the face of apocalyptic threats, Jesus reminds the disciples, "By your endurance you will gain your lives" (Luke 21:19). It becomes something of an axiom: to be faithful is to endure (Heb. 10:36; Rev. 3:10; 13:10; 14:12).

Nor is this the mindless endurance that simply clings for the sake of clinging, or presses on with no clear vision of the destination. In our case, "our eyes [are] fixed on Jesus, on whom faith depends from start to finish" (verse 2, NEB). Ours is a faith that rests in the One who, given a choice between giving up and holding up, held up: he "endured the cross," as disgraceful as it was (verse 2).

At the middle of Holy Week, this Wednesday meditation draws us into the middle of Christ's own suffering, urging us to endure it with him. It is a struggle against rank opposition from sinners (verse 3). Not only was it an inward struggle with his own self-doubts and fears in the face of death, but mustering the power to resist face-to-face those bent on destroying him, whether Judas (as in today's Gospel text) or Satan's other minions. Endurance, then, requires us to fight against ourselves as well as others who conspire, perhaps with us, against the life of faith.

In a word, our text today calls for clear, focused vision on a solitary goal—the life of obedient faith relentlessly pursued. We should know that others—many others—have preceded us in this race, and have run well. To them we look for confidence and assurance. We should also know that the One in whom we trust and for whom we live both "leads us in our faith and brings it to perfection" (verse 2, JB; cf. Acts 3:15; 5:31; Heb. 2:10).

John 13:21-30

More than any other Gospel, John gives attention to the departure of Jesus from the circle of his disciples. The absence of Jesus of Nazareth constituted the first major problem for the church and forced the believers to come to clarity about the nature and form of his continued presence among them as the living Lord. It also forced the church to deal with the problem of false messiahs who, in the wake of Jesus' departure, rushed into the vacuum claiming to be Christ returned.

This Gospel addresses the problem of Jesus' departure (even Easter with its message of triumph over death carries the pathos of a farewell) in the lengthy section, 13:1–17:26. This narrative consists of a farewell meal (13), farewell discourses (14–16), and a farewell prayer (17). Compressed into the time frame of his last night on earth, this section contains all the elements of the classical farewell of a great leader: the announcement of approaching death, the circumstances of it, the effect it will have on his followers, reflections on his exemplary behavior which they are to emulate, with encouragement and instruction on their life together after his death (compare this narrative with two other farewells: Luke 22:14-38 and Acts 20:17-35).

The immediate setting for today's lection is the farewell meal. That this is not the Passover as in the Synoptics (Mark 14:12 and parallels), John makes clear in 13:1. In this Gospel, Jesus does not eat the Passover with his disciples; he *is* the Passover, dying as the Passover lamb (19:31-37). The supper functions as the setting for washing the disciple's feet (13:2-5), an event not understood (verse 7), and for pointing out the betrayer (verses 21-27), an event also not understood (verses 28-30). The writer wants the reader to understand what those early disciples did not, that Jesus knows what is going on (verses 1-4) and that he is completely in charge. He not only knows that one of the Twelve will betray him (verse

11) and who the one is (verse 26), but Jesus actually commands him, "What you are going to do, do quickly" (verse 27). This portrait of Jesus not only strengthened faith later (verse 19), but encouraged those believers who, during their own nights of betrayal and arrest, could look back upon Jesus' experience as neither defeat nor tragedy. But the church could also reflect upon this night and be preserved from arrogance and triumphalism; after all, it was from within the inner circle that Jesus was betrayed.

Three phrases in verses 21-30, while not central to the thrust of the passage, deserve comment because they give insight into the writer's thought and also stir the reader's curiosity. The first occurs in verse 21: "He [Jesus] was troubled in spirit." This statement can be understood as similar to 11:33, 38 and 12:27; that is, as descriptive of Jesus' disturbed emotional state due to the events immediately before him. This is the closest John comes to picturing Jesus having a Gethsemane experience. But the statement "troubled in spirit, and testified" could be descriptive of the prophetic state. The very next words (verse 21) are a prophecy: "one of you will betray me."

The second unusual phase in this passage is the reference to "one of his disciples, whom Jesus loved" (verse 23). This unnamed disciple appears in six scenes in chapters 13–21, and in all except one (19:25-27) in the company of Simon Peter (13:21-26; 18:15-18; 20:1-9; 21:4-7; 21:20-24). In every case, this disciple is presented in a more favorable light than Peter. If these were Johannine and Petrine circles of Christianity, then there is no question in this writer's mind which apostle was closest to Jesus and provided the church with certain continuity with Jesus.

The third and final unusual phrase concludes this passage: "and it was night" (verse 30). No doubt the writer here again has a double meaning; "night" gives both the time and the nature of Judas' act. It is interesting that the earliest known tradition related to the Last Supper preserves the same sense both of time and of mood: "on the night when he was betrayed" (I Cor. 11:23). Even in the inner circle, even at a meal together, even on the last night of Jesus' life, the community of faith is in need of grace.

Holy Thursday

Jeremiah 31:31-34; Psalm 116:12-19; Hebrews 10:16-25; Luke 22:7-20

The Holy Thursday readings for this year are Eucharistic texts. In this context, Jeremiah's promise of a new covenant is applied to Christ on the occasion of the Passover and in each celebration of the Lord's Supper. The passage from the letter to the Hebrews explicitly interprets the Old Testament text in terms of God's purposes through the death of Jesus. The psalm's references to "the cup of salvation" (verse 13), "the death of his saints" (verse 15), and "sacrifice of thanksgiving" (verse 17) are particularly appropriate for the occasion. The Gospel lection is the Lucan account of the Passover meal and the institution of the Eucharist.

Jeremiah 31:31-34

This reading, which is assigned also for the Fifth Sunday of Lent, Year B, is an unqualified announcement of salvation. It contains the only explicit Old Testament reference to the New Testament, that is, new covenant. The lesson stresses a particular aspect of the good news of Holy Week and Easter, that God will transform human hearts. But just as Easter comes only after the death of Jesus, so in Jeremiah's vision of the future the new covenant comes only through and beyond suffering, in this case that of the Babylonian Exile. Thus these hopeful words come from a time of crisis and transition, when many people would have been asking if God's covenant with the people has come to an end. Jeremiah insists that judgment is not God's final word.

104

Consider the context of Jeremiah 31:31-34. It is part of a collection of announcements of hope and restoration (Jer. 30–31). Following the collection in chapter 32 is the report of an action by the prophet during Nebuchadrezzar's siege of Jerusalem. Jeremiah had been imprisoned in the court of the guard for announcing a Babylonian victory. Even while he was in prison for announcing bad news, he bought a field in Anathoth from his cousin to act out symbolically God's future. Even before Jerusalem was destroyed he announced: "Houses and fields and vineyards shall again be bought in this land" (Jer. 32:15). A powerful spiritual vision of changed lives and obedient hearts is followed by, of all things, a real estate transaction. The point is clear and consistent with the biblical tradition: So long as they are on this earth, even the people of the new covenant will need places to live, actual ground for growing food, and even a marketplace where things are bought and sold.

The introductory words of our passage, "Behold, the days are coming," emphasize that Jeremiah does not expect his vision to be fulfilled immediately, but in the future, with the end of the Babylonian Exile. Elsewhere in the book we learn that the prophet thought the Exile would last some seventy years. It thus seems clear that he did not expect to live to see this divine promise fulfilled.

The old covenant, which the people of Israel broke (verse 32), was the one established at Mount Sinai under Moses following the Exodus. There had been many others as well, including earlier ones with Noah, Abraham, Isaac, and Jacob and later ones in the times of Joshua and Samuel. Like Jeremiah's new covenant, the old ones had been initiated by God, and included the language of promise.

Few texts employ more intimate language to characterize the relationship between the Lord and those with whom he makes a covenant. In the past, the Lord says, "I took them by the hand," like a mother leads her children. The metaphor changes, but not the point: "I was their husband." While announcing a new covenant on the heart, the prophet knows that intimacy between God and people is nothing new.

All this intimate language attempts to describe the "covenant," a special kind of relationship in which parties

105

pledge themselves to one another. The two basic parts of the Old Testament covenants were a promissory oath or conditional self-curse and the stipulations or contents of what was promised. In the covenant at Sinai, the stipulations were the laws given to Israel. In Jeremiah 31, the emphasis falls upon the stipulations, the law written on the heart. But no list of laws is given here. Instead we hear the simple sentence that stands at the foundation of the Old Testament understanding of the covenant, "I will be their God, and they shall be my people" (verse 33).

It is worth emphasizing that the making of a covenant with God was not an individual, but a communal, act—both the work of the community and that which made them a community. It was Israel's covenant with God at Mount Sinai that made them a people, the people of God, binding them both to God and to one another.

What is new about the new covenant? That God initiates the covenant, that the Lord forgives sins, and that Israel will "know" the Lord intimately had been essential features of older covenants. What is unprecedented is the law written on the heart, the covenant at the core of one's being. The newness is a special gift, the capacity to be faithful and obedient. That signals the importance of the fact that the new covenant will be written on the heart. In ancient Israel, the heart was the seat of the will (see Jer. 29:13; 32:39; Ezek. 11:19; 36:26); consequently, the special gift here is a will with the capacity to be faithful. God thus promises to change the people from the inside out, to give them a center, a will to be faithful. This covenant will overcome the conflict between knowing or wanting one thing and doing another. In the new covenant the people will act as if they are owned by God without ever reflecting upon it.

Which laws, then, are written on the heart? All the laws of Moses? Just the Decalogue? The answer is all of these things, and none of them. Just these words will suffice: "I am yours, and you are mine," says the Lord. In the understanding of Jeremiah, this new covenant, by which the people of God know who they are, is set into motion as God forgives iniquity, forgets sin (verse 34).

Psalm 116:12-19

Psalm 116 was composed as a thanksgiving psalm to be offered by someone who had escaped the clutches of death, who had stood at the doors of Sheol, but who had recovered from sickness and could again worship and celebrate in thanksgiving at the temple.

In early Judaism, at the time of Jesus, this psalm along with 113–115 and 117–118 was sung in the temple by the Levites at the time of the slaughter of the Passover lambs and again at dinner when the Passover meal was eaten in a family celebration.

Three features have made this psalm especially appropriate to Holy Week in addition to the tradition of the psalm's association with the Passover season in Jewish ritual.

1. First of all, the reference to the cup in verse 13 has closely tied this psalm to services of the Eucharist on Holy Thursday. At the Passover celebration, the participants drank four cups of wine in the course of eating the evening meal which was completed by midnight. (The Mishnah stipulates that a person too poor to buy this much wine for the ritual could get the money from the temple welfare fund.) This psalm was recited probably at the drinking of the third or fourth cup.

2. Verse 15 speaks of the death of one of God's saints or pious ones. This text should not be interpreted as saying that death can be a good thing in the sight of God. (In spite of the tradition in the RSV or the NEB which reads: "A precious thing in the Lord's sight is the death of those who die faithful to him.") The sense of the Hebrew seems to be: "A weighty (or serious) matter in the sight of the Lord is the death of his pious ones." God too suffers in the death of the righteous, in the death of his worshipers. For ancient Israel, this would have been seen as referring to the fact that there would have been one less worshiper of God around.

3. The psalm refers to the sacrifice that the worshiper brings (verse 17). In the earliest use of the psalm, the sacrifice would have been part of a meal eaten in the temple as a service of celebration for renewed health. When the psalm came to be associated with Passover, the sacrifice was re-understood as the sacrificial lamb killed and eaten as part

of the national holiday. In Christian tradition, the sacrifice can be seen in relationship to Jesus, who offers himself as the sacrifice on behalf of others.

Hebrews 10:16-25

Today's epistolary lection opens with a quotation from Jeremiah 31:33-34, the well-known prophetic promise of a new covenant that also serves as today's Old Testament lesson. It has already served a major role earlier in the epistle (8:8-13).

Actually, these Old Testament verses bring to a conclusion the extended argument that encompasses 9:11–10:18, which is a full exposition of the sacrifice of Christ. We have already been told that the death of Christ is a sacrifice and that its cleansing effect extends to all. It is his sacrificial death that has made possible the fulfillment of the prophetic promise: "I will remember their sins and their misdeeds no more" (verse 17). Through his death, true and lasting forgiveness has been achieved, and for this reason sin offerings are no longer needed. They were necessary only as long as forgiveness was partial.

What, then, are the consequences of Jesus' blood being shed as the final, ultimate sacrifice for sin? First, it provides a basis for genuine confidence (4:16; 10:35; Eph. 3:12; I John 3:21), because it opens up a way of access to God heretofore impossible (7:19, 25; 10:1; Rom. 5:2; Eph. 1:4; Col. 1:22).

In our text today, this is visualized as our being able to enter the sanctuary, the sacred area of the tabernacle that was off limits to the ordinary worshiper. But through the once-for-all sacrifice of his life, Christ has become the supreme high priest over the house of God (2:17; 3:1; 4:14; 5:5, 10; 6:20; 7:26; 8:1; 9:11; 10:21; cf. Zech. 6:11-12). In this supreme role, his resurrected body provides an opening in the curtain separating the Holy Place from the Most Holy Place (6:19; 9:13).

As high priest over the house of God and as one who has opened the way of access to the very presence of God, Christ becomes a "new and living way" of access (7:25; cf. John 14:6). Not only has he entered the sanctuary (9:11-12), he has also made it possible for us to follow him in. Through him, we are able to enter the sanctuary, draw near to God, and have unprecedented access to God's very presence.

But such access is never casual. It rather requires proper preparation, and calls for at least three exhortations, introduced with the familiar words, "Let us ..."

First, *an exhortation to moral purity* (verse 22). We are able to approach God fully assured in our hearts (4:16; Isa. 38:3), but it is a prerequisite that we do so with purified hearts and bodies. The former refers to our having a clean conscience, free of the guilt of sin (9:14; 10:2; 13:18; cf. I Tim. 1:5, 19; 3:9; II Tim. 1:3; Acts 23:1). The latter recalls the custom of ritual purification through washing the body with water before entering the sanctuary, and here probably refers to Christian baptism (cf. Exod. 29:4; Lev. 16:4; Ezek. 36:25; I Cor. 6:11; Eph. 5:26; Tit. 3:5; II Pet. 1:9).

Second, *an exhortation to fidelity* (verse 23). Here we are urged to hold fast to the confession (3:1; 4:14). This is to be done hopefully (Rom. 5:2; Col. 1:23), because our God is not only a God who promises but a God who is faithful in keeping those promises (I Cor. 1:9; 10:13; II Cor. 1:18; I Thess. 5:24; II Thess. 3:3; II Tim. 2:13; Heb. 11:11; Rev. 1:5).

Third, *an exhortation to fellowship* (verses 24-25). Personal purity and fidelity is not enough. We are also encouraged to stir up within one another a deeper level of love for the community of believers as well as urge one another to do good deeds (cf. Tit. 2:14; 3:8, 14; I Pet. 3:13). Essential to this are times of meaningful corporate worship, when we "meet together." Such times, our text reminds us, are not to be neglected, even though it had already become the habit of some to prefer privacy to church attendance. But these times together become meaningful only insofar as they are occasions for encouraging one another (3:13; 13:22). Even more important than mutual upbuilding, they serve as occasions to prepare for the coming of the Lord, the approaching day (cf. I Cor. 1:8).

Luke 22:7-20

In most traditions the lections for this service will be used in connection with a Eucharistic meal. There will also be a service of footwashing in those communities that take the commandment (*mandate* from *mande*, our source for *maundy*) of this night to refer to washing feet (John 13:14) as well as to the Eucharistic meal (Luke 22:19-20). As for the meal, the Lukan text, joined here with Jeremiah 31 and Hebrews 10, calls for a strong emphasis on the fellowship of the participants and on covenant with God.

Luke 22:7-20 falls naturally in two parts: the preparation for the meal (verses 7-13) and the meal itself (verses 14-20). Luke's account of the preparation follows Mark 14:12-16 quite closely with a few stylistic changes and the identification of Mark's two disciples (14:13) as Peter and John (Luke 22:8). The similarities between this story of preparation and that prior to the entry into Jerusalem (19:28-34) are evident. In both cases we are not dealing with intriguing prearrangements but with the prophetic powers of the Son of God. There is some question about the accuracy of time reference in verse 7 since it was customary for the paschal lamb to be sacrificed on the day before the beginning of the Feast of Unleavened Bread. That we are dealing with a Passover meal, however, is fully certain in Luke (verses 8, 15), whereas in Matthew (26:17-29) and Mark (14:12-25) all references to the Passover are in the preparation and not in the meal itself.

In Luke's account of the meal itself (verses 14-20), several characteristics reflect the interests and concerns of this Evangelist. At table with Jesus are the apostles (verse 14), a designation preferred by Luke over Matthew's disciples (26:20) and Mark's Twelve (14:17). The pointing out of the betrayer, which Matthew (26:20-25) and Mark (14:17-21) place prior to the institution of the Lord's Supper, is delayed by Luke (verses 21-23). In so doing, Luke not only assures that Judas receives the bread and wine, very important in a Gospel that extends forgiveness to a prodigal, the crucifiers, and a thief dying beside Jesus, but Luke also fits the table talk of Jesus into a classical farewell form. By this arrangement of the materials and by the insertion of sayings found elsewhere in Matthew and Mark, Luke makes of the occasion a farewell by the leader of the group: first, the meal (verses 14-20), and then a discourse on what will happen and how his followers are to conduct themselves (verses 21-38).

It is quite evident that the sacramental practices of early Christian communities have affected Luke and all the other traditions of this last meal. Even so, the accents of each writer are still discernible. Luke's record of the meal itself consists of two parts: verses 15-18 and 19-20. The preacher will notice by footnotes to the text and in the discussions in commentaries that verses 19*b*-20 have created a problem for transmitters of the text. Even though most manuscripts contain verses 19*b*-20 they have been the subject of debate for two reasons: they give the occasion two cups (cup, bread, cup), and they include words of institution very close to those of I Corinthians 11:24-25. It can reasonably be argued, however, that Luke has combined here two traditions related to the meal, each consisting of a set of parallel sayings. In verses 15-18, the two sayings are associated with the Passover ("for I tell you I shall not eat it until it is fulfilled in the kingdom of God") and with the cup to be shared among them ("for I tell you that from now on I shall not drink of the fruit of the vine until the kingdom of God comes"). Taken alone, this unit stresses historical linkage with the Jewish Passover, table fellowship (the sharing of the cup was fellowship or "communion"), and eschatological expectation.

The second table tradition here (verses 19-20) centers on two other sayings: "This is my body which is given for you" and "This cup which is poured out for you is the new covenant in my blood." Even though "given for you" and "in my blood" came eventually to be interpreted primarily in sacrificial terms as atonement for sin, it must be said that Luke's is not atonement language. He insists that the meal is a Passover, which commemorates a covenant extended to the faith community by a God who liberates. He says they shared a cup, an act of table fellowship joining life to life; and he speaks of Jesus' blood in relation to the sealing of a covenant, not as a sin offering.

Celebration of God's liberation; table fellowship among the people of God; the enactment of a covenant bond: these are messages that have never lost their appropriateness or their promise.

Good Friday

Isaiah 52:13–53:12; Psalm 22:1-18; Hebrews 4:14-16; 5:7-9; John 18:1–19:42 or *John 19:17-30*

The first lesson is the most appropriate of Old Testament texts for this day. The mood and tone of the fourth Servant Song as well as its contents enable the church to fix its attention on the suffering of the Servant of God. Psalm 22 is an equally obvious text for the occasion, since Jesus called out its initial words from the cross. It is an account of personal suffering and distress and is cited (verse 18) in the Gospel lection (John 19:24). The reading from Hebrews is an interpretation of the obedient suffering of Jesus as high priest and one who was fully human. The long version of the Gospel lesson reports the events from the arrest of Jesus to his burial; the short version is the report of his crucifixion and death.

Isaiah 52:13–53:12

In the context of Second Isaiah (Isaiah 40–55), within the Old Testament as a whole, and even among the four Servant Songs (Isa. 42:1-4; 49:1-6; 50:4-9), this text is exceptional. While there is no reason to doubt that it was composed by Second Isaiah just before the end of the Babylonian Exile, it is remarkable for both its style and contents. The poetic language is rich, even extravagant, complicating the problems of interpretation. When is the language to be taken literally and when metaphorically? How much is intentionally vague or hidden? Who is, was, or will be the servant?

When the Servant Songs are considered together and in their context, the most likely candidate for the servant is Israel. Among the roles of the servant, those of the prophet

112

stand out. The servant is the one who, through word and life, proclaims the word of God to the nations. The corporate interpretation is the most difficult to sustain with the song before us because its poetic account of the suffering of an individual is so personal. However, the corporate understanding is possible if one sees the language as metaphorical, taking the humiliation of the servant as the suffering of Israel through the Exile.

We may fruitfully explore the meaning of the poem in terms of the different voices that speak and of the one of whom they speak. The first of these is the Lord, who speaks at the beginning (52:13-15) and the end (53:11b-12). The point of these addresses that bracket the account of the servant's suffering is to make the divine intention clear. From the very first it is affirmed that God will "exalt" and lift up his servant. While this exaltation is in the future, it is to take place before "nations" and "kings" who will be startled that one whose appearance was "so marred, beyond human semblance" (52:14) is exalted by God. Those in highest authority will bow to him. The concluding divine speech strikes the same note and gives the reason for the triumph of the servant: his obedience to death through which he bore the sin of many. The divine purpose, then, is to reverse the expectations of the world.

The second voice is that of the members of the community who speak in the body of the poem (53:1-11a). They seem to address themselves ("Who has believed what we have heard?" 53:1) in patterns that are reminiscent of the complaint or lament Psalms (such as Ps. 22), but even more similar to the dirge, or funeral song (II Sam. 1:17-27). The community mourns the suffering of the servant, giving an account of his life, his unfair trial, his suffering and death. They are in awe of his innocence (53:9), his quiet acceptance of his fate (53:7), and the fact that his suffering was on their behalf (53:4, 5, 10). Another aspect of the community's response is extremely important: In the presence of the suffering of this innocent one they are confronted by and confess their own sins (53:3, 4-6, 8). They recognize that, although they have now come to acknowledge him, during his suffering they did not stand with him.

113

Finally, there is the suffering servant himself. Throughout the entire poem he is not heard to speak a single word. This servant is described at every turn as a human being, exceptional in the breadth and depth of his unmerited suffering. That suffering was both emotional and physical, including deformity or disfigurement (52:14), rejection by the community (53:1-3), and corporal punishment (53:4-7). What is special about the suffering of the servant is that it is vicarious, on behalf of others: "He was wounded for our transgressions, he was bruised for our iniquities"; and efficacious: "And with his stripes we are healed" (53:5). No wonder the text has been cited so frequently in the New Testament as an explanation of the meaning of the passion and death of Jesus (Acts 8:34; Rom. 5:21; I Cor. 15:4).

Thus on Good Friday this text helps us encounter human suffering, especially of those who are innocent, and in particular the genuinely human suffering of Jesus. And, after all, before one can hear the good news of Easter one must hear the suffering—and the good news—of the cross.

Psalm 22:1-18

Since the days of the early church, if not already in the life of Jesus himself, this passionate lament imbued with the pathos of human suffering has been interpreted as the prayer of the suffering Messiah. This secondary reading of the psalm, its christianization, has been encouraged by the assertion that Jesus intoned it upon the cross (Mark 15:34) and by the similarity of details spoken of in the psalm with incidents reported about the trial and crucifixion of Jesus.

Like the story of the Messiah, the psalm moves from misery and suffering to assurance and thanksgiving, from abandonment and isolation to fulfillment and acknowledgment. The lection for Good Friday stops on the downward movement, on the dark side of the equation, on the bewildered and disoriented aspects of existence.

In these eighteen verses, we encounter an opening address shot through with a complaint against God (verses 1-2), a statement of confidence (verses 3-5), a description of distress (verses 6-8), a second statement of confidence (verses 9-10), a plea for help (verse 11), and a second description of distress (verses 12-18). One way of viewing the content of the psalm is to analyze the trouble in terms of its theological, anthropological, and sociological statements.

Many laments, like this one, allowed the worshiper not only to describe the distress of a bad situation but also to lodge a complaint against God and even to accuse him. The psalm opens this way in verses 1-2, which lament the unaccountable absence of God, and raises the suspicion about whether the Divine is acting responsibly. The worshiper declares that, if prayer is the means, the fault lies with God. The forsakenness of God (verse 1) is contrasted with the persistence of the worshiper (verse 2). Suffering and endurance in the presence of the Deity are one thing; the two in the absence of God are another thing. The first statement of the distress may then be seen as a theological issue.

The anthropological description is found in verses 6-8. Here the depiction speaks of the worshiper as a worm, scorned and despised. Compared to the fathers of the past who were aided in their endeavors and strengthened by the Divine (verses 3-5), the worshiper is a nobody, a subhuman. Again the theme of being God-forsaken appears, even calling into question the divine reputation as well.

The sociological dimensions of the distress are developed in verses 12-18. Enemies are described as everywhere; life has no refuge; no safe place remains; even the living is treated as the dead. Fear (verse 14) and weakness (verse 15) are described as the petitioner's condition: confronted with enemies spoken of as bulls, lions, dogs, and evildoers.

One could compare the imagery of the text with that of the accounts of creation in Genesis 1–2. The person in the psalm is a worm, hardly the upright image of God—a potsherd, a piece of broken pottery—not a special creation of God sustained by divine spirit but at the mercy of the animals— not one who rules with dominion over creation. Life has become chaos; cosmos is called into question. Darkness awaits the dawn; the *tohu wavohu* (the formless and the void) await the dawn.

Hebrews 4:14-16; 5:7-9

On Good Friday, as on no other day of the year, our attention is riveted on Jesus "in the days of his flesh" (5:7). On this day we confront the inescapable fact that Jesus died. For some, it would have been a sure sign of his divinity had he been able to bypass death. After all, the Old Testament had known figures, such as Enoch and Elijah, who had bypassed this event. And when those we know who have loomed larger than life finally die, we realize once again that death is the event that establishes our common link with all humanity.

Both of today's texts honor Christ as our great high priest, neither self-appointed nor self-exalted, but so designated by God (5:10; cf. 2:17; 3:1; 5:5; 7:26; 8:1; 9:11; 10:21). His was not an ordinary Levitical priestly appointment, but unprecedented and unparalleled—"after the order of Melchizedek" (5:10; cf. 6:20). It was through exaltation that he acquired this position, having "passed through the heavens" (4:14). To be sure, the great high priesthood of Jesus, as envisioned in Hebrews, is an exalted position far "above the heavens" (7:26; cf. Eph. 4:10).

Our text boldly states that the "religion we profess" (4:14, NEB) is grounded in this triumphant exaltation of the risen Lord. But there seems to be the awareness that exaltation can be understood as distance, that the exalted Lord can easily become an inaccessible Lord. As we multiply our images of a triumphant Lord penetrating the very regions of heaven itself, we can find ourselves confessing faith in a heavenly Christ remote and far away.

As a way of counterbalancing this portrait of an elevated high priest, officiating in the heavenly temple, our text firmly anchors our thoughts on earth and calls us to think of Jesus "in the days of his flesh" (5:7). We are first reminded of Christ's capacity to sympathize with our human weakness (2:17; 5:2). As one who became fully human, it was his lot to experience temptation of every kind and at every level (4:15). This may recall the Synoptic tradition of his temptation by Satan (Matt. 4:1-11 and parallels), and perhaps as well the Gethsemane experience (Matt. 26:41; cf. also Luke 22:28).

Yet it is the firm Christian conviction that tempted though he was, he endured "without sin" (4:15; 7:26; John 7:18; 8:46; II Cor. 5:21; I Pet. 2:22). His was the capacity to confront temptation squarely yet remain steadfastly obedient to the divine will—and to do so as no one else had done, or could do. As one who was genuinely in touch with human temptation, he becomes one who is genuinely sympathetic. Even though he sits enthroned, we are bold to approach him to "receive mercy and in his grace find timely help" (4:16, NEB). Our text insists that we should do so with confidence (cf. 3:6; 10:19, 22, 35). Our approach should be neither timid nor hesitant, but forthright and direct. We should know that whatever our struggle, it is not beyond his own experience.

Our second text is even more vivid in its depiction of the human agony of Christ. We are told that Jesus "offered up prayers and supplications, with loud cries and tears" (5:7). Most likely, this is a reminiscence of the Gethsemane tradition (Matt. 26:38-46 and parallels; cf. also John 12:27-28). Also possible is a reference to the cry of dereliction in the Synoptic tradition (Mark 15:33-39 and parallels). There could hardly be a more human image than that of Jesus crying out loud, shedding tears, praying to God for deliverance.

As the psalmist was promised, God hears the cries of the afflicted when they cry out to him (Ps. 22:24). It was finally through his suffering on the cross that his obedience was fully tested (5:8; Phil. 2:8). Through his obedience, he became perfected (7:28). As a result, he became the mediator of eternal salvation (9:12; Isa. 45:17).

It is impossible to read today's epistolary text in the context of Good Friday without squarely confronting the humanity of Christ. To be sure, exaltation is a central theme, but it is exaltation through obedience. It also speaks of salvation: God reaches out "to save him from death" (5:7), but only in the sense that God finally raised him from the dead. He was not saved from suffering, nor was he saved from death on the cross. The temptations that he resisted in life were of a piece with his final temptation: to escape suffering and death. But this, as with the others, he resisted, so that his death finally became more than a testimony to his full humanity. It also certified him as the true Son of God.

John 18:1–19:42 *or* John 19:17-30

The Fourth Gospel does not move directly from the last meal to the garden of Jesus' arrest. Instead, four chapters are devoted to farewell discourses and a final prayer before returning at 18:1 to the series of events leading to Jesus' death. Beginning at 18:1, the events move swiftly to their conclusion. This section is strikingly similar to its parallels in the Synoptics, testifying to the early formation of a passion narrative. That fact should not blind us, however, to the peculiar accents of this writer's telling of it.

The lectionary offers a choice in the Gospel lections for today's service. If tradition calls for a three-hour Good Friday service, then the entire narrative from arrest to death could be read with appropriate comments. However, for a single service of usual length, one could well choose to use only the portion dealing with the crucifixion and death (19:17-30). If the entire narrative is used, it would be important that the preacher not offer a sketch of these events but that the story be told *as John tells it*. In other words, what witness does this Evangelist make concerning Jesus' arrest, trials, and death?

With that in mind, chapters 18:1–19:42 can easily be divided into units which have their own integrity but which move the entire story along. One way of doing that is provided below, along with the perspectives on the narrative peculiar to this Gospel and hence worth attention when John's Gospel is the source of Good Friday preaching.

The Arrest (18:1-12). Gethsemane is here a garden, without agony. Jesus is fully in charge, knowing all that will happen (verse 4), reducing Judas to a presence that is just standing there, not needing Simon Peter's protection, and causing the arresting officers to fall back before him. Later when this Gospel was written, the details of who cut off whose ear, and which ear it was, were included in the story. The presence of a cohort with a captain (verses 3, 12), along with officers of chief priests and Pharisees, is the writer's witness to the conviction that secular and religious authorities, church and state, are arrayed against the Lord's anointed and are conspiring in his death.

Interrogation by Religious Leaders (18:13-27). In this Gospel, the only official action by the Jews is the questioning before Annas. Caiaphas is mentioned four times but there is no description of action by him or before him. Caiaphas had already determined without hearing or trial that Jesus should die (verse 14; 11:49-51). By speaking of two high priests when there could be but one, and by treating them so sketchily, John ironically is affirming 10:18: Jesus gives his life, no one takes it. Of more interest to this writer is the "trial" of Peter (and of the church symbolically) going on at the same time (18:15-18, 25-27).

Interrogation by Pontius Pilate (18:28–19:16). For all his flaunting of power, Pilate and the state are portrayed as impotent. In seven episodes, Pilate shuttles between the calm and in-charge Jesus inside and the crowd outside. Racing back and forth between private judgment and public pressure, Pilate succeeds only in getting religion, already dressed for holy services, to confess its Lord is Caesar. At Passover, commemorating freedom from pharaoh, the pharaoh is embraced.

The Crucifixion (19:17-30). Notice the brevity of the account, briefer than Mark's. Notice the absence of multitudes, passersby, conversation with the thieves, mocking, earthquake, or splitting of the temple veil. Nothing is here for sighing and despair. Jesus is in charge, carrying his own cross, fulfilling Scripture, caring for his mother, and giving his life. Others contribute unwittingly: the soldiers fulfill Scripture and sarcastic Pilate announces in three languages not an accusation but a truth: "Jesus of Nazareth, the King of the Jews."

The Burial (19:31-42). The corpse and burial receive almost as much attention as the crucifixion. Why? Perhaps as a polemic against early spiritualist heresies which denied that Christ was really in the flesh (I John 4:2-3). More certain is the writer's concern to show that Jesus died as the Passover lamb (Exod. 12), bringing to fulfillment Judaism's ritual life and offering a new Passover, a new exodus. Very likely the writer has used in the description of Jesus' corpse with its

119

outpouring of blood and water the church's language of eucharist and baptism. With sacramental words, the corpse of Jesus has become the Body of Christ.

If it is the choice of the preacher to focus only upon 19:17-30, the suggestions above concerning the crucifixion could certainly be expanded into a message. The Johannine images in the passage are two: Jesus is the Good Shepherd who gives his life, it is not taken from him (10:11-18), and Jesus is king. Self-serving crowds had tried to make him king (6:15); curious crowds had hailed him king (12:13); and now unwittingly Pilate proclaims him king. By his crucifixion, Jesus is lifted up, enthroned by executioners and glorified by those who think they are getting rid of him. But God is able to turn even the wrath and violence of the unbelieving world into the means of that world's salvation.

Easter Eve, Easter Vigil, or the First Service of Easter

Genesis 1:1–2:2; Psalm 33;
Genesis 7:1-5, 11-18; 8:6-18; 9:8-13; Psalm 46;
Genesis 22:1-18; Psalm 16;
Exodus 14:10–15:1; Exodus 15:1-6, 11-13, 17-18;
Isaiah 54:5-14; Psalm 30;
Isaiah 55:1-11; Isaiah 12:2-6;
Baruch 3:9-15, 32–4:4; Psalm 19;
Ezekiel 36:24-28; Psalm 42;
Ezekiel 37:1-14; Psalm 143;
Zephaniah 3:14-20; Psalm 98;
Romans 6:3-11; Psalm 114;
Luke 24:1-12

(Easter Vigil is traditionally a service of readings with little or no homily.)

Genesis 1:1–2:2

Ordinarily the Old Testament lessons for the Easter Vigil are simply read, not preached, taking the worshiping community through a summary of ancient Israel's history. Read in this order and on this occasion, these texts present a history of salvation in preparation for the death and resurrection of Jesus. The story begins with the first chapter of the Bible.

This reading contains all but a verse and a half of the Priestly Writer's account of creation. The mood of the story is solemn and measured; the repetition of phrases lends a liturgical dignity to the recital. If the account was not actually put into this form for worship, it certainly was shaped by persons with a deep interest in liturgy.

In terms of structure, the report consists of two uneven parts, Genesis 1:1-31 and Genesis 2:1-3, that is, the six days of creation and the seventh day of rest. One of the purposes of the story in its present form is to account for the sabbath rest. It was divinely ordained from the very first, and thus is taken by our writer as the most universal of laws.

Creation is not ex nihilo, out of nothing, but out of chaos. Before creation there were the primeval waters, within which God established the world. Moreover, as the Priestly account of the flood indicates (Gen. 7:11), the waters of chaos stand as the alternative to creation. If God withdraws his hand, the waters can return. In that sense, then, this chapter actually understands God as both creator and sustainer of the world.

In sharp contrast to the other account of creation which begins in Genesis 2:4b, God is transcendent and distant. The only actor or speaker in this chapter is God, by whose word or act all things that are come into being. Human beings certainly occupy an important place. They are created last of all, and then given stewardship over the creation. If this moving and majestic account can be said to have a major point, it is in the divine pronouncement that recurs throughout: "And God saw that it was good." The natural order is good not only because God created it, but also because God determined that it was so.

Psalm 33

This psalm, as a responsorial reading to the Priestly account of creation, stresses the role of the word of God and especially the creation of the world through the word. The description of God's creating acts are much more poetic and metaphoric in expression in the psalm than in the Genesis account; for example, God is depicted as gathering the sea as in a bottle (verse 7). In addition, the psalm stresses God's continuing interaction with and governance of the world. God's relationship to the world is not a once-for-all creation but a constant guiding and governance.

Genesis 7:1-5, 11-18; 8:6-18; 9:8-13

Like Genesis 1, the account of the flood is part of the primeval history, the story not just of Israel but of the entire human race. Between that initial chapter and Genesis 7 a great deal transpired. There was the second account of creation coupled with with story of the fall, ending with the expulsion of the original pair from the garden. Next came the story of Cain and Abel, when a brother kills a brother. Then follow genealogies along with short reports of events in the lives of the earliest generations. The immediate background of the flood story is the little account in Genesis 6:1-4 of how the "sons of God" took the "daughters of men" and gave birth to a race of giants. From the accounts of creation to the time of Noah the story is basically one of human sin and disorder, culminating in God's decision to put an end to the race, with the exception of Noah and his family.

The flood marks an important turning point in biblical history, but as the Book of Genesis is organized, it is not the most decisive one. Following the flood, the history of human sinfulness continues, with the story of the tower of Babel. The critical event is reported in Genesis 12:1 ff., the call of Abraham. To be sure, sin continues, but now, with the promise to Abraham, the direction of history is known. It becomes a history of salvation.

The verses for this reading comprise a rather full account of the flood, with the exception of the report of God's decision and his instructions to Noah. The assigned text comes mainly from the Priestly Writer, but some of it is from the Yahwist, whose name for God in most translations is LORD. It is also the Yahwist who reports that seven pairs of clean and one pair of unclean animals went into the ark; P has one pair of every kind. Moreover, in P the water comes when the floodgates of heaven are opened; the Yahwist speaks of rain. But according to both writers, God put an end to all human beings except that one family, and afterward vowed not to do it again. The reading appropriately ends with the good news that the natural order will abide and the rainbow will be a sign of God's promise.

For further comment on the conclusion of the flood story, see the notes on the Old Testament reading for the First Sunday of Lent in this volume.

Psalm 46

This psalm praises God for his divine care for his people and especially for Jerusalem, the City of God. With its emphasis on security in the midst of great turmoil and disruptions in the earth, it provides a proper response to the narrative of the flood. The worshipers confess, as Noah and his family may have, that they have nothing to fear should the mountains quake and the whole of the cosmos become chaos again.

Genesis 22:1-18

One must keep in mind the framework in which this reading is placed—both in the Book of Genesis and in the Old Testament—or important aspects of it will be missed. The context is the narrative of the patriarchs, Abraham, Isaac, Jacob, and the sons of Jacob, the leading theme of which is the promise that their descendants will become a great nation, will own their land, and will be a blessing to all the peoples of the earth (Gen. 12:1-3). The fulfillment of those promises comes first with the Exodus and then with the occupation of the land of Canaan as reported in the Book of Joshua.

The immediate prelude to this story is the report in Genesis 22:1-7 of the birth of Isaac. The promise of descendants had been repeated to Abraham and Sarah over and over. Just when it appeared that all hope was lost, they are given a son in their old age. Isaac is not simply symbolic testimony that the divine promise is trustworthy, he is also actually the first step in the fulfillment of that promise.

And then comes the account in Genesis 22:1-18 of God testing Abraham, by means of a command which threatened to take away the child of the promise. It is certainly one of the most poignant and moving stories in the Bible, and all the more so because of its restraint. Emotions are not described or analyzed, but the reader or hearer can sense the fear and grief. Even though we know how the story comes out, each time we read it we can experience the rising tension, feeling that the results may still be in doubt. Will Abraham go through with the sacrifice of Isaac? Will the angel speak up before it is too late?

The story is so meaningful and fruitful and has been told in so many ways over the centuries that it would be a serious mistake to reduce it to a single point. At one level, in the old oral tradition, it probably dealt with the question of child sacrifice. Being among cultures where child sacrifice was a genuine possibility, some early Israelites could well have asked, "Does our God require that we sacrifice our children?" The answer, through this account, is a resounding no. Our ancestor was willing, but God did not require it. The sacrifice of a ram was sufficient. In the framework of the Easter Vigil one is reminded that God gave his Son.

The leading theme of the story, as recognized through centuries of interpretation, is faith. It is, as the initial verse says, the test of Abraham's faith. What is faith? The biblical tradition answers not with a theological statement, or with a set of propositions, or with admonitions to be faithful, but with a story. It is the story of Abraham who trusted in God even when God appeared to be acting against his promise. Faith is like that. Faith in this sense is commitment, the directing of one's trust toward God. And it entails great risk, not in the sense of accepting a set of beliefs, but by acting in trust. Did Abraham know that the God he worshiped would not require the life of Isaac? We cannot know. We are told only how the patriarch acted, and how God acted.

Psalm 16

This psalm, probably originally used as a lament by an individual during a time of sickness, contains a strong statement of devotion to God and thus can be read as a theological counterpart to the narrative of Abraham whose faithfulness led him to the point of sacrificing his son Isaac. Like Abraham, the psalmist shows confidence in whatever fate or lot God might assign him. This psalm came to be understood in the early church as a prediction of the resurrection, especially Christ's resurrection, and was quoted in this regard by Peter in his sermon at Pentecost (see Acts 2:22-28).

Exodus 14:10–15:1

With this reading we come close to the heart of the Old Testament story and the Old Testament faith. In ancient Israel's faith no affirmation is more central than the confession that the Lord is the one who brought them out of Egypt. Traditions concerning the Exodus provide the fundamental language by which Israel understood both herself and her God. The basic focus of most of those traditions is upon the saving activity of the Lord; the history is a story of salvation.

The account in Exodus 14 actually follows the Exodus itself. The departure from Egypt had been reported in chapters 12 and 13; the rescue of the people at the sea happens when they are already in the wilderness. The two themes that mark the stories of the wandering in the wilderness are already present in this chapter, namely, Israel's complaints against Moses and the Lord (14:10-13), and the Lord's miraculous care (14:13-18, 30-31). The report does mark, however, Israel's final escape from the Egyptian danger, and this relates directly to the theme of the Exodus itself.

This reading, like the flood story, is the combination of at least two of the sources of the Pentateuch, those of the Priestly Writer and of the Yahwist. Two virtually complete accounts have been combined. The writers tell the story differently, with P reporting a dramatic crossing of the sea between walls of water (verse 22), and J speaking of a "strong east wind" (verse 21) and the chariots clogged in the mud as the water returns (verse 25). But a more important implication of the source division for our use of the text in the context of worship is the recognition that the sources place very different theological interpretations upon what happened. For the Priestly Writer, the emphasis is on revelation. The Lord "hardened the heart of Pharaoh" (verses 8, 17) to pursue the Israelites in order to "get glory over Pharaoh and all his host" (verse 17). That is, the Lord's purpose is for the Egyptians to "know that I am the Lord" (verse 18). For the Yahwist, the purpose is the salvation of the people (verse 13), and their consequent faith, not only in the Lord, but also in

Moses (verses 30-31). In the combined report, both themes are important. God acts in order to reveal who he is and also to save his people.

Exodus 15:1-6, 11-13, 17-18

The psalm text overlaps with the Old Testament reading and continues where it left off. Moses, having led the Israelites in their escape from the Egyptians at the sea, now leads them in worship. The expression of praise is generally identified as the song of Moses, and much of it is in the first person singular, "I will sing to the Lord." But the introduction points out that it was sung by Moses and the people, and its communal, congregational character is evident throughout. While the song is not in the Psalter, it is a psalm nonetheless and probably was used in worship by faithful Israelites through the centuries. The initial lines are placed in the mouth of Miriam in Exodus 15:21, except that they are in the second person instead of the first; she calls for the people to sing to the Lord.

The song is a hymn of praise, specifically praise of the Lord for saving the people at the sea. The hymn is for the most part narrative in form; that is, it praises God by recounting the story of his mighty deeds. In one sense what emerges is another interpretation of the rescue at the sea, different in some respects from the accounts in Exodus 14. But the language is at points highly metaphorical and rich in imagery which goes beyond the immediate events.

Recollection of the Lord's saving activity at the sea evokes two leading themes in the hymn. The first concerns God's awesome power over events and nature. The specific form of that theme here stresses the image of the Lord as a warrior who triumphs over his enemies. But it also emphasizes that the God praised here is incomparable; there is none like this one (verses 11, 18). The second theme of the hymn concerns God's love and care for the people whom he has redeemed. God is strength, song, salvation (verse 2), the one who cares for his people out of steadfast love (verse 13). Moreover, his past care for the people gives rise to hope that he will continue to act on their behalf in the future (verse 17), and will reign forever (verse 18).

Isaiah 54:5-14

The central message of Second Isaiah (chapters 40–55) is the announcement that the Babylonian exile is coming to an end; the Lord will bring the people back to Jerusalem. This text incorporates that theme but goes beyond it to proclaim and characterize the new era in Israel's history with her God. In this passage, which actually begins with Isaiah 54:1, the unnamed prophet of the exile employs a wealth of metaphors to characterize the new relationship between Israel and Yahweh. He is "husband," "Redeemer," the "God of the whole earth" (verse 5). These three expressions remind the hearers that the God who created all that is and acts in historical events to save is also as close to the people as a husband is to a wife.

God speaks (verses 6-10) to assure Israel that he has forsaken her, but only for a moment. He then declares what is in effect a new covenant, like the one sworn in the days of Noah. God now vows not to be angry again and establishes a "covenant of peace" (verse 10). Israel has in no sense earned this new covenant; it is simply that the Lord has compassion on those whom he had rejected. The concluding lines (verses 11-14) are addressed to the city of Jerusalem, which will be reestablished in righteousness for an era of peace.

Psalm 30

This psalm was originally a thanksgiving psalm offered by a worshiper who had recovered from sickness. As thanksgiving, it celebrates the transition from a time of sickness and destitution to a time of celebration and joy. Just as Easter marks the transition from death to life so this psalm marks the worshiper's transition from sickness to health. Its two keynote expressions of this transition are: "Weeping may tarry for the night, but joy comes with the morning," and "Thou hast turned for me my mourning into dancing."

Isaiah 55:1-11

Again, as is so often the case in the lectionary as a whole, and especially during Easter, the words of Second Isaiah come before us. This text from the end of the Babylonian exile was a call for hope and trust and a promise of salvation to the hearers; it reiterates that same call and promise during the Easter Vigil.

The passage has two distinct parts, verses 1-5 and 6-11, which are similar in both form and content. In the first section God is the speaker throughout, addressing the people of Israel as a whole. He begins with a series of imperatives (verses 1-3a) which resemble on the one hand Lady Wisdom's invitation to a banquet (Prov. 9:5), and on the other hand the calls of street vendors. The invitations to come for what the Lord has to offer are both literal and metaphorical: God offers actual food, and "food" which enables one to live the abundant life ("that your soul may live," verse 3a). What the people are invited to "come, buy and eat" is the proclamation of salvation which follows in verses 3b-5. God announces that the ancient covenant with David (II Sam. 7) now applies to the people as a whole. Again, Israel has in no sense earned this new covenant; it is a free act of God's grace. Moreover, as the Lord made David a witness to the nations, now all nations will come to the people of Israel. The proclamation of salvation, then, is ultimately directed toward all peoples.

The second section (verses 6-11) also begins with imperatives, calls to "seek the Lord" and to "call upon him." The "wicked" and "unrighteous" are invited to change their ways and "return to the Lord." These invitations, while addressed to the human heart, are quite concrete. To "seek" and "call upon" the Lord refer to acts of prayer and worship. For the wicked to "forsake his way" is to change behavior. The foundation for the imperatives is stated at the end of verse 7, "for he will abundantly pardon." The remainder of the section (verses 8-11) gives the basis for responding to God's call. God's plan for the world ("ways," "thoughts") is in sharp contrast to human designs. That plan is the announcement of salvation which the prophet has presented throughout the book, the redemption and renewal of the people. The will of God is effected by the word of God, another theme found throughout Isaiah 40–55. That word is the one uttered at creation (Gen. 1:3 ff.), and it is the divine announcement of the future through the prophets. In its emphasis on the word of God and its contrast between human and divine wisdom this concluding section of Second Isaiah alludes to the beginning of the work (Isa. 40:1-11).

Isaiah 12:2-6

Not all Old Testament psalms are found in the Psalter. Isaiah 12 actually includes two, along with traces of the liturgical instructions (verses 1*a*, 4*a*). The songs conclude the first section of the Book of Isaiah and suggest that the prophetic book was used in worship even before an official canon of scripture was established. Both psalms are songs of thanksgiving. The first (verses 1-3) celebrates and gives thanks for deliverance from trouble. In verse 2 it echoes the vocabulary of the Song of Moses (Exod. 15:2), moving from thanks for a specific divine act to generalizations about the nature of God as the one who saves and who is the strength, song, and salvation of the worshiper. The second psalm (verses 4-6) consists almost entirely of calls to give thanks and praise (verse 4). God is praised especially for his mighty deeds. Because God, the Holy One of Israel, is great, all the earth should know, and those who live in the shadow of the temple in Zion should sing for joy.

Baruch 3:9-15, 32–4:4

This passage, often characterized as a hymn to wisdom, is not actually a song of praise such as those in the Book of Psalms. While it does characterize and praise wisdom, it is basically an admonition to the people of Israel to listen to and learn from wisdom.

The book of Baruch is attributed to Jeremiah's scribe and placed in the Babylonian exile, but it actually stems from a later time. The section from which this reading comes is like other late wisdom literature such as the Wisdom of Solomon and Ecclesiasticus. It identifies wisdom with the law of Moses, "the commandments of life" (3:9), and "the way of God" (3:13; see also 4:1). Behind that answer stands a question that became prominent in the so-called intertestamental period, Is there a conflict between the truth which can be discerned by human reflection and that which is revealed in the law?

Our text alludes to the Babylonian exile (3:10-13), but it is characterized as a spiritual situation of separation from God rather than the actual exile. The verses not included in the reading (3:16-31) also contain somewhat spiritualized allusions to the history of Israel. The reading finds its place in the Easter Vigil, first because of the references to death and its alternative. Israel, growing old in a foreign land, is as good as dead (3:10-11), because the people have forsaken "the fountain of wisdom" (3:12). If they will attend to wisdom they will gain strength, understanding, life, and peace (3:14). All who hold fast to wisdom will live, and those who forsake her will die (4:1). The second reason for the use of this passage in the Easter Vigil is its theme of wisdom as the gift of God which reveals the divine will to human beings. This is quite explicit in 3:37, which is echoed in John 1:14, and has been taken as a reference to the coming of Jesus.

Psalm 19

This psalm of hymnic praise of God declares that God has communicated his will and himself through nature—verses 1-6—and through the law or Torah—verses 7-13. Without speech, God's voice is heard in the world of nature, and his communication, like the light of the sun, falls everywhere and nothing can hide from it. In the Torah, God's will is embodied in commandment and precept and offers its blessings to those whose ways it directs and guards.

Ezekiel 36:24-28

This reading is the central section of a passage in which Ezekiel presents the divine announcement of a new Israel. God, through the prophet (see verses 22, 32), is the speaker. This dramatic announcement of good news presupposes that the people of God are in trouble. The description of that trouble is given in the context (verses 16-21) and alluded to in our reading. Israel is in exile, away from the sacred land, but the trouble is even deeper. Separation from the land corresponds to separation from their God. They are in exile because of their sin, their disobedience which led to uncleanness. Now God is about to act, not because Israel deserves it, but for the sake of his "holy name" (verse 22).

There are two aspects to the coming work of salvation, one external and one internal, corresponding to Israel's present plight. First, the Lord will gather up the people and return them to their land (verse 24). But if they are to remain there (verse 26), a major transformation must occur. That is the second aspect of the good news, the establishment of a new covenant (see Isa. 54:10; 55:3) with a new Israel. This transformation is spelled out in terms of three distinct steps: (1) the Lord will sprinkle (cf. Exod. 24:6) the people with water, purifying them from their uncleanness; (2) he will give them a new heart and a new spirit, replacing their heart of stone with one of flesh (cf. Jer. 31:31); and (3) God will put his own "spirit" within them. "Spirit" here represents both the willingness and the ability to act in obedience. The promise is summarized by the reiteration of the ancient covenant formula, "You shall be my people, and I will be your God" (verse 28). The radical difference between this new covenant and the old one is that the Lord himself will enable the people to be faithful.

Psalm 42

This psalm can be closely associated with the sentiments of Ezekiel 36:24-28, the Old Testament lesson to which it is a response. Ezekiel predicts the coming rescue of God's people from exile and the transformation of the human personality and will. The psalm, originally used as an individual lament, early became associated with the Easter Vigil because it expressed the people's longing for redemption and their lamenting over being absent from the sanctuary. The psalm presupposes that the speaker is living away from the Sacred City. The psalmist's thought about former days when the worshiper went on a pilgrimage to Jerusalem only intensifies the depression and despair that accompany living in a foreign and hostile land and heightens the desire to be at home again in the temple.

Ezekiel 37:1-14

Ezekiel's vision of the valley of dry bones, like so many other Old Testament readings for this season, stems from the era of the Babylonian Exile. That it is a vision report is indicated by the introductory formula, "The hand of the Lord was upon me," which the prophet uses elsewhere to begin reports of ecstatic experiences (Ezek. 3:22). The report is in the first person and, like most prophetic vision reports, consists of two parts, the description of what was revealed (verses 1-10) and the interpretation (verses 11-14). Throughout there is dialogue between Yahweh and Ezekiel.

The message from the Lord communicated through the report is the response to the problem stated in verse 11. The people of Israel are saying, "Our bones are dried up, and our hope is lost; we are clean cut off." Ezekiel sees himself carried by the spirit of Yahweh to a valley full of bones, like the scene of an ancient battle. When the Lord asks if the bones can live again, Ezekiel gives the only possible answer, "O Lord God, thou knowest" (verse 3). While the nuance of the response is not immediately plain, it becomes clear in the context; the God of Israel can indeed bring life in the midst of death. When the prophet obeys the command to prophesy to the bones a distinct sequence of events transpires: bones to bones, sinews to bones, flesh on the bones, and then skin covering them. The importance of the next step is emphasized by a further divine instruction. The prophet calls for breath to come into the corpses and they live. The view of human life as physical matter animated by the breath that comes from God is found throughout the Old Testament (cf. Gen. 2:7).

The interpretation (verses 11-14) emphasizes that the vision is a promise of national resurrection addressed to the hopeless exiles. In no sense is the seriousness of their plight denied. They are as good as dead, and death in all possible forms is acknowledged as a reality. But the word of God in the face of and in the midst of death brings to the people of God a new reality, life. It is a free, unconditional, and unmerited gift. When read on the eve of Easter, this text is a strong reminder that God is the Lord of all realms, including that of death. Moreover, the promise of life is addressed to the people of God, and resurrection is a symbol not only for a life beyond the grave but also for the abundant life of the community of faith this side of physical death.

Psalm 143

Originally used as an individual lament by worshipers suffering from illness, this psalm prays for God's intervention and rescue. The condition of the worshiper's distress is described in terms of death, of going down to the pit. Such depictions fit well with the description of the exile as a graveyard in Ezekiel 37. Like those awaiting Easter morning, the psalmist asks to "hear in the morning of [God's] steadfast love."

Zephaniah 3:14-20

The last of the Old Testament readings for the Easter Vigil is a shout of joy and an announcement of salvation to Jerusalem. The passage begins with a series of imperatives addressed to the Holy City, calling for celebration (verse 14). The remainder of the unit in effect gives the reasons for celebration. These reasons include the announcement that the Lord has acted on behalf of the city and is now in its midst as king (verse 15) and a series of promises concerning the renewal of the city and the return of its people (verses 16-20). Both the mood and contents of the text anticipate the celebration of Easter.

Our unit is the fourth and last section in the book of Zephaniah and stands in sharp contrast to the remainder of the book. The section which immediately precedes this one (Zeph. 3:1-13) had announced a purging punishment upon the city and its people. But now darkness has become light; fear and terror have become hope and celebration.

The prophet Zephaniah was active in the seventh century, not long before 621 B.C. He was concerned with the coming judgment upon his people, particularly because of their pagan religious practices. It is possible that this concluding section of the book was added in a later age, perhaps during the Babylonian Exile (cf. 3:19-20), by those who had actually been through the fires of destruction and who looked forward to celebrating God's forgiveness, which the return from exile represented. But in any case the theological interpretation presented by the structure of the book in its final form is quite clear. The celebration of God's salvation follows the dark night of judgment and suffering.

Psalm 98

Like Zephaniah 3:14-20, this psalm is an exuberant affirmation of divine triumph and success. This affirmation is noted by the word "victory" in each of the first three verses. The psalm proclaims the victory of God and calls upon the whole world to break forth into song and the sound of musical instruments. As part of the Easter Vigil, this psalm contributes its call for a celebration of salvation and for the recognition of God as king.

Romans 6:3-11

This text serves as the epistolary reading for the Easter Vigil or the First Service of Easter in all three years. Psalm 114 serves as the response to this text in which Paul discusses Christian baptism as the sacramental act of dying and rising with Christ.

It is a most appropriate text to be read in this liturgical setting. The community gathers either on Easter Eve or Easter morning. In either case, the text straddles the death and resurrection of Christ. Like the Roman god Janus, this liturgical moment looks in both directions: back to his death, forward to his life. In one case, the tomb serves as the focus of our attention; in the other, it is the stone rolled away. As we visualize the closed door, our mood is somber, for we can only think of the entombed, lifeless body. As we visualize the open door, we are amazed, if not buoyant, for we feel despair giving way to resurrection hope.

As our thoughts oscillate between death and life in this service, so does today's epistolary text. Interestingly, these remarks from Paul are prompted by a question of ethics. One of the objections raised against his theology of justification by faith was that it failed to provide an adequate moral imperative. In fact, it could be construed as encouraging a form of moral relativism. If we are saved by grace through faith, and not by keeping laws or the Law, what then is the motivation to be good?

Paul's response is to interpret for his readers their own initiation rite into the Christian faith and to press its implications to the full. The place to begin is to realize that baptism actually plunges us into the death of Christ not merely as a symbolic reenactment but as an act of sacramental entry and participation. Jesus had asked his disciples whether they, like he, would actually be willing to undergo a baptism of death, that is, to plunge themselves headlong into violent death (Mark 10:38; Luke 12:50).

As a way of underscoring the completeness of our reenactment of the death of Christ, Paul repeatedly uses the language of participation—"buried . . . *with* him" (verse 4), "united *with* him" (verse 5), "crucified *with* him" (verse 6), "died *with* Christ . . . live *with* him" (verse 8, italics added). We miss the point if we see our baptism as an event symbolically analogous to the historical event of Christ's death and resurrection. It is not that we die *like* he did, are buried *like* he was, and are raised *like* he was. It is rather that we are co-participants *with* him in that event in which death gave way to life.

Only when our union with Christ is seen in such starkly realistic terms, when the deepest part of our selves has actually undergone death, do we experience and enter a new form of existence. There is no other way to describe it than resurrection life. Its radical newness marks it off from every other mode of existence. It is not the old redirected or retreaded but transformed—a new creation (II Cor. 5:17; Gal. 6:15). It is the creation of what did not exist before—service in the new life of the Spirit (Rom. 7:6; cf. 12:2; Eph. 2:15; also. Isa. 43:18-19).

So radical is this redefinition of our selves that our form of living is transformed. Quite literally, who we are changes. And consequently, what we do changes as well. The "old personality" dies (Eph. 4:22; Col. 3:9) as the sinful self is destroyed (Gal. 2:19-21; 5:24). With the destruction of the self comes liberation from the hold of sin (verse 7; cf. Acts 13:39; I Pet. 4:1).

What is born in the new creation is a living hope (I Pet. 1:3). Infused with the Spirit of new life, we begin to experience moral renewal, knowing all the while that full participation in resurrection life lies ahead in the future (verse 8; cf. I Thess. 4:17; II Tim. 2:11).

For all this, the implications of dying and rising with Christ are not merely postponed to the future. Both death and life are present realities. Christ's death was final, "once for all," and just as final is the life he lives to God (verse 10). Final, but ongoing. Even so are we to regard ourselves as "dead to sin and alive to God in Christ Jesus" (verse 11; cf. II Cor. 5:15; I Pet. 2:24; also Gal. 2:19).

So it is, then, that the death and resurrection of Christ is not only ours to ponder but to enter. And having entered, there to live.

Psalm 114

This psalm, read as a response to Paul's discussion of the association of Christian baptism with the death of Jesus, is a celebration of the Exodus from Egyptian bondage and of the entry into the Promised Land. Typologically, one might say that the Exodus, like Christ's death, symbolizes the end of an old state of life and the dawning of a new state. The entry into the Promised Land, like Christian baptism, was a time when the benefits of redemption became real. In this psalm, Exodus from Egypt and entrance into the Promised Land are closely joined so that parallel events are seen as characteristic of the two episodes. At the Exodus, the sea fled and the "mountains skipped like rams"; at the Jordan, the river rolled back and the hills skipped like lambs (verses 3-4). The address to the sea and river, the mountains and hills in verses 5-6 which is continued in the address to the earth in verses 7-8 serves as the means for making contemporary the Exodus and entrance events. Thus the users of the psalm, which was always read at the celebration of Passover, "became" participants in the past events of salvation as the Christian in baptism becomes contemporary with the death of Jesus.

Luke 24:1-12

Luke 24:1-12 will appear as an alternate lesson for Easter Sunday. If used here for the Easter Vigil, it is important that the sermon, in fact, the entire service, be one of restraint and anticipation, resisting the temptation to borrow the joyful proclamation from the next day.

It is evident that both Luke and Matthew had access to Mark 16:1-8, although both made changes in substance and form in contouring the empty-tomb story to their own theologies and their readers' needs. Luke introduces the women as "they" (verse 1), delaying until the end to give their names (verse 10). What is important for Luke is that these women witnessed the crucifixion (23:49) and the burial (23:55) and the empty tomb (24:3). Only after they enter the tomb and discover the body missing does Luke introduce the messengers in dazzling apparel (verse 4). Luke's simple reference to "two men" (instead of Mark's one, 16:5) joins this passage to the Transfiguration (9:30) and to the Ascension (Acts 1:10) and may indicate how Luke wants the reader to classify and understand this story. Even though our earliest tradition of the resurrection (I Cor. 15) centers entirely on appearances of the risen Christ and does not include the empty tomb as part of that tradition, it is clear from Luke's account here and the repetition of it in 24:22-24 that he regarded it as part of the Easter story. The witness of an empty tomb, taken alone, is hardly persuasive, but joined to appearance narratives, it both strengthens and heightens the dramatic force of the church's proclamation.

Luke's account of the message of the two men to the women differs from Mark at four important points.

First, Luke makes Galilee the place where Jesus instructed his followers concerning his death and resurrection (verse 6) whereas in Mark (16:7) Galilee was to be the site of an appearance to his disciples. For Luke, Galilee is now past and Jerusalem is the center for Christ's appearances (24:13-43) and for the subsequent mission of the church (24:44-53).

Second, the women are reminded of Christ's words which in Luke constitute a brief formula or creedal statement about betrayal, crucifixion, and resurrection (verse 7). Essentially the same statement is repeated in verses 26 and 46.

Third, the women are not treated simply as messengers. They are reminded of what Christ had taught them, and they recalled the teaching. This is to say, they are treated as disciples in and of themselves and are not told to go tell the disciples.

And finally, the women do go tell the eleven (verse 9; apostles in verse 10), but Luke also includes "all the rest" (verse 9). The group of believers from Galilee is, Luke says later, about one hundred twenty persons (Acts 1:15).

It is now that Luke names some but not all the women who report their experience (verse 10). Among those named, Joanna (8:3) replaces Mark's Salome (16:1). "The other women" had followed Jesus from Galilee and would be present at the beginning of the church in Jerusalem (Acts 1:14). That the apostles did not believe the women (verse 11; repeated at verse 41) may be understood in one of two ways: either as a dramatizing of the burden which the resurrection placed upon faith even among those closest to Jesus, or as Luke's way of minimizing the empty-tomb story as generative of faith. Both interpretations are reasonable and appropriate to Luke's message.

In many translations, verse 12 is omitted from the text and placed in the footnotes. The reasons do not lie in the lack of support in the Greek manuscripts; the weight of evidence is strongly in its favor. Its questionable status is due rather to the widespread judgment that verse 12 is an interpolation from John 20:3-10, and its presence here creates a contradiction with verse 34. However, it could reasonably be expected that the various resurrection traditions would quite early intermingle and influence one another.

The preacher is on solid ground to include verse 12 in this lection, and, needless to say, will find in this verse a most fitting close to the Easter Vigil. Simon Peter, who was later to see the risen Christ in a special appearance (I Cor. 15:5), at this point goes home, "wondering at what had happened." With him the whole church waits until tomorrow.

Easter Day or the Resurrection of the Lord or the Second Service of Easter

Acts 10:34-43 or Isaiah 65:17-25; Psalm 118:14-24; I Corinthians 15:19-26 or Acts 10:34-43; John 20:1-18 or Luke 24:1-12 (If the first reading is from the Old Testament, the reading from Acts should be the second.)

The *New Common Lectionary* provides the passage from Isaiah 65 for those churches which use an Old Testament reading on Easter Day and do not celebrate the Easter Vigil with its long list of Old Testament readings. Isaiah 65:17-25 still anticipates the eschatological rejoicing which Easter inaugurates. The responsorial psalm, the same for all three years of the cycle, is a song of thanksgiving for deliverance. In it death is the vanquished enemy. The New Testament readings include instances of all types of early Christian literature concerning the resurrection. The passage from Acts is the proclamation of the gospel—the life, death, and resurrection of Jesus—in almost creedal form. Luke 24:1-12 and John 20:1-10 are accounts of the discovery of the empty tomb, and John 20:11-18 reports Mary Magdalene's encounter with the risen Lord.

Acts 10:34-43

If there is any day of the Christian year when the message of the universal love of God is heralded to the whole world, it is Easter. All the more fitting, then, that this sermon summary from Acts be read. It is the first clear instance in Acts of the gospel heralded to a Gentile. It occurs on the lips of Peter, one of the earliest witnesses of the Easter faith (cf. I Cor. 15:5). In a few broad strokes, it gives us the essence of the Christ story (verses 37-41).

We should note first that our text begins with a bold proclamation of God's impartiality: "The truth I have now come to realize . . . is that God does not have favorites" (verse 34, JB). It is an axiom of Judeo-Christian faith that God shows no partiality (Deut. 10:17; II Chron. 19:7; Sir. 35:12-13; Gal. 2:6; Rom. 2:11; Eph. 6:9; Col. 3:25; I Pet. 1:17; cf. also I Clement 1:3; Epistle of Barnabas 4:12; Polycarp to the Philippians 6:1). Among other things, this means that God cannot be bought, either with money or human favor.

If God is impartial, it follows that the love of God is unbounded, universal in its scope. Thus, the terms of God's acceptance are for "any one who fears [God] . . . and does what is right" (verse 35; Acts 10:2, 22; 13:16, 26; Ps. 15:2, 4). The language here is sacrificial (cf. Lev. 1:3; 19:5; 22:19-27). Those who live in the fear of God and do what is right become an acceptable offering, even if they are Gentiles (Isa. 56:7; Mal. 1:10-11; Rom. 15:16; Phil. 4:18; I Pet. 2:5).

True enough, God's word was sent first to Israel (Acts 13:26; Ps. 107:20; 147:18-19), and in keeping with the prophetic promise it was an announcement of peace (Isa. 52:7; Nah. 1:15; cf. Eph. 2:17; 6:15). But it was not as if Jesus was the Messiah of one nation or people. He is rather "Lord of all" (verse 36; Matt. 28:18; Rom. 10:12; cf. Wisd. of Sol. 6:7; 8:3).

We can see, then, how our text confronts the question of God's impartiality: if God shows no favorites, why did the gospel first come to Israel? Peter's concern is to show that the Easter faith is truly universal in scope.

At this point, we have a concise summary of the Christ story.

1. John the Baptist represents the beginning point (verse 37). This conforms to the way the Gospel of Mark begins, and scholars have noted the similarity of this summary with the overall outline of the Gospel of Mark. Given the importance of John's prophetic preaching, it is little wonder that in some traditions Christians drove down the first peg here (Acts 1:22; 13:23-24; Luke 3:21-22 and parallels; 16:16).

2. The baptism of Jesus (verse 38*a*). The various strands of the gospel tradition agree in seeing Jesus' baptism by John as his "chrism," the time when God poured out the Holy Spirit on him as an expression of divine favor and approval (Matt. 3:13-16 and parallels; also Luke 4:18; Acts 4:27). It was both a prophetic fulfillment (Isa. 61:1) and a reminiscence of God's appointment of earlier messiahs, such as David (I Sam. 16:13). Whatever else it signified, it was an expression of power.

3. The healing ministry of Jesus (verse 38*b*). One of the least contestable aspects of Jesus' life on earth is that he went about healing the sick and exorcising demons (cf. Matt. 4:23-25 and parallels). The name of Jesus itself conveyed healing power (Acts 9:34). His power to perform deeds of kindness toward the afflicted only attested the presence of God within him: "for God was with him" (cf. Isa. 58:11; John 3:2; 8:29).

4. His death by hanging on a tree (verse 39). All the Gospel passion narratives echo this brief statement. "Death by hanging" was no more honorable then than now, and it carried with it the curse of the Law (Gal. 3:13; Deut. 21:23).

5. Raised by God on the third day (verse 40). Here we shift to the central focus of our celebration on Easter Day. We should see it as the day God acted decisively not only in behalf of Jesus but in behalf of all humanity (Acts 2:24,32; 3:15; 4:10; 5:30; 13:30, 34, 37; 17:31). The "third day" is part of the very substructure of Christian faith (cf. I. Cor. 15:4-7; Hos. 6:2).

6. Made manifest to select witnesses (verses 40*b*-41). Part and parcel of the Easter faith is the conviction that the risen Lord appeared, or was made visibly manifest, to a circle of disciples on Easter morning. As those who had "seen," they became his witnesses (Luke 24:48; John 14:19-22; 15:26-27; Acts 1:8, 22; 5:32; also I Pet. 5:1). That true recognition occurred in the context of eating and drinking with the risen Lord gives all the more meaning to a Eucharistic Service celebrated on Easter Day (Luke 24:30, 43; John 21:13).

And what are the implications for those who are privy to this Easter revelation? An irresistible urge to proclaim it abroad (verse 42; Acts 1:8; 4:20). But ours is not simply the message: "He is risen!" As victor of both death and life, the risen Lord now becomes the one who is to judge both the living and the dead (Rom. 2:16; 14:9-10; II Tim. 4:1; I Pet. 4:5). He has been appointed to this special task by God (verse 42; also Acts 17:31).

But there is more: the risen Lord is everything the prophets expected and hoped for (verse 43). Through him forgiveness is now universalized (Isa. 33:24). Faith in Christ becomes the means through which all humanity is able to share in the unbounded, universal love of God. He is indeed "Lord of all."

Isaiah 65:17-25

These are hopeful words from a difficult and troubled time. They are associated with the anonymous prophetic figure or figures responsible for most of Isaiah 56–66, active in the early postexilic period. Many Judeans had returned from Babylon to their homeland, the temple almost certainly had been rebuilt, but the future of the people was by no means secure. In addition, there is evidence of sectarian conflict within the community.

In the context of which our reading is a part there is a somewhat liturgical pattern. Isaiah 63:7–64:12 gives a series of prayers, mainly of complaint and petition, and then Isaiah 65:1-25 records the response. This movement, however, is probably the work of an editor who organized earlier materials.

Isaiah 65:17-25 is a prophetic address, an announcement of salvation. God is the speaker throughout, and the contents concern the future. There are two opening or introductory formulas, in verses 17*a* and 18*b*, "For behold, I create. . . ." First the prophet hears God announce the new era (verses 17-19*a*), and then he hears God present a description of the circumstances of life in that time (verses 19*b*-25). The description of the new age is crafted in a pattern that alternates negative and positive, what will not be and what will be. Verses 19*b*-20*a* report that there will be no weeping and no early death, then verses 20*b*-21 describe the positive side: long life and fruitful labor. Verses 22-25 continue such an alternation of negative and positive descriptions.

To characterize this passage as a prophetic address is to observe that the vision of the future is not yet an apocalyptic one. Our writer—or speaker—knew himself to be in the tradition of Second Isaiah as well as Isaiah of Jerusalem from the eighth century B.C. He quotes and alludes to both of them. The style of address is especially similar to that of Second Isaiah, and the expression "former things" (verse 17) comes from him. Most important, the announcement of a "new heaven and a new earth" is quite different from the vision that will appear several centuries later in apocalyptic literature such as Daniel, Isaiah 24–27, and—still later—Revelation 21:1 and II Peter 3:13. As the subsequent description makes quite clear, the announcement in Isaiah 65:17 has in view a transformation of circumstances on this earth, and within history, not beyond them.

The vision here concerns a new age of salvation, specifically focused upon Jerusalem. It will be inaugurated with rejoicing, a celebration in which even God participates (verse 19). "Weeping" and "distress" will be ended (verse 19), but death itself will not. Rather, infant mortality and other forms of premature death will be ended (verse 20). It is only death that comes too soon that is perceived as the enemy. Obviously, even in the age of salvation people will work at construction and agriculture (verses 21-23), but it will be productive and fruitful labor, in which efforts and results coincide (see Amos 9:14; Ezek. 28:11). There will be no need to fear enemies who would take over the fruits of one's labors. Moreover, women will not labor to bring children into a world full of "sudden terror" (verse 23, RSV fn). With regard to death, work, and childbirth, the vision of the future appears to reverse some of the curses of Genesis 3:16-19.

But there is more. The very foundation of the situation in which peace prevails is the blessing of the Lord. There is no talk of the new age as a reward for righteousness or the like. Rather, it is a gift of God, who promises to answer prayers even before they are expressed out loud. Finally, the concluding verse anticipates an even more dramatic transformation of the natural order, with natural enemies living in peace with one another, the lion eating straw, and the snake eating dust. These lines, which certainly depend upon Isaiah

11:6-9, stress again that the center of the new age will be the holy city Jerusalem on God's "holy mountain."

To be sure, the future envisioned here is far short of the Easter kerygma. Nevertheless, it deserves to be heard. In Isaiah 65:17-25, death is present, but it does not ruin life. People will still work, but in a situation in which justice is present. And it would be good news indeed if women everywhere could bring children into a world that did not present them with the sudden terrors of war or famine.

Psalm 118:14-24

Portions of this psalm are used in the *Common Lectionary* for Palm Sunday throughout the three cycles (see pages 71-72). As we noted above, the psalm seems to have been composed for and utilized as the litany in a public thanksgiving ceremony. As is typical of thanksgiving psalms, much of the wording is human-to-human address. In this psalm, the king has returned victoriously from battle, reports to the human audience on his triumph, enters the temple amid acclaim and jubilation, and offers a prayer of thanksgiving and sacrifice.

The portion of the psalm selected for the Easter lection contains several of the components of the litany (for the full outline of the psalm, see the discussion under Palm Sunday). Verse 14 begins with the description of the sufferer's triumph and the lessons learned from that (verses 14-18). The returning victor, in verse 19, requests the opening of the gates (to the temple, probably); is responded to by the priests (verse 20); offers a prayer of thanksgiving addressed to the Deity (verse 21); and is answered/responded to by the assembly of people or a choir (verses 22-24).

The king's description of his distress and redemption begins in verse 5 and extends through verse 18. The monarch describes his suffering as being surrounded by the nations and attacked by fierce enemies. It is uncertain whether the psalm describes an actual battle or whether this description was sort of a standard version that could be used from time to time, that is, on those occasions when the king returned from battle as a winner not a loser. The battle can, of course, be seen as one of the representative battles of good/God's elect against the bad/the enemies/the nations. In some Near Eastern cultic dramas, the king and his god fought the powers of evil and chaos at the New Year celebration. In Christian tradition, Jesus is said, according to the old form of the Apostles' Creed, to have "descended into hell." Jesus' "harrowing of hell" involved his invasion of Satan's domain and thus a struggle with hostile powers. In this psalm there are parallels to this harrowing of hell and the king's fight against his enemies.

Verse 14 summarizes the confessional point of the previous verses, affirming that God is the origin of the ruler's strength and the source of his song. Verses 15-16 note the victory songs sung by the king's forces following their triumph which is ascribed to the right hand (the clean hand, the strong hand) of Yahweh. After an actual battle one can image the troops feasting, dancing, and celebrating at the site of their triumph.

The struggle of the king—like the struggle of Jesus—is depicted as a struggle with death, in verses 17-18. The real enemy, the final annihilator, is death. Thus the king can explain his success in battle as God's not letting him fall into the power of death. Again, the parallels with Easter should be obvious.

The litany of entering the temple gates (verses 19-20) can be compared with similar entry liturgies in Psalms 15 and 24. Inside the temple precincts, the monarch offers thanks (verse 21). Verse 22 may be seen either as part of the king's thanksgiving and thus a continuation of verse 21 or else as part of the community's response and proclamation and thus a link with verses 23-24. At any rate, the theme of verse 22, like the Easter theme, emphasizes the movement from humiliation/rejection to exaltation/glorification. A stone (= the king = Jesus) which has been rejected by the builders (= the nations = the Jews/Romans) as unworthy and a possible structural defect has been elevated to a place of prominence (= the corner of the building = the king's victory in battle = Jesus' resurrection).

The congregation responds to the new reality as "marvelous" and "the Lord's doing" in verses 23-24. Thus the psalm lection closes out with a confessional affirmation.

I Corinthians 15:19-26

The notion of resurrection has never been easy to accept, even for Christians. Clearly, some within the Corinthian church found it an incredible notion (15:12). Apparently, they found it easier to believe that Christ was raised from the dead than that they themselves would be similarly treated.

Today's epistolary text occurs in the middle of Paul's discussion of the resurrection, where he responds to the doubts of the Corinthian Christians.

The first verse of our lection actually concludes the thought begun in verse 12. It is generally treated as the final thought of the previous paragraph. It is Paul's final stroke against the desperate thought of life that ends with our last breath. The faith that impelled him to preach was not for hope in this life only, though that might be an improvement. Nor was the Easter faith laced with an element of uncertainty, as if we had to wonder and waver about the hope to which we have committed our selves and our lives. To proclaim Christ apart from the Easter faith is to proclaim no Christ at all. Such would be a most unfortunate message and ours would be a pitiable state of self-contradiction undermined by doubt.

The linchpin of Christian faith and identity is the single proclamation that Christ has in fact been raised from the dead (verse 20; 15:4; Rom. 6:4; 8:11; cf. Matt. 16:21 and parallels). This is not only the essence of Easter, it is the essence of Christian existence. How this is conceived may be, and has been, furiously debated. What happened we do not know. That it happened we firmly believe.

Paul insists that Christ's resurrection was not an isolated instance, an event "back there." It is rather an event whose rippling effect has reached all humanity. The metaphor he uses is that of "first fruits," an image drawn from the Old Testament in which that which was first harvested symbolized the full harvest that was to come later (Lev. 23:10). It was as if he was the first full plant to spring forth from the ground, the sure sign that others would spring to life in due course (15:23; Col. 1:15, 18; Rev. 1:5; 3:14; also Rom. 8:29; Heb. 1:6). When we see the first daffodil of spring, we know that eventually others will follow.

147

But how can an event in the life of one person typify the destiny of all persons? We might grant that Christ was raised, but does it follow that we too will be raised? Is it possible for the act of a particular individual to have universal significance—for all time? Genesis 1–3 provided Paul the solution to the problem of Christ's particularity. Its message is clear: through the deed of one man, Adam, death came to all humanity. Through one individual, the destiny of us all was affected (Gen. 3:1; Wisd. of Sol. 2:24; Sir. 25:24).

If we can conceive that death passed to us all through the first Adam, we can also imagine that life is ours through the last Adam (I Cor. 15:45-49). If death came to us through one man, so can life.

The order is clear: first Christ, then "those who belong to Christ" (verse 23), literally "those who are of Christ" (Gal. 5:24). Through our participation with him in his death and resurrection, we become sharers in his destiny (Rom. 6:3-11). This occurs not now, but at his coming (Matt. 24:3; I Cor. 1:8; I Thess. 2:19; 3:13; 4:15-16; 5:23; II Thess. 2:1; James 5:7-8; II Pet. 1:16; 3:4, 12; I John 2:28).

At the end, Christ hands over to God the reign that has been his (Dan. 2:44; Eph. 1:21-22), but only after vanquishing all hostile forces and powers (I Cor. 2:6; Eph. 1:21; Col. 1:16; 2:15; I Pet. 3:22). In the words of Psalm 110:1, he reigns until every enemy has been put under foot (cf. Matt. 22:44 and parallels; Luke 19:27). The final enemy to be destroyed is death itself (verse 26; Rev. 20:14; 21:4).

The force of this text read on Easter Day is to confront us and reassure us that our destiny—those who are "of Christ"—is indissolubly linked with Christ's own destiny. Death is an enemy. It can be viewed no other way. But what we lost in Adam we have gained in Christ. Our vision of the future can be none other than that of the risen Christ, Conqueror of Death and Bringer of Life.

John 20:1-18 *or* Luke 24:1-12

Since Luke 24:1-12 was the Gospel for Easter Vigil, we will here attend only to John 20:1-18. One may, of course, use

Luke 24:1-12 for this service; if so, comments on that reading can be found in the Vigil lessons.

John 20:1-18 belongs to that body of New Testament material referred to as resurrection narratives. Like Matthew 28 and Luke 24, John joins both elements of those narratives, the empty tomb and the appearance of the risen Christ. Mark 16 has only the empty-tomb portion (if the text ends at verse 8), and I Corinthians 15:3-8, our earliest resurrection narrative, has only the appearances, but none, strangely enough, to women. Unlike the Synoptics, this Evangelist speaks of only one woman at the tomb (20:1), but she is the one common to all the Gospels, Mary Magdalene (of Magdala). Luke says (8:2) seven demons had been exorcized from her; legend portrays her as a beautiful woman redeemed by Jesus from a life of illicit love.

If chapter 21 is regarded as an epilogue, then 20:1-18 is one of two resurrection narratives in this Gospel, the other being 20:19-31 (the Gospel lection for next Sunday). In each of the two, the writer has interwoven a story of an appearance to an individual in the presence of some of the Twelve, the former involving two disciples and Mary; the latter, ten disciples and Thomas. The structure of today's lection is the split story, a form quite common in Mark: the account opens with Mary Magdalene at the tomb, shifts to the two disciples, then returns to Mary.

Verses 1-10 preserve the empty-tomb tradition. This tradition, while containing variations among the four Gospels, seems to have been fixed quite early. Its principal components are: (1) it is early on the first day of the week; (2) women (woman in John) come to the tomb; (3) the stone has been removed; (4) a messenger appears (two messengers in Luke 24:4 and John 20:12; this element is delayed in John and made a part of the appearance story); and (5) confusion, doubt, fear, and joy follow.

And what is the testimony of the empty tomb? For Mary, it means the body of Jesus has been moved. Stolen? Matthew (28:11-15) develops this substory. Taken to a more permanent burial site? Perhaps. Removed by the gardener for some reason? Mary surmises as much (verse 15). For Simon Peter, who arrives after the other disciple but enters the tomb first (verses 4-7), the tomb contains burial cloths but no body. No response from him is recorded except that he returned home (verse 10). For the disciple whom Jesus loved (13:22-25; 18:15-16; 19:26-27), the same evidence was more persuasive: he believed (verse 8). This favorable word about this anonymous disciple is consistent with the other references to him (see above), especially in scenes in which he is paired with Simon Peter. Chapter 21 records another such scene. Here is a case of the empty tomb alone, without any other witnesses, angelic or human, generating faith. It is important to keep in mind, however, that such belief, needing very little evidence or support, is congenial to the portrait of a disciple who lay against Jesus' breast at the Last Supper and to whom Jesus committed the care of his mother. But even so, the disciple did not know what to do with this faith and he, too, went home. Obviously, he has at this point only added another line to his creed: "raised on the third day."

The appearance story (verses 11-18) is quite different. In the account before us the components are: (1) Mary's hesitation, even resistance to belief; (2) Jesus' appearance to her, which did not produce faith immediately; (3) Jesus speaks her name which promptly renews their former relationship (Jesus knows his own, calls them by name, and they know his voice, 10:3-4); (4) Jesus informs her that the old relationship can no longer be the same, because he is glorified and available, not to the former circle of friends alone, but to the world (12:20-31); (5) Mary is commissioned to tell the disciples; and (6) Mary obeys the command. The story is complete.

That which Mary is to tell Jesus' brethren is the message of the ascension, not simply of the resurrection (verse 17). For this Evangelist, the death, resurrection, and Ascension constitute the glorification of the Son, the return to God, the triumph over evil forces, and the gift of the Holy Spirit to his followers (12:20-32; 14:16-17; 15:26; 16:7-15). Easter is completed at Pentecost.

Easter Evening

Acts 5:29 or Daniel 12:1-3; Psalm 150; I Corinthians 5:6-8 or Acts 5:29-32; Luke 24:13-49
(If the first reading is from the Old Testament, the reading from Acts should be the second.)

The notes sounded in the readings for the Easter Evening service are those of joy and triumph. The Acts passage contains an early formulation of the central message of Easter, God's resurrection and exaltation of Jesus. The alternate first reading contains one of the two unambiguous Old Testament expressions of a belief in the resurrection from the dead. First Corinthians 5:6-8 calls for the celebration of the sacrifice of Christ as the paschal lamb, and Psalm 150 is an uninhibited expression of praise. The Gospel lection is the account of the appearance of Jesus to the disciples on the road to Emmaus and his evening meal with them and their recognition that "he was known to them in the breaking of the bread" (Luke 24:35).

Acts 5:29-32

The setting for today's text is the confrontation between the apostles and the Jewish Sanhedrin. It records one episode in a series of events occurring within the precincts of the temple (4:12-42). After the incident involving Ananias and Sapphira, the apostles continued their ministry of signs and wonders (4:12; cf. 2:19, 22, 43; 4:30; 6:8; 7:36; 8:13; 14:3; 15:12). In doing so, they were continuing the healing ministry of Jesus (cf. 4:16-19; 7:21-23). So astonishing were the results of their ministry that increasing numbers joined the faith.

In response to this outburst of messianic mercy, the authorities took the appropriate measures, even more severe than when they had previously resisted the work of Peter and John (4:5-23). Yet as hostility and resistance increase, so does God's capacity to vindicate the cause of the gospel, and the apostles are miraculously freed (4:17-21). It is a matter of sheer wonderment to the authorities that the apostles could have escaped (5:21-26). Once again, they are accosted and brought before the Sanhedrin (4:27-33). As before, the case is decided in their favor, this time through the words of Gamaliel who cautions his colleagues against obstructing what might possibly be the will of God (5:38-39). Even so, the apostles are punished, but this only serves as an occasion for intensifying their efforts (5:41-42).

Here we see an example of a pattern typical of Luke-Acts. First, there is a powerful display of the gospel, either in prophetic word or miraculous deed. Inevitably, this is met with resistance, usually by the authorities. But with the resistance comes divine vindication visibly displayed: the case is thrown out, the disciples are miraculously released. This then serves as an occasion for an even more powerful display of the gospel. We see this pattern begin to unfold in chapter 4, and as the story progresses, the level of resistance and vindication gradually intensifies. By the end of Acts, it becomes clear that the gospel is irrepressible. Nothing is really able to obstruct the progress of God's Word.

In today's text, we are first presented with the standoff between the Sanhedrin and Peter and the apostles. Earlier they had been warned (4:18), and they will be warned again (5:40). At issue, as the Sanhedrin saw it, was where to place the responsibility for Jesus' death (Matt. 27:25).

In response, the apostles insist that theirs is a higher loyalty: "We must obey God rather than men" (verse 29). A similar display of courage before the authorities is seen earlier (4:19), and many others will follow (Stephen, 6:8–8:3; Peter, 12:1-19; Paul, 16:25-40; 18:12-17; 19:23-41; 21:27–26:32). It is a classic confrontation with many precedents (cf. Dan. 3:16-18) and successors (Martyrdom of Polycarp 14).

There follows a succinct summary of the Christian message: Christ hanged on a tree (10:39; 13:29; Gal. 3:13; I Pet. 2:24; cf. Deut. 21:23) whom God raised and exalted to a right-hand position of preeminence (Acts 2:33; cf. Ps. 110:1;

118:15-16). As exalted Leader and Savior, he extends repentance and forgiveness of sins (2:38; cf. 4:12). To this there is a double witness: the apostles themselves (1:8) and the Holy Spirit (John 15:27-28) whom God bestows on the obedient (verse 32).

In this episode, the gospel clearly wins, as it does throughout Acts. It is all too easy to read these accounts and become triumphalist in our thinking. In this liturgical setting, we may forget that the Easter faith can require defense as well as celebration. The scene Luke sketches is drama no doubt, but episodes like this could and did occur. What we have is an account of courageous witnesses digging in their heels against the intimidating threats of those in power. Even if we celebrate Easter in peace, others may do so at high cost. And so ultimately may we.

Daniel 12:1-3

Certainly it is appropriate that this text, one of the two Old Testament expressions of a belief in resurrection, should serve in Christian worship on Easter. The other text is Isaiah 26:19, like Daniel a late passage, but unlike Daniel which speaks of a double resurrection, of "some to everlasting life, and some to shame and everlasting contempt" (verse 2). With this reading we approach the earliest stages in the articulation of that belief in Israelite, Jewish, and subsequent Christian reflection on the question.

We should bear in mind both the historical and the literary contexts to which this reading belongs. The Book of Daniel, and this part of it in particular, can be dated with some precision on the basis of historical allusions to the short period when the Jerusalem temple had been taken over by Antiochus Epiphanes IV, 167–164 B.C. It comes from the time of the Maccabean revolt against the Hellenistic despot, before victory was attained in December, 164 B.C. The era saw, in addition to struggles against the foreign power, sectarian conflict within Judaism. The literary context of the lection is the fourth and final vision report in the book, Daniel 10–12. Daniel's vision begins with a lengthy introduction (10:1–11:1), presents an account of historical events (11:2-39), a revelation of the end time (11:40–12:3), and concludes with instructions to "seal the book" (12:4). The verses that follow (12:5-13) probably are secondary reflections concerning the time of the end.

It is characteristic of the apocalyptic visions in Daniel and elsewhere to begin with the "prediction" of events already known to the visionary and to organize history into a series of eras, culminating in the increasingly evil final age just before the end. History is a struggle between the forces of good and evil. In this case the transition from events that have occurred to those yet to come takes place between Daniel 11:39 and 11:40, with the key phrase, "At the time of the end . . . ". When one translates the vision into history, it becomes clear that most of the events predicted in 11:40-45 did not happen as expected.

Daniel 12 presents a vision of the culmination of the present struggle, and of history itself. The visionary expected that culmination to take place in the near future. "At that time" (verse 1) indicates a particular point in time, right after the events just predicted in 11:40-45. This much is clear about the visionary's expectations: The power of God will be manifest through Israel's guardian angel Michael, there will be a time of tribulation unlike any of the past, and the faithful ("your people," "every one whose name shall be found written in the book") will be delivered. There will be a resurrection of the dead, some to "everlasting life" and others to "shame and everlasting contempt." Moreover, "those who are wise" are singled out for special honor.

Note, however, what is not said, or what is left uncertain. There is no schedule for the time of tribulation in relation to the resurrection. It is not clear whether history continues afterward or not. The indication that "many of those who sleep in the dust of the earth shall awake" (verse 2) leaves open the question of a general resurrection of all who have died in the past. What is the basis for having one's name "written in the book," and are "the wise" who shall shine the same as the ones whose names are found there or a special group among them? What is the resurrection "to shame and everlasting contempt"? These and other questions have opened the door for a great deal of speculation about the end times and the judgment day, but they indicate that one should be cautious about building a full-blown theology on such a narrow and ambiguous foundation.

We should not lose sight of the fundamental point and purpose of this passage. The reports of apocalyptic visions are addressed to real human beings in times of crisis. Their purpose is to reassure and encourage people, especially those experiencing persecution. The visionary is convinced that the forces that oppose the will of God, powerful as they may appear, will be defeated in the end. It is the end of history, its culmination in the reign of God with the vindication of the righteous, that gives meaning to all of it. The new age is breaking in, and the knowledge that this is so gives not only hope but direction for lives lived out in the light of that future. The belief in resurrection belongs within this apocalyptic hope. It is an expression of faith, not in the natural immortality of human beings, but in the power and gracious will of God who is able even to bring the dead to life.

Psalm 150

This final psalm in the Psalter concludes the book with a great and universal call to praise God. As such, it may be seen not only as the fitting conclusion to the book as a whole but also as a statement of faith and confidence in the future. How different the Book of Psalms would have been had it concluded with a moaning and depressing lament!

The tenfold repetition of the call to praise in the body of the psalm is the most characteristic feature of this psalm. Like other examples of the number ten in the Bible, it was probably chosen deliberately both as a memory device (note that we have ten fingers) and as an affirmation of completion or fullness. The two hallelujahs ("Praise the Lord") at the beginning and end are opening and closing liturgical statements which bring the number to twelve.

Three factors in the praise of God are noted: the places of praising (verse 1), the reasons for praising (verse 2), and the means of praise (verses 3-5).

The places of praising are the temple, which was considered the center point of the universe in late Jewish thought, and the firmament, which was considered the dome or heavens encircling the universe. Praise should thus extend from the center outward to the whole of creation and include every living thing (see verse 6).

The reasons for praise are God's "mighty deeds" and "his exceeding greatness." Thus both divine action and divine being are stressed.

The means of praise are multiple musical instruments of all types. This call to orchestrated adulation suggests something of what went on in festive worship services in the temple. The one medium of praising God that is noted, which is not a musical instrument, is the dance. Throughout the Bible, dancing is associated with celebration and joy (see Exod. 15:19-21; Ps. 30:11), and it probably played a significant role in Israelite worship.

The appropriateness of this psalm for the Easter Evening service is based on its call to and emphasis on praise, since Easter is the central day of celebration in the Christian year.

I Corinthians 5:6-8

In I Corinthians 5 Paul responds to an anonymous report that he had received. Word had it that one of the Corinthian members was living with his father's wife, or stepmother (5:1). Such a relationship was strictly forbidden by Jewish law (Lev. 18:8; 20:11). Roman law also prohibited such a union.

The actions of the offenders themselves are of less immediate concern to Paul than the church's actions—or lack of action! The man and woman remained unnamed, and Paul does not address them directly. Rather he addresses the church. Theirs was not merely an attitude of tolerance and liberality, but one of arrogance (verse 2). Apparently, they actually boasted of their tolerant spirit, and perhaps even of their ability to devote their time and energy to matters more spiritual than mere physical relationships.

Paul, of course, is shocked and immediately calls for the removal of the offender from the congregation (verse 2). Such acts of excommunication from the community of faith had firm precedent in the Old Testament (Num. 5:3; Deut. 17:2). Similar procedures existed among the Qumran separatists.

It is in the context of Paul's dealing with this problem of sexual immorality within the Corinthian church that he introduces the subject of leaven. After reminding them once again that their smugness little befits them (cf. 5:2; also 4:6), he reminds them of an everyday truism: "A little leaven leavens all the dough" (verse 6, NEB; also Gal. 5:9). This commonplace of popular wisdom has been repeated in many forms, such as, "One bad apple spoils the barrel." The point is always the same: give rot a start and soon it will ruin everything.

It is the Old Testament that provides the background of the imagery here. The Israelites were instructed to remove all leaven from their homes as they prepared for the celebration of Passover (Exod. 12:19; 13:7; Deut. 16:3-4). The fermenting power of yeast rendered it unclean and unsuitable for the celebration of a holy event. Only bread that was devoid of yeast was to be eaten.

Paul reminds the Corinthians that it is out of character for them to harbor such gross immorality in their midst, much less to boast of it! Christ, the Passover lamb, has been sacrificed (verse 7; John 1:29; I Pet. 1:19; Rev. 5:5). In effect, the Christian Passover has begun, and the appropriate manner of life for Christian observers is one from which all forms of corruption (leaven) have been removed. It is presupposed that observers of the Christian Passover have "unleavened" character, one that is sincere and true (verse 8).

In the context of Easter Evening, today's epistolary text calls us to recognize the moral implications of the paschal mystery. Above all, we are required to leave behind "malice and evil" and pursue "sincerity and truth" (verse 8). We are likewise cautioned against the bane of arrogance and human presumption. If nothing else, our own arrogance often blinds us to the simplest truths of life that even everyday wisdom knows and teaches. We may scoff at established conventions and mores, and even ridicule the popular proverbs of the masses, but first we should be sure our own morality and wisdom exceed theirs. But it seldom does.

Luke 24:13-49

Blessed is the church which has an Easter Evening service. Of course, everyone is tired: to accommodate the large crowd of worshipers in the morning, preachers, readers, singers, liturgists, and many others pressed into service, have done double and triple duty. Some have even participated in sunrise services. But the very conditions that argue against an evening worship argue more persuasively in favor of it. Especially those who have spent the day serving others need now to sit down and be fed. The day needs to be reflected on, gathered up, appropriated. It is a fine evening for a walk; why not to Emmaus?

The resurrection narratives in the four Gospels are similar enough to lose their distinctive traits; they are different enough to demand that their distinctiveness be recognized and preserved. The preacher's first task is to come to clarity about the components of the narrative in the Gospel before us. Luke 24 falls broadly into five parts: (1) verses 1-12, the women at the tomb; (2) verses 13-35, the Emmaus story; (3) verses 36-43, Jesus' appearance to the eleven and others; (4) verses 44-49, instruction and commission; and (5) verses 50-53, the departure of Jesus. Within this material, one can see how the various resurrection narratives had begun to influence one another. For example, verse 12 reflects John 20:6-10; verse 34 confirms I Corinthians 15:5; verse 40 seems to be a borrowing from John 20:20; and to verse 51 some manuscripts add a line from Acts 1:9-10. Since verses 1-12 were discussed as the Gospel lesson for Easter Vigil, and since verses 44(46)-53 will be the reading for Ascension Day, we will here consider the second (verses 13-35) and third (36-43) components of Luke's resurrection narrative.

Luke 24:13-35, like other stories told by Luke (the prodigal son and the sea voyage of Paul, among others), bears the marks of skill and artistry in narration. The beauty and completeness of such stories do not invite interrupting comments, but their significance in the church's faith demands some discussion. The appearance to the two disciples on the way to Emmaus is not in the list of Jesus' appearances in I Corinthians 15:3-8, nor does the story have a parallel in the other Gospels. As it is Luke's style to echo Old Testament stories in his accounts about Jesus (for example, I Sam. 2 lies behind Luke 2:41-52), very likely Genesis 18:1-15 was in Luke's mind here. In this appearance of the risen Christ, as in the others, faith comes slowly. In fact Luke says, "But their eyes were kept from recognizing him" (verse 16) until faith was born in response to witnessing which included explaining the meaning of Scriptures. At the Transfiguration, the disciples' eyes were dulled with sleep (9:32), and at the Ascension their vision was blocked by a cloud (Acts 1:9-11). Faith is not coerced or overwhelmed by revelations to the unprepared.

Here the disciples are prepared by the opening up of appropriate Scriptures (verse 25). The role of Scripture in the removal of ignorance and the generation of faith is a strong theme in Luke (16:31; 24:44-47; Acts 2:14-36). And joined to Christ's "opening the Scriptures" is his self-revelation in the breaking of bread (verses 31, 35). The meal is clearly described in the language of the Lord's Supper (verse 30), making the story one of experiencing the risen Christ in word (interpreting the Scriptures) and sacrament ("he was known to them in the breaking of bread"). It is quite possible that the story in verses 13-35 was shaped with Christian worship in mind.

The return of the two disciples from Emmaus to Jerusalem links verses 13-35 to verses 36-43 which record Jesus' appearance to the eleven and others with them (verse 33). Even though the two narratives are in many ways different, they are framed on the same pattern: the risen Christ appears, the disciples do not recognize him, they are scolded for doubting, food is shared, Jesus enables them to understand the Scriptures, and they respond in amazed joy. In verses 36-43, however, a new theme emerges: the corporeality of the resurrected Christ. The offering of hands and feet for examination and the eating of fish are the writer's insistence that Christian faith in the resurrection of Christ cannot be reduced to a vague Greek notion of the immortality of the soul. Neither can the risen Christ be separated as a different being from the historical Jesus: the one raised is the one crucified. "See my hands and my feet" (verse 39) is

Christ's word to the church: Easter is forever joined to Good Friday and to follow the risen Christ is to follow the One who bore the cross. Those whom Luke addressed with this clear affirmation are still among us, preferring a Christ without scars.

Second Sunday of Easter

Acts 5:27-32; Psalm 2; Revelation 1:4-8; John 20:19-31

Motifs for this day include the exaltation of the risen Lord and the response of followers to him. The first reading carries on this season's semicontinuous readings from the book of Acts and includes the passage from the Easter Evening service. In it the disciples bear witness before the council to their faith in Jesus: "God exalted him at his right hand . . ." (Acts 5:31). Psalm 2 is a royal psalm that likewise emphasizes the exaltation of the Lord's anointed and the certainty of his triumph over the kings and rulers of the earth. The second reading is the salutation of the book of Revelation, John's doxological greeting in the name of Jesus Christ, "the first-born of the dead, and the ruler of kings on earth" (Rev. 1:5). The Gospel lection is the Johannine account of the appearance of Jesus on the evening of resurrection day and the encounter with Thomas.

Acts 5:27-32

This text has already been treated in the Easter Evening service. It is one of the texts for this service in Years A, B, and C, and the reader may wish to consult our remarks in Years A and B.

Psalm 2

The association of this psalm with the Easter Season and Christian interpretations of Jesus was early and widespread in the early church. The Gospel accounts of the baptism of Jesus and the Epistle to the Hebrews are heavily dependent on this psalm in their christological formulations. In many ways, the New Testament writers were justified in their utilization of this text since it is messianic through and through. By "messianic" we mean it reflects aspects of the ancient Israelite understanding of the reigning king (their messiah).

Two features of the royal theology (messianic theology) are paramount in this psalm: the king's relationship to Yahweh and his place in the world of other nations. One form of interpretation sees this psalm as part of the spoken components of the royal coronation ceremony. It was thus used when a new king was crowned in Jerusalem. If this is the case, then the twofold relationship of the king—to God and to the other nations—focused on in this psalm is clearly understandable.

The first six verses may be seen as two stanzas in which the lines of the second are responses to those of the first. The opening stanza describes the planning and plotting of the nations (these represent historical chaos) against Yahweh and his messiah, the Jerusalem king (God and the king represent divine order and divine institutions). Placing the lines of the two stanzas in tandem gives the following parallels between the lament or description of distress in verses 1-3 and the description and response of God in verses 4-6: The nations conspire and plot grandiose plans to deal with the problem of the Judeans—God in heaven chuckles; the kings busy themselves with implementation of their plans (building arms and raising armies)—God will speak to them in wrath and fury; and they desire to free themselves from God and his anointed, to proclaim their independence from divinely ordained orders—God reaffirms the role of the Davidic messiah and the holy city of Jerusalem in the world of the nations. In these stanzas, the Davidic ruler is depicted as God's special, the anointed/the messiah, whose role in history sets bounds upon the nations of the world.

In verses 7-9, the messiah-God relationship is more fully spelled out. The king speaks, describing the conditions of his rule granted by God at the time of the coronation—the "today" of verse 7c. The king is declared to be the son of Yahweh, a son of the God. The Hebrews probably understood such sonship in terms of adoption rather than in terms of God's having sired the new monarch. (This may also be the perspective of the earliest Christology in Mark; Jesus was adopted as the Son of God at the baptism which was understood as his anointment and coronation.)

According to verses 8-9, the king was promised that he would rule over the nations of the earth and smash them in pieces like a person breaking pottery with an iron rod. Such imagery of a universal rule no doubt draws upon the monarchical braggadocio fostered in ancient Near Eastern royal palaces and courts. That this is the case can be seen from the following assertions the Assyrian king made about himself:

I, Ashur-nasir-apli, strong king, king of the universe, unrivalled king, king of all the four quarters, sungod of all people, chosen of the gods, beloved of the gods, the pious who rules all people, strong male, who treads upon the necks of his foes, tramples on all enemies, the one who breaks up the forces of the rebellious . . .

This claim to a universal rule, however, laid the foundations for the belief that the Messiah in God's kingdom would rule over the whole cosmos.

The final stanza of this psalm (verses 10-12), probably with the new king speaking, calls upon the nations of the world to recognize God's act in establishing the new king in Jerusalem and to offer obeisance to the Judean monarch. Part of the call is a warning that failure to heed could bring divine retribution. Even in the ancient world, the issue of how one related to God's messiah on the throne in Jerusalem was of ultimate significance.

Revelation 1:4-8

In the cycle of Sundays of Easter, the epistolary readings for Years A, B, and C are taken from First Peter, First John, and Revelation respectively. In keeping with the buoyant mood celebrated in the great Easter octave, the fifty-day period that extends from Easter to Pentecost, they are intended to elicit emotions of confidence, joy, and hope.

We should also note that this text serves as the epistolary reading in Year B for Proper 29 (Christ the King). The reader may wish to consult our remarks there.

As a text for the Second Sunday of Easter, this highly stylized lection from the first chapter of the Johannine apocalypse exudes a feeling of triumph and confident hope. We might first note its structure. It is in the form of an epistolary greeting: "John to the seven churches that are in Asia" (verse 4). To these churches, grace and peace are extended from a threefold source: God, the seven spirits, and Jesus Christ (verses 4-5). Then follows an acclamation to Christ for what he has done in our behalf (verses 5*b*-6). At this point, there is a shift from his past work to his eschatological work. In words reminiscent of the vision of the coming Son of Man in Daniel 7, our eyes are directed toward the future when Christ will appear on the clouds, visible to all. His will be the last word. Finally, in verse 8, our text concludes with the note on which it began: a declaration of the Lord God, the Alpha and Omega, the one who encompasses all of time.

Clearly, the Spirit plays only a minor role in this magnificent text. We receive greetings from "the seven spirits who are before [God's] throne" (3:1; 4:5; 5:6). This is most likely a way of underscoring the fullness of God's Spirit as it is variously manifested.

The God who greets us is defined with respect to time. The present, past, and future are God's in an absolute sense. The formulation here represents an extension of the declaration in Exodus 3:14, "I AM WHO I AM." At the end of the passage, this is amplified with God's own confession as the "Alpha and Omega" (verse 8). Just as these letters respectively begin and end the Greek alphabet, so does God stand at both the beginning and end of time. As such, God is to be understood as both the source from which time and history derive and its *telos*, the polestar toward which all history moves.

But the setting in the ring is provided by Christ. He is first proclaimed, or confessed, in a threefold manner: (1) as faithful witness, (2) firstborn of the dead, and (3) ruler of kings on earth (verse 5). The progression of thought here seems to be chronological. In his earthly life, he demonstrated complete fidelity even as he died as a witness, or martyr of the faith (5:9). The second stage points to his resurrection. As one raised from the dead, he became the first to experience resurrected life. Among all the dead, his "birth" to new life made him the first child of life. The third stage points to the dominion that is his as exalted Lord. It is one in which he reigns preeminently over every earthly ruler: King of kings, Lord of lords (17:14; 19:16).

Our text does not merely attest the preeminence of Christ; it also unfolds the ways in which he has benefited us. He is the one "who loves us and has freed us from our sins by his blood" (verse 6). Indeed, his own reign he has transferred to us (cf. Col. 1:13-14), and we have become his own priests officiating in his behalf (cf. I Pet. 2:5). Because of this, we ascribe eternal glory and dominion.

The text does not end, however, until we are confronted with the future. It is a time of both promise and threat, but especially of threat to those who conspired against him. His judgment will be universal: "all the peoples of the world shall lament in remorse" (verse 7, NEB).

The language of today's text is confessional through and through. We are hearing the early church at worship as it acclaims God as Alpha and Omega and Christ as faithful witness, firstborn of the dead, and ruler of all the kings of the earth. But these words are addressed to churches in crisis that are under threat, and thus they assure them that the enemies of Christ will eventually be confronted by him in judgment. Those who are being threatened with extinction must be reminded that God stands both at the beginning and end, else their hope vanishes.

John 20:19-31

Perhaps this is an appropriate time to remind ourselves and the congregation that this is the Second Sunday of Easter, not the First Sunday After Easter. Easter is not a day but a season, concluding at Pentecost. The lections for these Sundays and the messages drawn from them are vital for sustaining the meaning of Easter in the life and faith of the church.

The preacher would do well to review the comments on

John 20:1-18, the Gospel for Easter Day. Verses 19-31 constitute the second half of the resurrection narrative in this Gospel, each part consisting of two stories: the two disciples and Mary Magdalene (verses 1-18), the ten disciples and Thomas (verses 19-31). Today's lection may be divided into the following units: Jesus' appearance to the disciples (verses 19-23); transition to the Thomas story (verses 24-25); Jesus' appearance to Thomas (verses 26-29); conclusion (verses 30-31).

Very likely verses 19-23 originally existed as a resurrection story apart from verses 1-18. There is no acknowledgment of the appearance to Mary, or of Peter and the other disciple going to the tomb, or of the other disciple already believing (verse 8). On the other hand, verses 19-23 are strikingly similar to Luke 24:36-43. Obviously, many resurrection appearances in Mark and Matthew are in Galilee, while in Luke and John they occur in Jerusalem.

The record of the appearance in verses 19-23 makes several statements important in John's theology.

First, the one risen is the one crucified (verse 20). While there probably was in the statement "he showed them his hands and his side" a response to those who denied Jesus Christ had come in the flesh (1:14; I John 4:2), a primary emphasis of this Evangelist is that the risen and glorified Christ is the same Jesus who was with the Twelve prior to the crucifixion (14:18, 25-26). To believe in Christ is to believe in *Jesus* Christ and to have a Christ cult or a Spirit cult which does not heed and follow Jesus of Nazareth is to distort the gospel.

Second, Jesus gives to his followers the peace that he had promised (verses 19, 21; 14:27; 16:33).

Third, Jesus gives to his disciples the Holy Spirit that had been promised (14:16-17, 25-26; 15:26; 16:7-11, 13-15).

And finally, verses 19-23 contain the commission and granting of apostolic authority (verses 21-23; Matt. 16:19; 18:18). For this Evangelist, authorization for the gospel comes from God through Christ to the apostles whose word makes disciples and preserves the continuity of the message. Within the space of these five verses, one recognizes major themes which are more elaborately treated in Matthew and

Luke: the risen Christ comes to his followers, grants authority, gives the Holy Spirit, and sends them into the world.

Verses 24-25 provide a bridge to the Thomas story. This is not to say these two verses are unimportant; on the contrary, they are the key not only to the Thomas story but to verse 29. The disciples have been given the Holy Spirit and sent out with the word. The first person to whom they speak it does not believe; he insists on palpable evidence. Hence, the appearance to Thomas.

The appearance to Thomas (verses 26-29) offers him the evidence he wants, but it is no more than the others had been given (verse 20). Furthermore, there is no indication that Thomas actually touched Jesus when invited to do so. His confession, "My Lord and my God!" (verse 28) is a burst of praise which may have been used in early Christian worship. After all, these are Sunday stories (verses 19, 26). Jesus' response to Thomas (verse 29) may contain a mild reprimand, but more importantly it contains a blessing on the contemporaries of the writer and on all of us who have not seen and yet who believe. Jesus had prayed for all those who would believe through the apostles' word (17:20). They spoke that word to Thomas and he did not believe, and so the risen Christ repeats and confirms that the word spoken is sufficient for faith and those who believe that word are no less blessed than those who saw Jesus in the flesh.

The conclusion (assuming chapter 21 is an epilogue) simply makes two statements: what is written here has been selected from a multitude of signs performed by Jesus (verse 30), and the purpose of writing (only one other Gospel states its purpose, Luke 1:1-4) is to generate faith in Jesus Christ the Son of God, for it is faith in him as the revelation of God which gives life (verse 31; 17:3). All who believe have passed out of death into life (5:24).

Third Sunday of Easter

Acts 9:1-20; Psalm 30:4-12; Revelation 5:11-14; John 21:1-19 or
John 21:15-19

The texts for this season help us recall the beginnings of the church. In that context the readings for today concern the call and commissioning of two apostles by means of encounters with the risen Lord. The first lesson gives us the account of the conversion of Saul of Tarsus and his designation as a "chosen instrument" of the Lord (Acts 9:15). The psalm responds in particular to Saul's blindness and healing. The second reading is part of the vision of angels around the throne of God, singing praises to the Lamb who was slain. The Gospel reports the appearance of the risen Lord to Peter, whom he commissions to feed his sheep.

Acts 9:1-20

In today's text, Luke presents us with a narrative account of the conversion of Saul of Tarsus. It is the first of three tellings of this dramatic confrontation with the risen Lord. The other two occur as part of Paul's defense speeches (22:3-21; 26:9-23). Paul himself does not give us such a detailed, full-blown account, but he does insist that his prophetic call to be God's messenger to the Gentiles was a dramatic reversal in his life (Gal. 1:12-17).

As the opening text for the Third Sunday of Easter, this account of Paul's conversion serves as Luke's reminder to us that the appearances of the risen Lord were not confined to Easter Day. Not only does the Lord appear to Saul, but to Ananias as well (verse 10), and this is only one of many such dramatic visions in Acts (10:3, 17, 19; 11:5; 12:9; 16:9-10; 18:9; 22:17-21; 23:11; 27:23). In Luke's view, Easter is not confined to a single day. Instead, the risen Lord continues to be the energizing force in the church.

There is some question whether this is best read as an account of Paul's "conversion" or as his prophetic call. Certainly, Paul interprets this experience in terms reminiscent of Old Testament call narratives (Gal. 1:15; cf. Isa. 49:1; Jer. 1:4-5). Luke's accounts also exhibit similar features. The risen Lord employs the double address, "Saul, Saul" (verse 4; also 26:14), which recalls similar instances in the Old Testament where Yahweh issues a summons to Jacob (Gen. 46:2), Moses (Exod. 3:4), and Samuel (I Sam. 3:4). In a later account, Paul relates that he was divinely commissioned while praying in a trance in the temple (Acts 22:17-21). This bears close resemblance to the famous prophetic call of Isaiah (6:1-10). It is also profitable to compare Saul's conversion with that of Heliodorus recorded in II Maccabees 3:22-40 (cf. also IV Macc. 4:1-14).

In any event, Paul's record as a persecutor of the church is well established, both by his own testimony and that of Acts (I Cor. 15:9; Gal. 1:13, 23; Phil. 3:6; Acts 8:3; 22:4, 19; 26:10-11). We are on firm historical ground at this point.

The basic elements of the story are well-known. Saul is introduced as the archenemy of the church, described here as "the Way" (cf. 18:26; 19:9, 23; 22:4; 24:14, 22). Raging with fury, he searches out Christian men and women, and drags them tied and bound before the authorities in Jerusalem (cf. I Macc. 15:21). En route to Damascus, he is knocked to the ground by a lightning bolt from heaven, and out of the dazzling light hears the voice of the risen Lord. The text makes it clear that Paul alone experienced this "appearance" (verse 7; cf. I Cor. 15:8).

Blinded and dazed, he is led to Damascus where he encounters Ananias, God's appointed messenger who trembles at the thought of meeting this persecutor whose reputation has preceded him. Ever obedient (verse 10; cf. I Sam. 3:1-9), he listens to God's charge, which serves as a cameo portrait of the Paul who is presented in Acts 13–28. He is a "chosen vessel" (KJV) destined to be God's witness before Gentiles (13:47; 26:17; 28:18; cf. Rom. 1:5, 14, 16; 11:13; 15:16-18; Gal. 1:16; 2:2, 8, 9; Eph. 3:8; Col. 1:27; I Tim. 2:7), kings (25:13, 23; 26:1; 27:24), and Israel (13:16-43; *passim*). His will also be a mission of suffering (verse 16), which is elaborately attested in Luke's story of Paul (e.g. 14:19-23).

Ananias finds Paul, lays his hands on him (cf. 6:6; 8:17-19; 13:3; 19:6; 28:8) and bestows on him the Holy Spirit (cf. Luke 1:15, 41, 67; Acts 2:4; 4:8, 31; 9:17; 13:9, 52; 19:6). In response, Paul submits to baptism for the forgiveness of his sins (cf. 22:16), and after regaining his strength begins immediately to proclaim in the synagogues of Damascus Jesus as the Son of God (13:33; Luke 22:70).

Even though Luke clearly regards Paul's conversion as a special case and describes it as a way of underscoring his unique role as the apostle to the Gentiles, beyond that it is also instructive. Luke sketches for us a portrait of one prepared by God for a special mission. Thus Paul emerges as another in a long line of divinely commissioned designees who moves out in obedient response, even when it means radically departing from his past and being plunged into suffering as a way of life.

Psalm 30:4-12

This psalm of thanksgiving was originally composed for use in a worship service celebrating a worshiper being healed from some life-threatening illness. As a thanksgiving song, it calls upon the audience accompanying the worshiper (family, friends, fellow villagers) to join in the celebration (verse 4) and to listen to the testimony and preaching of the one healed (verses 5-6).

Verses 1-3, for some reason not included in the lectionary, spell out part of the experience undergone by the worshiper. As usual, the sickness/healing are described in very general categories since the psalm would have been employed on numerous occasions for different persons with different conditions of illness involved. Sheol and Pit in verse 3 refer to the realm of the dead. Here they do not mean that the individual died but are used metaphorically. To be subject to any form of sickness was already to be in the grip of Sheol, to be under the power of death. Weakness in life could be spoken of as being under the power of death. The verbs speaking of the rescue—"drawn me up," "healed," "brought up," "restored"—also use spatial images. These factors allowed such psalms as 30 to be used in the early church when talking about the resurrection (note the use of Ps. 16:8-11 in Acts 2:25-28).

The verses for this lection begin with a call to fellow participants to join in the festivities of the thanksgiving celebration. Verse 6 seems to imply that the worshiper had gone through a phrase of life unconcerned with the Deity. This would have been in a period when things were prospering well and before the onset of trouble (see Deut. 8:11-20). If this is the case, one may assume that this attitude was one the worshiper was warning against. "Don't be like I was"—assuming that nothing could threaten life's prosperity. This may be said to be the anthropological lesson, what the case shows about human nature. The second lesson is theological, having to do with the character of God (verse 5). God's anger may be bitter and the reality of divine punishment strong but these are transitory. It is divine favor and goodwill that are lasting. Tomorrow and the dawn can bring a new day. (This last description is probably based on the fact that worshipers spent the night in the temple and were given divine oracles in conjunction with the morning sacrifice.) This same imagery has impressed itself indelibly in the Christian vocabulary as a consequence of the Easter story.

Verses 7-12 of the psalm are direct address to the Deity—a thanksgiving prayer perhaps offered in conjunction with a thanksgiving sacrifice. As in most thanksgiving psalms, the speaker or psalm-user rehearses the "before" conditions and then what happened. That is, the psalm contains a statement of the distress from which one was saved and sometimes, as in verses 8-10, a summary of the prayer offered at the time of the sickness. The substance of these verses reflects something of a plea bargaining—the worshiper suggests that nothing was to be gained by his death, in fact, it would result in a loss to the Deity, namely, the loss of a faithful worshiper who could no longer offer praise to God in the dust of death.

The "after" vocabulary dominates in verses 11-12. Sackcloth and mourning have been replaced with dancing and gladness. The tears of nightfall have been replaced with the joy that comes in the morning.

Revelation 5:11-14

In today's epistolary reading, we hear the angelic hosts of heaven singing praise to God and the Lamb. It occurs as the last panel of the grand heavenly vision that stretches through two chapters (4:1–5:14). This is the first of several such visions depicted in Revelation. It occurs after the letters to the seven churches of Asia (2:1–3:22). At the outset, we get a glimpse of what is to come as John unfolds his vision of the Son of Man (1:9-20). But the scope of this vision in chapter 1 is far more narrow than the vision of chapters 4–5.

We are introduced to the vision through a door opening into heaven itself (4:1). We are first shown the magnificent heavenly throne splendidly furnished (cf. 4:2, 9-10; 5:1; 6:16; 7:10, 15; 19:4; 20:11; 21:5; also I Kings 22:19; II Chron. 18:18; Ps. 47:9; Isa. 6:1; Sir. 1:8). Surrounding this central throne are twenty-four other thrones on which are seated twenty-four elders clad in priestly attire (4:4, 10; 5:5-8, 14; 7:11, 13; 11:16, 14:3; 19:4; cf. Isa. 24:23). Flashes of lightning and peals of thunder around the throne interrupt the quiet tranquility we might expect. It is clear that we are in the presence of the Divine before whom all the elements quiver and shake.

The heavenly court includes more than the twenty-four elders. Encircling the throne are the four living creatures, that is, animals (4:6; 5:6, 8, 11, 14; 6:1; 7:11; 14:3; 15:7; 19:4). They resemble a lion, a bull, a human, and an eagle respectively. Each has six wings and is literally covered with eyes. They pour out unceasing praise to God who sits enthroned, and as they sing the twenty-four elders bow down in unison. We see an elaborate, lavishly furnished heavenly court genuflecting in unison as they honor the One at their center: the eternal God who made the universe.

Next our eyes are drawn to the right hand of the enthroned God. It holds a scroll written on both sides and sealed with seven seals. A book so thoroughly sealed can only contain the deepest of mysteries, but alas there is no one in the entire heavenly court who is able to break the seals. Then, out of the misty background there emerges the figure of the Lamb with all the signs of having been slaughtered. It has seven horns and seven eyes. As he moves toward center stage to take the scroll, those in the heavenly court pay him the homage they had previously given to God. Their song expresses their confidence in his ability and worthiness to break the seals (5:9-10). His sacrificial slaughter in which his blood was poured out has qualified him to break the seals and open the book.

It is at this point that today's text begins. First, the heavenly court has lavished praise on God who sits enthroned. Then, it directs its attention to the slain Lamb of God. Now, the chorus of voices widens to include thousands upon thousands of angels, heavenly figures who are not included in the immediate heavenly court (cf. Dan. 7:10; I Enoch 14:22; 40:1; Heb. 12:22). This host of angels is seen as an endless host circling the throne, the animals, and the elders. It is, as it were, a never-ending set of adoring heavenly beings arranged in concentric circles with their attention riveted toward the center.

The angels' song simply echoes that of the twenty-four elders and the four animals: praise to the slaughtered Lamb who is now ascribed every imaginable accolade: "power, riches, wisdom, strength, honor, glory and blessing" (verse 12, JB; cf. 7:12; 11:17; 12:10; 19:1-2; also I Chron. 29:11).

But the circle widens even farther to include not only the twenty-four elders, the four animals, and the angelic hosts, but every living creature "in heaven and on earth and under the earth and in the sea" (verse 13). The language encompasses every imaginable region (cf. Exod. 20:4; Deut. 5:8; Ps. 146:6; also Phil. 2:10).

As this breathtaking, opening vision reaches its conclusion and we are prepared for the scene in which the Lamb breaks open the seven seals (chapter 6), the combined chorus of voices that includes every species of aerial, terrestrial, subterranean, and aquatic animal, pays honor both to the God who sits enthroned and the slaughtered Lamb. This serves as a means of calling our attention, in closing, to the two chief figures of the vision: God and the Lamb. As a final gesture, the four animals say, "Amen," and the twenty-four elders bow down.

If we allow ourselves to resonate with the imagery of this vision, we find that we are truly overwhelmed. This attests the immense power of apocalyptic language to engage us. If we allow it to work the way it was intended to work, as we move through the vision we find that we too are being "taken up" into heaven to peer through the open door along with John the Seer. Before long, we find ourselves singing the song of the heavenly host and bowing down in reverence and awe before the eternal God and Christ, the slain Lamb of God whose cause has finally been vindicated. We soon see ourselves as among those of "every race, language, people and nation" who are made *"a line of kings and priests"* destined to serve God and rule the world (verses 9-10, JB). The Seer's vision, in other words, becomes our own vision.

John 21:1-19 *or* John 21:15-19

Today the preacher is offered an alternative reading, but since it consists of verses which lie within the longer lection, we will here comment upon the whole of 21:1-19 and thereby attend to the alternate in the process. But first a few words need to be said about John 21 as a whole.

John 21 is often referred to as an epilogue. To do so is not to imply lesser quality or authority but to indicate its literary relationship to the remainder of the Gospel. Clearly the writer drew the Gospel to a conclusion at 20:30-31, and 21:1, "After this" only loosely joins what follows to what precedes. In addition, verses 24-25 can be taken as the signature of a later hand, perhaps a disciple of the writer of chapters 1–20. But whether by the same or a later writer, a more pressing question has to do with the purpose of this chapter. What does it seek to achieve? To correct a rumor in the early church that the beloved disciple would never die, say some commentators. Verses 20-23 certainly explain the origin of the notion and set the record straight, but there is much in the chapter unrelated to that matter. To rehabilitate Simon Peter, say others. Perhaps; the one who denied Jesus three times here is given an opportunity to affirm his love three times (verses 15-19). Simon Peter is certainly a prominent figure in most of the scenes in the chapter. The story confirms I Corinthians 15:5 and Luke 24:34 which speak of a resurrection appearance to Simon, and verses 4-8 have a parallel in Luke 5:3-7 in which attention focuses on Peter. In addition, the shepherd imagery of verses 15-19 is echoed in I Peter 5:1-5, a text associated with Simon Peter. However, this theory hardly fits the less than complimentary portrait of Simon, especially in verses 4-8 and 20-23, and the more favorable view of the beloved disciple (verses 7, 20). Another common theory is that this chapter was added by someone favorable to Galilean Christianity who wished to end the Gospel with a resurrection appearance in Galilee (21:1), as do Mark and Matthew, rather than in Jerusalem. Again, the theory is not adequate for all the material in the epilogue. Perhaps multiple purposes rather than a single one best fit the chapter.

The portion of chapter 21 providing today's lesson may be divided as follows: the setting (verses 1-3); Jesus' appearance to the disciples (verses 4-8); breakfast with Jesus (verses 9-14); Jesus and Simon Peter (verses 15-19). The scene at the Sea of Tiberias (Galilee) is more Synoptic than Johannine. In Mark 1:16-20, Jesus calls his first disciples from a life of fishing; according to John 1:35-42, the first disciples came to Jesus from following John the Baptist. John 1:43-45 agrees, however, that they were Galileans. The return to fishing implies the disciples were unable to sustain Easter beyond resurrection appearances. Belief in the resurrection was an item of faith but it had not been translated into life and mission in the world. The radical decline in church attendance and activity after Easter Sunday indicates the problem is still with us. When Jesus appeared again (verse 4), it is as though the disciples had not seen the risen Christ before, even though this is the third appearance (verse 14). That which stirs them to faith is Jesus' supernatural knowledge (1:47-49; Luke 5:3-7) concerning the fish. As one has come to expect by now, the beloved disciple is the first to recognize Jesus (verse 7), just as he was the first to believe in the resurrection (20:8).

The breakfast by the sea (verses 9-14) not only confirms

that the risen Lord is the historical Jesus (he eats bread and fish), but recalls some of the most meaningful moments shared during Jesus' ministry. Although not a major theme in John, the other Gospels frequently portray Jesus at table. Early in the thinking and practice of the early church, eating together was an occasion for experiencing the presence of Christ (I Cor. 11:23-24; Luke 24:28-35, 41-43). Fish and bread quickly came to have symbolic significance far beyond their value as staples of the common diet. Eating together confirmed and encouraged faith for living in the face of immense obstacles.

If the meal with Christ reflects early Christian worship, then worship was also a time of being confronted with Christ's penetrating question, "Do you love me?" (verses 15-19). The exchanges between Simon and Jesus reveal several strong accents in the theology of this Evangelist: faith is a personal relationship with Christ (15:1-8); this relationship has its expression not only in words but in obedience (14:15); one particular form of this obedience is caring for others as Christ did (10:1-17; 20:21); for some such as Simon Peter, this obedience will result in martyrdom (16:2); but to all, wherever it may lead, the word by which discipleship began is the final word: "Follow me" (verse 19).

Fourth Sunday of Easter

Acts 13:15-16, 26-33; Psalm 23; Revelation 7:9-17; John 10:22-30

It is the season of the beginning of the church, and this took place through the proclamation of the "message of this salvation" (Acts 13:26), the "good news" (Acts 13:32) that God raised Jesus from the dead. So, our first reading reports that Paul preached in Asia Minor. The psalm does not respond directly to the first reading, but the theme of the Lord as shepherd anticipates the Gospel lection. The second reading is a portion of that vision of the redeemed before the throne of God. The passage from John has Jesus respond to a challenge by asserting that his sheep hear his voice, he knows them, and they follow him.

Acts 13:15-16, 26-33

The setting for today's opening text is Paul's missionary sermon in the synagogue at Antioch of Pisidia. It occurs within the larger setting of his mission work in Syria, Cyprus, and in central Asia Minor, what is sometimes called his first missionary journey. Upon entering Pisidian Antioch, Paul and his entourage go to the synagogue, which provides the occasion for Luke to present an example of Paul's preaching to a Jewish audience. As the first full-length sermon that appears on the lips of Paul (13:16-41), it is intended to provide us with one of his typical synagogue sermons. In some respects it reminds us of Peter's sermon in Acts 10:34-43, which we treated earlier as the opening lection for Easter. But this sermon has its distinctive contours.

It is crafted for an audience of Jews and God-fearing Jewish proselytes (verse 16). It begins with God's election of Israel and rehearses their stay in Egypt (verse 17), their Exodus from Egypt (verse 17), and the forty years of wilderness wandering (verse 18). It moves on to the period of conquest (verse 19), the judges and the monarchy (verses 20-22). Specifically mentioned are Saul and David, and here the historical survey stops (verse 23). We soon see that the summary of Israel's history has been moving toward David as a way of getting to Jesus, David's progeny.

At this point, the Christian phase begins as we are told of the ministry and preaching of John the Baptist (verses 24-25). Here begins the portion of the sermon selected for today's opening lection. The story that began with Abraham is seen to have its logical fulfillment in the Christian movement—"to us has been sent the message of this salvation" (verse 26; cf. 10:36; also Ps. 107:20; 147:18). The Jews of Jerusalem and their leaders are charged with failing to read the prophets carefully. They have inadvertently fulfilled what the prophets predicted by their rejection of Jesus. It was a mistake of ignorance (verse 27; 3:17; 17:30; cf. Luke 23:34; I Cor. 2:8; also I Tim. 1:13).

Paul insists on the innocence of Jesus (verse 28)—a recurrent Lukan emphasis (Luke 23:4, 13-15, 22, 41, 47). The Jewish leaders enlisted Pilate to kill him (verse 28; cf. 2:23). All of those who had a hand in his death were unwittingly fulfilling the prophets, even as they took him down from the cross and laid him in a tomb (verse 29; cf. Luke 18:31; Matt. 27:59-68 and parallels).

It was God who reversed this miscarriage of justice by raising him from the dead (verse 30; cf. 3:15; 4:10; 5:30; 10:40; 13:37). Afterward, he appeared "for many days" to those who had followed him from Galilee to Jerusalem, and in doing so became his witnesses (verse 31; 1:22; I John 1:1-6). This section ends with the good news that God's promise has been fulfilled (2:24; Rom. 1:4). The Son begotten by the Father mentioned in Psalm 2 can be none other than Jesus, the Son of David (verse 33).

The final section of the sermon futher expands on Christ's resurrection (verses 34-37) and moves to the offer of forgiveness through his name (verses 38-39). The final word is a word of warning that his Jewish audience take heed lest they once again become the unwitting fulfillment of the prophetic scriptures (verses 40-41).

As it stands, the lection has an awkward transition. Moving directly from verse 16 to verse 26 is slightly redundant. This can be remedied simply by omitting 16*b*.

The portion of Paul's speech selected for the opening lection provides us with a concise summary of the early Christian kerygma as presented to a Jewish audience. As we read it in the context of the Fourth Sunday of Easter, it places us squarely within the storyline of Jewish history. The theological claim being made is that the Christian story is the proper ending to the story begun with Abraham and Moses and that moves through David to Christ. Even though the sermon occurs on the lips of Paul, it embodies Lukan theology: the Christian movement is the fulfillment of the divine promise. At every stage, it shows us God's promise coming true and God's word being kept.

Psalm 23

The choice of this psalm to accompany the reading from the Gospel of John is based on the psalm's utilization of imagery drawn from shepherding and on the sense of confidence that permeates the entire composition.

In spite of the fact that Psalm 23 is perhaps the best known of the Psalms and that its overall thrust is quite clear, many questions still puzzle scholars about the original considerations that went into its writing. Was it a song of confidence and assurance for general use by the people? Or originally only by the king? Or by someone who had taken asylum and sought protection in the sanctuary because of some accident (perhaps manslaughter)? How is God described in the psalm? Only as a shepherd? Or as a shepherd and a dinner host? Is the psalmist described only as a sheep or also as a dinner guest?

In spite of such uncertainties, the psalm's emphasis on the nature of God and his actions as the source of human trust is quite clear. The psalmist faces the future unafraid because of confidence based on trust in Yahweh.

Two sets of images can be seen running throughout the

psalm: images of trouble and danger and images of assurance and tranquility. The psalm does not assume a Pollyanna attitude that reads all of life optismistically and expects good everywhere. The writer takes no sunshine, everything-will-be-okay attitude toward existence.

The following are the terms and images used to speak of the negative aspects, the troubles of life: (1) The "shadow of death" or, better, "the valley of deep darkness" (see RSV margin); (2) evil; and (3) enemies. The very fact that troubles are given such a place in the psalm has contributed to its appeal. It rings true to life.

The positive images of protection and assurance predominate in the psalm. Note the following: "green pastures" and "still waters" which provide food and drink to restore one's physical vitality and life (RSV: "restores my soul"); leads along proper paths (RSV: "paths of righteousness") so as to avoid danger; a rod and staff offer protection against predators and direction to the would-be prey; "a table" spread with all the accompanying accouterments like oil for the body and wine for the spirit; and finally a dwelling in the house of Yahweh (the temple) to the length of a person's days (not "for ever" as in the RSV). To dwell in the temple might be taken literally and understood to refer to a manslayer claiming asylum (see Deut. 19:1-10), to some cultic personnel who served continuously in the temple (see I Chron. 9:33), or it might be a metaphorical way of expressing the opportunity to visit the temple (see Pss. 15:1; 24:3).

Revelation 7:9-17

Before we look at today's text, perhaps we should fill in the gap between this and last week's epistolary reading. After the panoramic vision of God enthroned amid the heavenly court is completed (4:1–5:14), the Lamb proceeds with his appointed task of opening the seven seals of the scroll (5:1). The opening of the first six seals is described in chapter 6. But before the opening of the seventh seal, which is related in 8:1-5, there is an interlude (chapter 7).

The interlude comprises two visions. The first is that of the 144,000 redeemed who enjoy divine protection (verses 1-8).

The second is that of a vast multitude of people who are gathered around the throne of God (verses 9:17). It is this second vision that serves as today's epistolary lection.

The scene is the same as that depicted in the earlier vision described in chapters 4–5: God sitting enthroned, encircled by the heavenly court of the twenty-four elders, the four animals, and the angelic hosts (verse 11). As before, they praise God and the Lamb as those to whom full and final salvation belongs (verse 10; cf. 5:13; 11:15, 17; 12:10; 15:3-4; 19:1-2, 5, 6-7).

What is different this time is that the host of worshipers is now extended even further. The earlier vision ended with all living creatures, probably animals, ascribing worship to God (5:13). But now there is a vast, innumerable, multitude drawn from all the peoples of the earth (verse 9; 5:9; 10:11; 11:9; 13:7; 14:6; 17:15). They are standing before the Lamb clothed in white robes (verse 9; 6:11; 3:4-5, 18; 4:4; 19:14). They are also holding palm branches in their hands (cf. Lev. 23:40, 43; also II Macc. 10:7). Their white clothing symbolizes purity and righteousness, the branches victory. As they ascribe salvation to God and the Lamb, the rest of the heavenly court bows in honorific response and pays similar tribute (verses 11-12).

The members of this vast multitude are still unidentified. So, one of the elders asks the Seer who these white-clad persons are and where they have come from (verse 13). We are told that they are those who have endured the "great tribulation" (cf. Dan. 12:1; Matt. 24:21 and parallels). Their robes have been purified through the blood of the Lamb (cf. Rev. 22:14; Gen. 49:11; Exod. 19:10, 14; also I John 1:7; Rev. 1:5; Heb. 9:14). They are, in other words, the martyred saints who have been vindicated by God and now form part of the heavenly company.

Their lot is now described (verses 15-17). This eschatological vision has three features:

1. Unceasing worship of God in the heavenly temple (verse 15). They now center their attention around the heavenly throne, serving in the temple night and day (cf. 3:12; 11:1-2, 19; 14:15, 17; 15:5-6, 8; 16:1, 17; 21:22). They now enjoy the divine protection of God's own presence (cf. Ezek. 37:27).

2. Absence of physical deprivation (verse 16). Life with God in the heavenly court excludes hunger, thirst, and scorching heat. The description here is a direct quotation of Isaiah 49:10. Also excluded are tears (verse 17*b*; cf. Rev. 21:4; Isa. 25:8; Jer. 31:16).

3. Presence of the Lamb in their midst as their shepherd (verse 17). The Lamb is now envisioned as the Shepherd who lives and walks among his sheep (5:6; Ezek. 34:23). In language reminiscent of Psalm 23, the Shepherd guides the saints to springs of living water (Ps. 23:1-3; cf. also Rev. 21:6; Isa. 49:10).

One of the most obvious features of this text is its thematic connection with Psalm 23 and the Gospel reading (John 10:22-30). All three of these texts speak of shepherds, each in its distinctive way, but the epistolary text, as well as the Gospel text, shows the way in which the imagery of Psalm 23 was appropiated by the early church.

For some, depictions of the eschatological age such as we have here are too distant, removed from the world we know and live in. In this text, however, the people of God are central. The martyred saints have moved beyond this life and have begun to participate in the triumph of the heavenly court. The life sketched for them in verses 15-17 may be an eschatological ideal, but it is one to which we have all aspired at one time or another, in one way or another. One of the preacher's tasks in treating this text is to establish some link of continuity between life as depicted here and life as we know it—or wish it.

John 10:22-30

It is still Easter, but even Easter does not relieve the church of the task of engaging opposition and unbelief. Hence our lection for today. John 10:22-30 lies within the long section on controversies between Jesus and various opponents (5:1–10:42). Several times in this section Jesus is threatened with death on the charge of blasphemy. Even if that word is not mentioned, that is the issue because Jesus made himself equal with God (5:18; 8:58-59; 10:30-31). This death talk, though real, is ineffective, because in this Gospel, no one takes Jesus' life, he gives it (10:18) when his hour comes (12:23).

Some scholars speak of 10:22-30 as a duplicate passage because it repeats events and conversations centering in the Feast of Tabernacles (chapters 7, 8). Here at the Feast of Dedication (verse 22) as during the Feast of Tabernacles, Jesus is in the vicinity of the temple; Jesus is pressed to declare openly who he is; Jesus refuses on the grounds that the people would not believe if he did; Jesus declares his unity with God; an attempt is made on Jesus' life. The lines of repetition are evident, but the time, place, and issue at stake still deserve attention.

The controversy in 10:22-30 occurs in Jerusalem, in Solomon's portico, during the feast of Dedication. This feast is the Feast of Hanukah, observed in the winter (verse 22), near the time of the Christian celebration of Christmas. Hanukah commemorated the Maccabean victory over the Syrians about 160 B.C, the recovery of the temple, and the consecration of the altar which had been profaned by the Syrians. Already in this Gospel, Jesus' signs, speeches, and controversies have been presented as occurring on other feast days: Sabbath, Passover, and Tabernacles. In this Evangelist's theology, Jesus fulfills and brings to an end Judaism with all its festivals and traditions. While the follower of Jesus celebrates this understanding, opposition to it and to Jesus by those who hold dear these traditions is to be expected. And it is important to keep in mind that in this Gospel, the Jews are not only the Jews but they represent "the world" which does not believe. Church history makes it abundantly clear that "the world" is inside as well as outside the circle of disciples. Our text addresses conditions within the church in which customs, places, traditions, and rituals are held so firmly that the total adequacy of Christ is obscured, if not denied.

Again Jesus is pressed to state clearly if he is the Christ (verse 24). He refuses to answer for two reasons: one, they would not believe even if he told them (verses 25-26). They have the witness of Jesus' works but they are unconvinced. In 5:30-47 the testimonies to Christ are listed—John the Baptist, the scriptures, God, and Jesus' works—and yet the controversy continues. As Chrysostom put it, they do not believe, not because Jesus is not a shepherd but because they are not sheep. The second reason Jesus does not tell them he is the Christ is that Christ or Messiah is not an adequate term to identify who Jesus is. He is the Messiah, but the term had been so shaped by the expectations and wishes of the people that it was hardly possible to say yes to the question without creating false hopes. When an expectation is distorted, the fulfillment of that expectation gets distorted. The first task of a messiah is to get people to quit looking for a messiah. Jesus moves his auditors beyond the idea of messiah to son of God. The crucial claim is stated in verse 30: "I and the Father are one." It is for this claim that attempts are made on Jesus' life (5:18; 8: 58-59; 10:30-31, 36-39).

The line of thought in verses 26-29 seems to be circular: my sheep are the ones who believe and those who believe are my sheep. Some light may be shed by two comments on Johannine theology. First, faith is a possibility for those who will to do the will of God (7:17). Although faith is a complex theme in this Gospel, one theme is consistent: for those who stand back, arms folded, waiting to be convinced, final proof is never enough. Those who enter the flock hear the shepherd's voice. Second, in this Gospel, Jesus is the revelation of God, from above, whose ministry is not contingent on any human act or word or request. Even toward his mother (2:3-4), his brothers (7:3-9), and his friends (11:3-6), Jesus behaves according to "his hour"; that is, all directives are from above. So complete is this initiative from above that even Jesus' disciples are those chosen, given of God. In our language, this is a radical understanding of grace: all is of God, not of our choosing. It is inevitable that strong statements of grace sound very much like determinism. Alongside such affirmations, however, are others which announce freely that whoever believes has life eternal (3:16-17). Christian faith lives by and witnesses to both statements: all is of God, and whosoever will.

Fifth Sunday of Easter

Acts 14:8-18; Psalm 145:13b-21; Revelation 21:1-6; John 13:31-35

The readings for this day are rich in their diversity. The first lesson continues the account of the spread of the gospel with the story of Paul and Barnabas at Lystra healing a man who was a cripple from birth and then of their being regarded as gods. The responsorial psalm is a hymn of praise that underscores the apostles' affirmation that worship belongs to God alone. John's vision of a new heaven and a new earth, with all things new, is the second reading. In the Gospel lection a great deal is presented in a few verses: Jesus' assertion that God is glorified in the glorification of the Son of man, his assertion that no one can go where he is going, his gift of the new commandment, "that you love one another," and the message that his disciples are known by their love for one another.

Acts 14:8-18

This opening reading has the same general setting as the text from Acts in last week's reading. Paul is engaged in his mission of central Asia Minor. Having been driven out of Pisidian Antioch, Paul and his company entered Iconium only to meet similar resistance from unbelieving Jews. Eventually, they arrive at Lystra, where Luke relates the incident described in today's reading.

It is the story of the healing of a man crippled from birth and its impact on the native population. In many respects, it is reminiscent of the healing of the lame man in the temple by Peter and John (3:1-10). As Peter had done, Paul fixed his gaze on the man (verse 9; cf. 3:4). The signs of his healing were visible (verse 10; cf. 3:8).

185

The form of the story exhibits the general outline of the miracle of healing stories that we find in the Gospels and other literature of the ancient world: (1) a description of the afflicted person (verse 9); (2) encounter with the miracle-worker, in this case, Paul who stares at him and sees some sign of faith (verse 9; cf. Matt. 8:10; Luke 5:20); (3) the healing itself, here expressed in Paul's command for him to stand up and walk (verse 10; cf. Acts 9:34; Ezek. 2:1); (4) visible proof of the healing—"he sprang up and walked" (verse 10; cf. 3:8); and (5) the impact on the crowds who are here inclined to elevate Barnabas and Paul to divide status (verses 11-13).

As is the typical pattern in Luke-Acts, a prophetic deed, such as a powerful sign or wonder, is often followed by a prophetic word. In Act 3, the healing of the lame man at the Gate Beautiful (3:1-10) provides the occasion for Peter's sermon in the temple (3:11-26). In chapter 14, though the healing of the lame man at Lystra is not followed by a full-blown sermon, it is followed by a short statement (verses 15-17).

The remarks attributed to Barnabas and Saul provide a counterpoint to the lengthy sermon Paul preached in Pisidian Antioch (13:16-41). There, Luke provides an example of a typical synagogue sermon. Here, we are given the gist of what Paul is likely to have said in contexts where the gospel confronts popular pagan superstition. The more full-blown version of a Pauline sermon before a pagan audience does not occur until he goes to Athens (17:22-31).

Several features of their remarks are worth noting:

1. Barnabas and Paul stoutly resist being elevated to divine status. They too are human like their audience (cf. Acts 10:26; also James 5:17; Wisd. of Sol. 7:1-6; IV Macc. 12:13). They are not to be regarded as gods who come down from heaven but as bringers of good news (14:7; 15:21).

2. Pagans with no previous contact with Jewish religion are urged to turn away from "vain things" and turn to a living God (verse 15). This seems to have been the basic pattern of early Chirstian preaching to Gentiles (cf. Rom. 1:21; Gal. 4:9; I Thess. 1:9; also Acts 15:19; 26:20).

3. The basic appeal is to recognize God as Creator. Naturally, this is a corollary of belief in the living God, but it

renders it more specifically (cf. 4:24; 17:24; Rev. 10:6; 14:7; Exod. 20:11; II Kings 19:15; Neh. 9:6; Isa. 37:16; Ps. 146:6).

4. God has not been without witness among all the nations (verses 16-17; cf. Rom. 1:20). Even though God has not coerced Gentiles to accept monotheistic worship, there has been abundant testimony of God's goodness, seen in the lavish provision of the natural order (verse 17; cf. Lev. 26:4; Jer. 5:24; Ps. 147:8).

Within Luke's overall literary purpose, this episode is intended to give us a glimpse of the gospel confronting popular pagan religion. All the elements of popular religion are here, such as the people's inclination to deify these itinerant preachers who heal one of their own (cf. Acts, 28:6). But their steadfast refusal to be turned into supermen is instructive. Empowered by the Spirit they may be, but gods they are not. Luke wants to make sure this line is clearly drawn. One of his messages is that the power of the Easter faith works through bringers of good news without turning them into gods. Their task is not to become God, but to proclaim God—the living God who is responsible for creating all things and providing us with rains, harvests, and satisfying food.

Psalm 145:13b-21

This acrostic or alphabetic psalm interweaves petition and proclamation, prayer and praise, speech to God and speech about God into a well-integrated and articulate composition. Petition/prayer/speech to God is found in verses 1-2, 4-7, 10-13a, 15-16, and proclamation/praise/speech about God is found in verses 3, 8-9, 13b-14, 17-21. This lection consists of prayer (verses 15-16) and proclamation (verses 13b-14, 17-21).

In some respects, this psalm comes as close as any Old Testament text to giving us a theological description of the Divine. The verses preceding our reading speak of the kingdom of God. Verses 13b-20 may be said to describe the nature of the king who rules over his domain. One of the linquistic features of these verses is the word "all" (Hebrew *kol*) which appears over a dozen times in these verses. The term indicates the inclusiveness and universality of the actions and sentiments of God.

Two things should be noted, in general, about this latter part of the psalm. (1) The author of the psalm, and thus all who used it, speak about God in a rather detached fashion. Theological speech is present in an almost unique form but there is little passion, little sense of intense feeling. This fits in with the teaching and didactic quality and alphabetic form of the psalm. (2) The theology of the psalm is one based on extreme confidence, assurance, and certitude. That is, the psalm seems to breathe the air of success in life, to reflect the positive outlook of one secure in the world, confident in the operations of the cosmos, and positive in outlook and perspective.

Verses 13*b*-21 may be viewed (and preached) in terms of two, almost synonymous, propositions that are stated and then further expounded and illustrated. The propositions are found in verses 13*b* and 17. God is "faithful [loyal] in [to] all his words, and gracious in all his deeds" and "just in all his ways, and kind in all his doings." Two characteristics of the Deity are emphasized: his fidelity to justice in actions and mercy (kindness) as the disposition, the motivating senti-ment, behind divine actions.

Verse 14 illustrates the principle that justice is characteris-tic of divine actions. Such justice is shown in God's rescue of the falling, his support of those bowed down. Those who suffer and are oppressed needlessly and without cause can find in God a defendant and one who rights the situations. (This is one of the reasons why the Old Testament, especially the Psalms, contains so many laments and complaints, so many "bitches" and gripes about the human situation. The expression and articulation of the human hurt is not only viewed as therapeutic but also it is assumed that ultimate reality, God, is disposed to give justice.) That God upholds the falling and raises the fallen echoes one of the major themes of the Bible: God as the special protector of the weak and oppressed, God as the one who "reverses human fate," who brings to fulfillment and realization the unpromising. (This is the Cinderella theme which can be seen as a dominant motif in so much of the Old Testament: Abraham and Sarah with no children, Moses as a babe afloat in the Nile, the Hebrews in slavery, David as a shepherd lad.)

Verses 15 and 16 illustrate the principle that God is gracious. All living things (good and bad, Israelite and foreigner, human and animal) are dependent on God and are not disappointed. God's providence and care sustain the whole of existence.

In verses 17-20, 17*a* is illustrated in verse 18 and 17*b* is illustrated by verses 19-20. (Verse 21 is a sort of closing benediction.) In verses 17-20, a few modifications and conditions enter the picture and slightly modify the more sweeping claims in verses 13*b*-16. Note that "in truth" is a condition in verse 18*b* and verse 20 claims that God preserves those "who love him" but destroys the wicked. Even in God's providence, moral factors are seen as playing their role.

Revelation 21:1-6

As we move through the epistolary lessons in the Sundays of Easter, we gradually progress towards the final vision of the last things, including the vision of the New Jerusalem. Today's epistolary lection consists of one part of that final, grand vision that stretches from 21:1–22:5.

Obviously, its liturgical setting is the season between Easter and Pentecost, and this will cause us to see certain themes more than others. But we should remember that this well-known text also figures in other parts of the lectionary, most notably as the First Lesson for the observance of All Saints Day in Year B and as the Second Lesson for the observance of January 1 as New Year's Day in Year A. The reader may wish to consult our remarks there.

We should begin by noting that this is an apocalyptic vision. We are invited by the Seer to share his vision of "a new heaven and a new earth" (verse 1). As such, it is the fulfillment of the prophetic promise (Isa. 65:17, 19-20; 66:22) towards which early Christian hope was directed (II Pet. 3:13). To the apocalyptic mind, cosmic scenery could change with one stroke of the brush. Mountains could be moved, rivers redirected. The earth, sky, and sea could vanish before one's very eyes (cf. 6:14; 16;20; 20:11; also Ps. 114:3-4, 7-8; II Pet. 3:7, 10, 12). The point is that the world we once knew is no more. All is new.

Our eyes are next lifted up to the open heavens from which we see "the holy city, new Jerusalem" descending. It had become proverbial to think of Jerusalem as the "holy city" (11:2; 21:10; 22:19; cf. Neh. 11:1, 18; Isa. 48:2; 52:1; Dan. 9:24; Matt. 4:5; 27:53). When Christians envisioned heaven, it became natural to do so as the heavenly Jerusalem (Gal. 4:26; Heb. 11:16, 12:22; also Rev. 3:12). The picture is enhanced even further with the introduction of bridal imagery, already used earlier (19:7, 9) and influenced by the Old Testament (Isa. 61:10; cf. Matt. 22:2).

We have already been introduced to the great white throne on which God is seated (20:11). From this throne comes a loud voice which utters an oracle that interprets the vision (verses 3-4). Two elements are worth noting:

1. God's presence is really meant to be within the people of God. Literally, God's tabernacle is with human beings (13:6; cf. John 1:14). This represents the fulfillment of the fondest prophetic hopes, namely that God and the people of God would find their mutual home in and with each other (Lev. 26:12, Ps. 95:7; Jer. 31:1, 33; Ezek. 37:27; Zech. 2:10-11; cf. II Cor. 6:16).

2. The presence of God among the people of God means the removal of all human hurt. Everything that pained us formerly and brought us to tears is now gone, again as the prophets had always hoped (Isa. 25:8; 43:18; 65:17-18; Jer. 31:16, cf. Rev. 7:17). In particular, there is no more death, the most painful of human realities (Isa. 35:10; 51:11; Rev. 20:4; I Cor. 15:26).

As if it were not clear how radically different this view of life is, the enthroned God continues the interpretation, proclaiming, "Behold, I make all things new" (verse 5). It had been an old promise (Isa. 43:19) now made possible through the Christ-event (II Cor. 5:17).

The Seer is instructed to write all this down and is assured that it is an absolutely reliable vision (verse 5). With a word of finality he further asserts, "It is done!" (verse 6; cf. 16:17), and is identified as the "Alpha and the Omega" (cf. 1:8;

22:13). The final words of reassurance in today's lection (which breaks off with verse 6, but could easily be extended through verse 8) are that God stands at the fountain of living water, dispensing water free of charge to the thirsty (cf. 7:16-17; 22:1, 17; John 7:37; Isa. 55:1; Jer. 2:13; Zech. 14:8).

Only those with anemic imaginations can fail to be gripped by this vision of the new heaven and new earth. There has never been a human soul steeped in the human condition who has not pined away for a radically new world. Whether it is Marx sketching the ideal economic state or Lennon crying for us to "imagine" a peaceful world, the hope is always for something different—and better. What is striking about the Seer's vision in today's text is that in this new world God is the central figure. Whatever else may be hoped for, the Seer sees no chance apart from the mutual indwelling of God and the people of God. The faith of Easter is that this is now possible through the risen Christ in a way otherwise unimaginable.

John 13:31-35

Our Gospel for today falls within that portion of John's Gospel generally referred to as the farewell materials. The public ministry of Jesus ended at 12:50, 13:1-30 records the farewell meal, and 13:31–17:26 consists of farewell discourses and prayer. This entire section is presented as occurring on a single evening, concluding in the garden where Jesus was arrested (18:1). As farewell material it is both the preparation of Jesus' disciples for his coming death and the message of the glorified Christ to the church preparing them for life in the world following his departure. No other Gospel so extensively deals with the absence of Jesus, the first major crisis for the disciples.

Today's lection consists of Jesus' words spoken at table following the last meal he had with the Twelve. According to John 13:1, the meal is before the Passover (Jesus dies on the day of Preparation as the Passover lamb, 19:31-37) and not the Passover meal as in the Synoptics (Mark 14:12, parallels). John alone records the footwashing (13:1-20) and joins the Synoptics in recording Jesus' indication of his betrayer (verses 21-30). Judas leaves the room (verse 30), and our lesson begins, "When he had gone out, Jesus said. . . ." Brief as it is, 13:31-35 consists of three parts: Jesus' announcement of his glorification (verses 31-32); Jesus' statement of his glorification in terms of departure from the disciples (verse 33); Jesus' instruction for their life together after his departure (verses 34-35).

Since the glorification of the Son in this Gospel refers to the death, resurrection, and return to God, verses 31-32 are John's equivalent of a passion prediction. Here as in the Synoptics the announcement meets with confusion among the disciples (13:36–14:11; Mark 8:27-33; 9:30-37; 10:32-35), but there the parallels end. In the Synoptics, the predictions are in private; here Jesus has already told the Jews (verse 33); in the Synoptics, the predictions are followed by instructions on cross bearing, service, and childlikeness; here the disciples are commanded to love one another (verses 34-35). Also unique to this Gospel is Jesus' translation of his announcement of glorification into terms that are personal and relational. "Little children, yet a little while I am with you. You will seek me. . . .'Where I am going you cannot come'" (verse 33). This is family talk; a group is about to lose the one who is their reason to be together. The key to their understanding what is happening and to their future is their relationship to Christ and to one another. The burden of Jesus' word to them is that their relation to him inform and determine their relation to one another. The "one another" here clearly refers to the members of the community of faith. There are, of course, texts urging love for all people, but that is not the thrust of this text. Here and in the prayer in chapter 17 the concern is for Christians relating to one another. The immediate need in the Johannine church was internal harmony. As is clear in I John 2–4, doctrinal disputes and differences in response to outside pressures were eroding the unity of the Johannine church. Love for one another was essential for the continued life of the community.

But in what sense is the command to love "new"? Certainly there is no implication that love was absent from their lives in the tradition of Judaism. Perhaps it was new in that the disciples were entering a new time of life in the world after Jesus' departure. Perhaps it was new in that only now had Jesus begun to talk this way to them. Or perhaps the nature of their love for one another was to be new: they were to love as he had loved them (verse 34). And what was the nature of that love? It was, according to this Gospel, a matter of telling the truth, being faithful in sharing the word of God, continuing to act *for* those who may not be responsive, and, if need be, to give one's life. If love is understood as acting toward one another as God has acted toward the world and as Christ has acted toward his disciples, then love is not simply a feeling. If love is a way of speaking and doing and being for one another, then it is not strange to speak of love for one another as a "commandment."

Sixth Sunday of Easter

Acts 15:1-2, 22-29; Psalm 67; Revelation 21:10, 22-27; John 14:23-29

One theme that runs through the texts for the day concerns the question of qualifications for membership in the community of faith. The background of the Acts passage is dissension and debate concerning the Jewish laws, specifically, Is circumcision necessary? The result is an apostolic decree concerning the admission of Gentiles. The responsorial psalm is a song of thanksgiving, including a call for all peoples and nations to praise God. The second lesson is the magnificent vision of the new Jerusalem, the gates of which are always open, "but only those who are written in the Lamb's book of life" (Rev. 21:27) will enter. In the Gospel reading Jesus promises that the Father will love those who love him and keep his word.

Acts 15:1-2, 22-29

The book of Acts unfolds the growth of the church as it moves beyond Jerusalem to the regions of the western Mediterranean. In one sense, it is a series of successes, even when met with resistance. But it is not without controversy. Luke's inclusion of an account of the Jerusalem Conference in Acts 15 attests this. The church may experience rapid growth but not without internal conflict. And when this occurs, the thing to do is to stop and resolve the conflict.

Chapter 15 has this function in the overall narrative. It is centrally located within Acts. The Jerusalem Conference occurs between Paul's mission in Syria and central Asia Minor and the next major stage of his work, his mission in Western Asia Minor and the Aegean. Until the question of the terms on which Gentiles become members of the church is resolved, further progress cannot be made.

The crux of the matter is stated in verse 2: some Jews from Judea had come to Antioch insisting that circumcision was a prerequisite to salvation (verse 1; cf. 15:24; 21:20-21; also Gal. 2:12). Put simply, in order to be included among the people of God, Gentiles had to become Jews.

This occasioned "no small dissension," Luke's understated way of saying that it sparked a major controversy (cf. 15:39; 23:7, 10; 24:5; also II Tim. 2:23). Paul and Barnabas argued the case of freedom from the law for Gentiles. Since the matter could not be resolved then and there, the church in Antioch decided to send a delegation to Jerusalem where they could take it up with the leadership of the church, that is, the apostles and elders (verse 2; cf. 15:4, 6, 22-23; 16:4; also 11:30; 14:23; 20:17; 21:18). Hence the calling of the first church council.

It is not clear whether the conference was limited and included only the delegation meeting with the apostles and elders (verse 6), or whether it included the whole church (verses 12, 22). In any case, as Luke reports it, the assembled group heard from Peter (15:6-11), Barnabas and Paul (15:12), and James (15:13-21). Because of his influential role in the Jerusalem church, James makes the proposal that carries the day (cf. Acts 12:17; Gal. 1:19; 2:12).

It is the proposal of James that is included in the letter embodying the apostolic decree (15:23-29), and this forms the heart of today's First Lesson. The final section (15:30-35) reports that the delegation returned to Antioch with the letter. When it was read to the congregation, it caused great joy. Then we move to another stage of the Pauline mission.

The compromise reached was as follows: circumcision will not be required of Gentiles, but they must observe certain minimal requirements. First, they are required to abstain from eating meat that had been sacrificed to idols (verses 20, 29; also Acts 21:25; cf. I Cor. 8-10; Rev. 2:14, 20; IV Macc. 5:2; Exod. 34:15-16). Second, they are forbidden to eat meat that had been improperly slaughtered. This excluded eating the meat of animals that had been strangled and still had blood in them (verses 20, 29; cf. Lev. 1:5). Third, "unchastity," or fornication is forbidden (verses 20, 29; cf Lev. 17-18).

This account poses several problems. First, as we have already noted, it is not altogether clear whether it was a closed session or open session (cf. verse 6 and verses 12, 22). Second, Paul's role remains disputed. According to chapter 15, he not only attends and speaks, but delivers the letter to Antioch. Yet in Acts 21:25, James appears to inform him of the agreement for the first time. Also, he makes no mention of this apostolic decree in his letters (cf. I Cor. 8-10; Gal. 2:6; Rom. 14). In fact, in some circumstances he allows for the eating of meat sacrificed to idols (cf. I Cor. 8:8; 10:27). Third, there is a question about the geographical area to which it applies, whether intended for the regions of Syria and Cilicia (15:23) or for all regions (15:19-21; cf. 21:25). Paul may not have mentioned it to the Corinthians because it was inapplicable there! Fourth, it is difficult to square Acts 15 with what Paul reports in Galatians 1–2.

Because of these difficulties, it has been suggested that Luke's account in Acts 15 actually combines two separate controversies: (1) one dealing with the terms on which Gentiles are to be admitted to the church, and (2) the other dealing with terms on which Jewish Christians and Gentile Christians are to live together and interact with one another socially.

In addition to the historical difficulties, Luke's account offers at least two features worth noting. First, it is an occasion when church leaders meet to resolve a major controversy facing the church. Besides the principals, such as Barnabas, Paul, Peter, James, the other elders and apostles, there were persons such as Silas, lesser known perhaps, yet playing a crucial role in the early chuch (cf. 15:22, 27, 32, 34; 15:40-18:5; II Cor. 1:19; I Thess. 1:1; II Thess. 1:1; I Pet. 5:12). Second, the solution reached is not merely a human compromise, but a decision influenced by the Holy Spirit (verse 28). Here, as elsewhere in Acts, it is the Spirit who is the guiding force in the life of the early church, not only in the work of mission (8:29; 10:19; 11:12; 13:2; 20:23; 21:11) but also in "practical" questions of church life, especially ones of major theological import.

Psalm 67

This psalm appears to look in two directions and to express two sentiments. Offering thanks, it makes request; celebrating the harvest, it looks forward to divine favor (verses 6, 1). One might assume that the psalm, like Psalm 65, was once used in a national ritual or communal thanksgiving. (Note the close connection of thanksgiving and confession in Deut. 26.)

Verse 1 with its threefold indirect request to the Deity—"be gracious," "bless," "make his face to shine"— is reminiscent of the Aaronic priestly blessing in Numbers 6:24-26. The rationale for the threefold petition in verse 1 is given in verse 2. The rationale for Israel's (the "us" in verse 1) blessing is the consequence that it would have in the world of the nations. God's blessing on Israel makes known his way (or "domain, manner") and saving power among the nations, among the goyim. This may sound like a bit of special pleading, in fact, a form of special greed, namely, to request one's own well-being for the impact it will have on others. Yet we must remember that the ancients were not ashamed to call attention to their God's reputation and to associate that reputation with the well-being of the God's worshipers.

The prayer for the nations (note the refrain in verses 3 and 5) gives expression to something of a universalistic outlook. (Verse 7 perhaps should be translated, "May God bless us; let. . . ," which would give it also a petitionary form.) The psalm certainly contains no narrow, nationalistic sentiment but confesses that God judges and guides the peoples of the world (verse 4) and thus they are his responsibility.

In the Christian scheme of things, the Easter experience and the exaltation of Jesus celebrated in the Ascension affirm the divine blessings poured out upon the church which radiated outward to the nations of the world. In addition, like the psalm, the Christian gives thanks for blessings received ("the already" of Christian faith) but looks forward to blessings to come ("the not yet").

Revelation 21:10, 22-27

In this epistolary reading, we are still in the midst of the final vision of the new Jerusalem (21:1–22:5). For discussion of the broader literary context, see our remarks on last Sunday's epistolary lesson.

One of the seven angels beckons the Seer, "Come, I will show you the Bride, the wife of the Lamb" (verse 9; cf. 19:7-8). With this, the Seer is carried away in the Spirit (1:10; 17:3; cf. Isa. 21:1) and taken to a high mountain. His vantage point is comparable to that from which Ezekiel sketches his vision of the restored temple (cf. Ezek. 40:1-2). But what he sees is the "holy city Jerusalem" descending from God out of heaven (11:2; 22:19; cf. Matt. 4:5; 27:53; Neh. 11:1, 18; Isa. 48:2; 52:1; Dan 9:24). There follows a magnificent description of the city's structure and measurements (verses 11-21).

Then begins the major section of today's reading. We are struck by the fact that the new Jerusalem has no temple, especially since such prominence was given to the temple in earlier visions (cf. 3:12; 11:1-2, 19; 14:15, 17; 15:5-6, 8; 16:1, 17). This may in fact be an allusion to the destruction of the Jerusalem temple in A.D. 70. In response to this, Christians had already interpreted the body of Jesus as the "new temple" (John 2:19-21). Thus, in this vision, the temple is replaced by the very presence of the Lord God Almighty (cf. 1:8; 4:8; 11:17; 15:3; 16:7, 14; 19:6, 15; also II Cor. 6:18; II Sam. 7:8; Amos 3:13) and the Lamb.

The city is lit up in dazzling light, but it is not light provided by sun, moon, and stars. It was expected that in the eschatological age the heavenly lights would be rendered obsolete, and that the radiant glory of God would alone be needed (Isa. 60:19-20; also 1–3; cf. 24:23; II Cor. 3:18; Rev. 22:5). It is thus a city that knows no night (verse 25*b*; cf. 22:5; Zech. 14:7). In similar fashion, Jesus had come to be identified with light and glory (John 1:1-18; 8:12; also II Cor. 4:6).

Its population includes the "nations," that is, the Gentiles (verse 24) as well as the kings of the earth. This too was part of the prophetic eschatological vision: God's light would extend to include the Gentiles (Isa. 49:6; 60:3, 11; Ps. 72:10-11). It is a city with an open door, with gates that would never be shut (Isa. 60:3, 11).

Everything unclean is excluded from the heavenly city, especially those whose ways are "false or foul" (verse 27, NEB; 21:8; 22:15; cf. Ezek. 33:29; Zech. 13:1-2; II Pet. 3:13). Membership is limited to those whose names are in the "Lamb's book of life" (3:5; 13:8; 17:8; 20:12, 15; also Luke 10:20; Exod. 32:32-33; Ps. 69:28; Isa. 4:3; Dan. 12:1; Mal. 3:16).

This vision of the heavenly city should not be viewed in isolation from the rest of chapters 21-22. In last week's epistolary text, we saw certain features that are not here, and this part of the vision has distinctive elements. We should also note that it continues on into chapter 22, with the description of the river of life and the tree of life.

Some of the elements here are continuous with the vision as a whole, most notably the insistence that it is the place where the divine presence is fully and finally realized. No place of worship, no temple, synagogue, or church building is needed any longer. To be this close to the center of God makes the temple redundant.

Also worth noting is its universal population—it is a place for all nations and peoples. Finally, all racial and ethnic barriers are broken, and the new humanity exists in its undifferentiated fullness.

Especially prominent is the stress on moral purity. Revelation makes no mistake about what constitutes good and evil. The line between virtue and vice is sharply etched here (21:8; 22:11, 15). But every Utopian vision recognizes that evil in all its forms obstructs the way to true life together. But if we have to live with it, and even have it live within us here, at least we can look toward a time when it is no more and to a place where it is finally out of place.

John 14:23-29

John 14:23-29 belongs to the section of this Gospel devoted to Jesus' departure from his disciples and his return to God (13:1–17:26). The comments on this material introducing last Sunday's Gospel (13:31-35) may be reviewed to get a sense of the larger context. The immediate context is the farewell discourse in which Jesus is elaborating on the meaning of his departure on the ongoing lives of his followers. It is difficult within these discourses to isolate a distinct unit of material having its own center because of the repetition and the absence of the usual literary clues that signal the beginning and ending of a unit. Verse 23 is in response to a question by Judas (not Iscariot), but verse 24 seems to begin a new line of thought. In order to isolate verses 23-29 as a distinct lection, one needs to focus on the subject matter and not on the literary form. Such an examination yields three themes: love as the bond joining God, Christ, an the disciples (verses 23-24); the promise of the Holy Spirit (verses 25-26); peace and joy appropriate to the return of Christ to God (verses 27-29). Since the three themes do not depend on one another or relate directly to one another, the preacher may wish to choose one of them for the sermon. The approach of Pentecost makes the second theme attractive but verses 25-27 will reappear on Pentecost Sunday, so the preacher will want to plan accordingly. We will discuss the three in the order of their appearance in the text.

Verses 23-24 continue the discussion of love from last Sunday but enlarge the arena of its activity. In response to the question concerning Christ's revealing himself to his disciples (verse 22), Christ speaks of love as the identifying condition existing among himself, God, and the disciples. The love of God for us and the love of Christ for us are common New Testament themes, but our loving Christ and loving God are relatively rare outside the Gospel. The Shema (Deut. 6:4) is repeated in Mark 12:29-30, but most often our relation to God and to Christ is characterized as faith and hope. In John, however, Jesus presses the question, "Do you love me?" (21:15-19). God is love and all relationships derived from that understanding are characterized as love. Fundamental to the union of God, Christ, and the disciples is love. As far as the disciples are concerned, love is formed and sealed by the word Christ has spoken to them, and holding to that word, obeying that word, is the evidence that the relationship of love pertains. When that is the case, God and Christ come and make their home with the disciples (verse 23). The expression "make our home" is the same as that of verse 2: in God's house are many "rooms" or "abiding places." Hence, just as the disciples are promised a room or home with God in the future, so in verse 23 they are promised that God and Christ will take rooms or dwell with them here and now. "I will not leave you desolate; I will come to you" (verse 18). The eschatology of John is both future and present and both should be claimed by the church. Pentecost and Parousia join and at times blend as both promise and presence.

Verses 25-26 contain the second of five statements in the farewell speeches in which the Holy Spirit is promised (14:16-17; 14:25-26; 15:25; 16:7-11; 16:13-15). Peculiar to this Gospel is the designation of the Spirit as Paraclete, that is, as Counselor, Comforter, Helper. In that the Spirit is *another* Counselor (verse 16), the Spirit is to the church what Jesus was to the disciples. In verse 26, four statements are made about the Holy Spirit: (1) God will send the Spirit (we do not have to do something to *get* the Spirit); (2) the Spirit is in Jesus' name (the experience of the Spirit does not permit the disregard or rejection of the historical Jesus); (3) the Spirit will teach the church, since Jesus had not yet fully said all that the church needs to understand (16:12); and (4) the Spirit will bring to remembrance the words of Jesus. The Spirit does not provide direct and unmediated experiences of God which contradict or render useless the tradition or the continuity of the faith community. The Christian faith is authorized by the line of continuity from God, to Christ, to the apostles, to the church (17:1-26). The Holy Spirit confirms and informs that tradition and enrolls disciples in the story of God's word in the world.

Verses 27-29 assure the disciples that peace and joy are appropriate to the events soon to transpire. Jesus' arrest and death are not a triumph of the world but are rather the operation of God's will in all things and the confirmation of the Son's love. The peace given is the confidence that God is God, that God loves the world, that God is for us, and that God makes that love real in acts of self-giving. Therefore, neither our pains nor our pleasures, neither our gains nor our losses are ultimate; they do not create nor do they annul the peace of God. To understand this is to rejoice (verse 29), as Paul would say, "Always" (I Thess. 5:16).

Ascension Day

Acts 1:1-11; Psalm 47; Ephesians 1:15-23; Luke 24:46-53 or *Mark 16:9-16, 19-20*

On the day that commemorates the Ascension of the Lord the paragraphs that begin the book of Acts will hold center stage. The psalm that responds to the account of the Ascension is an exultant hymn in praise of the Lord's coronation as king over all the earth. The text from Ephesians doubtless is chosen for this occasion because of its affirmation that God has made Jesus Christ "sit at his right hand in the heavenly places" (Eph. 1:20). The Lucan passage, an account of the final commissioning of the disciples by the risen Lord, immediately precedes the Acts passage in Luke's two-volume work. The alternate Gospel lection from Mark contains (16:19) a parallel report of the Ascension.

Acts 1:1-11

For the first few centuries, the church included the celebration of Ascension as part of Pentecost. According to Tertullian, Christ's ascension took place at Pentecost. But by the late fourth century, the celebration of Ascension and Pentecost had developed as two separate events.

The custom of celebrating the Ascension of Christ forty days after Easter, or on the Sixth Thursday during the fifty-day period from Easter to Pentecost, is largely attributable to the mention of "forty days" in today's First Lesson (verse 3). Strictly speaking, the observance of Ascension will be held on the Sixth Thursday, but as a matter of convenience can be observed the following Sunday, the Seventh Sunday of Easter.

In the *Common Lectionary* the same four texts are employed

for Ascension Day in all three years. But as we treat this First Lesson, we might note that in other lectionaries other passages have served as the First Lesson: Year A—Daniel 7:9-14; Year B—Ezekiel 1:3-5, 15-22, 26-28; and Year C—II Kings 2:1-15. All these appropriately bear on the theme of Ascension and may be consulted for additional perspective. The reader may also wish to consult our remarks on the texts for this day in Years A and B.

The first chapter of Acts is most appropriate as an opening lesson since Christ's ascension is specifically mentioned three times (verses 2, 9, 22). In the second part of today's opening lection (verses 6-11), we have Luke's narrative description of this event—the only such description in the New Testament (cf. Luke 24:50-53). Of course, the tradition of Jesus' ascension is known elsewhere, but it is usually referred to only briefly (cf. Mark 16:19; John 3:13; 6:62; 20:17; also I Tim. 3:16).

At the outset, we should note that quite often the New Testament does not clearly distinguish Jesus' ascension from his resurrection. Rather, we are often told simply that after his death, he was "exalted," or "taken up," as if his resurrection is itself his ascension (cf. Rom. 1:4; 10:6; Phil. 2:9; Eph. 4:8-10; I Pet. 3:22; Heb. 4:14; 7:26). By contrast, Luke sees the resurrection of Jesus and his ascension into heaven as two separate stages, separated in time by forty days.

Several features of today's text are worth noting in the context of our celebration of Ascension.

First, it is a time of recollection. We are told that during the forty days, the risen Lord presented himself to the disciples as alive and spoke to them concerning the kingdom of God (verse 3). Not only had this been one of the major themes of the preaching of John the Baptist (Matt. 3:2 and parallels) but of Jesus as well (Matt. 4:23 and parallels). This involved the announcement that the sovereign reign of God had now set in—a time of hope for the poor, the captive, the sick, and the oppressed (Luke 4:18-19).

But in spite of the abundant teaching of Jesus concerning the kingdom of God, especially through the form of parables, confusion still abounded. Those who heard his preaching found it next to impossible to disentangle God's promise of a new era of divine sovereignty from their own notions of nationalism. And the discussion almost inevitably turned to *when* (verse 6). They have to be told, once again, that establishing times and dates is God's exclusive prerogative (verse 7; also Matt. 25:34 and parallels; also Rom. 16:25; I Cor. 2:7; Eph. 1:4; 3:9, 11; Col. 1:26; II Tim. 1:9). Their task is not to predict but to wait.

Second, it is a time of anticipation. The disciples are instructed to "wait for the promise of the Father" (verse 4). The time when the Holy Spirit would be poured out in abundance is not far off, and when it occurs it would be a great outburst of power. In fact, the Spirit and power are always closely linked (cf. Luke 1:35; 24:49; Acts 10:38; Rom. 15:13, 19; I Cor. 2:4-5; I Thess. 1:5; Heb. 2:4). The book of Acts provides thorough documentation of the powerful energy unleashed by the Spirit beginning with the Day of Pentecost.

Our text moves beyond the expectation of the pouring out of the Spirit and also points to the ultimate return of Christ. The disciples are assured that his coming will be a manner similar to his departure (verse 11).

In both cases, the cast of the eye is forward. The disciples are now with the risen Lord, but their attention is directed towards a time when he will no longer be with them in the same way. He will be absent, but present with them through the Spirit. The power they now feel in his presence they will experience even when he is absent. They are thus instructed to stop gazing into heaven and be about the business at hand—waiting for the renewal that will begin in and with Jerusalem.

It is precisely this tension between recollection and anticipation that is felt in the celebration of Ascension. On the one hand, we want to hold on to Easter and the risen Lord, yet we are being beckoned to let go and look to the coming Spirit as the One who will lead us into the future.

Psalm 47

This psalm has long been associated with the Ascension celebration in the Christian church, a celebration which commemorates Jesus' exaltation in the heavenly world. In its original usage, Psalm 47 probably celebrated the ascension of God in the annual enthronement ritual.

The features in the enthronement ritual, as reconstructed by scholars, involved the removal of the ark (representing Yahweh the Israelite God) from the temple, the cleansing of the temple and people (the Yom Kippur or Day of Atonement ritual), and the return of the ark to the temple (see Ps. 24:7-10). The latter was understood as Yahweh's reenthronement, his ascension back to the throne and assumption of authority as king. Psalm 47 would have functioned in the liturgy as part of the celebration of Yahweh's reenthronement.

The psalm divides into three units, with verse 5 as the fulcrum balancing verses 1-4 and 6-9. Verse 5 affirms the cultic reality ("God has gone up"; that is, Yahweh has ascended with the ark into the Holy of Holies) and notes some aspects of the people's cultic reaction ("with a shout"; "with the sound of a trumpet").

The two units sandwiched around verse 5 are both calls to worship with statements giving the reason or motivation for such praise. The first summons—"clap your hands"; "shout to God"—is addressed to the peoples or foreign Gentile nations (verse 1). The motivation for clapping and shouting is twofold. (1) Yahweh a terrible (in the sense of awesome) God is the great king who rules over all the earth. (Note the claims made for the ascended Jesus; Phil. 2:10.) (2) This universal claim, however, is counterbalanced by the more nationalistic, particularistic claim of the elect people in verses 3-4. Jacob is the chosen, the elect and thus nations are under their feet (that is, subordinate to the special people of God). This tension between universalism and election runs throughout the Scriptures and is still today an issue in terms of the relationship of denominations to one another and in terms of Christianity and the church's relationship to other communities not to mention the issue of nationalism versus internationalism. The psalm sees this tension overarched if not overcome in the fact that God reigns as king over both.

The second call to praise, in verse 6, is simply a fourfold "sing praises." The opening line of this verse can best be translated, "sing praises, O gods." The sense of this reading would suggest that the gods of the nations are called on to offer praise to the Israelite Deity (see Ps. 82:1 for a similar concept). The motivation for such praise again notes that Yahweh is king over all the earth, reigning over the nations, enthroned on his holy throne (in the Jerusalem temple). Verse 9 contains two parallel lines with no connective (the "as" in the RSV has been added by the translators). The two parallel lines refer to the foreigners—"the princes of the people"—and to the Jewish community—"the people of the God of Abraham." The expression, "the shields of the earth," appears to be another way of saying, "the princes of the peoples," that is, the rulers of the world are said to belong to the God of Israel.

Ephesians 1:15-23

This text, at least portions of it, is also employed elsewhere in the *Common Lectionary*. It is the epistolary reading for the Second Sunday After Christmas in Years, A, B, and C. It is also the epistolary text for All Saints Day (November 1) for Year C. The reader may wish to consult additional remarks made in connection with those days.

Today's epistolary text should be read as a rich theological reflection on the exalted status of Christ. Throughout the text, Christ's absolute supremacy is assumed, and we may regard it as a fitting text to stimulate our thinking about the theological significance of Christ's ascension.

No clear distinction is made in the text between Christ's resurrection and his ascension. It may be, however, that we have the beginning of a two-stage distinction when we are told that God "raised [Christ] from the dead and made him sit at his right hand in the heavenly places" (verse 20; cf. I Pet. 1:21). The language is supplied partially by Psalm 110:1, which speaks of the elevation of the king to God's right hand. What is new is his location "in the heavenly places," an important phrase in Ephesians. But in Ephesians it is no longer the exalted Lord himself who shares this place of preeminent position. We who are "in Christ" are also envisioned as being elevated to the heavenly sphere where we will enjoy the numerous spiritual blessings mentioned in this opening prayer (1:3; 2:6). Our text, then, reports on ascension in two senses: Christ's and our own.

From this elevated position, we are in a unique position to receive the spiritual blessings God offers us in Christ. Among these is the capacity for spiritual discernment (verses 17-18). We are assured that the eyes of our understanding will be opened in the sense that our spiritual wisdom is deepened and our knowledge of God is enriched (cf. Col. 1:9-10; also I John 5:20; Isa. 11:2; Wisd. of Sol. 7:7). In particular, we are enabled to grasp the size and shape of the hope to which we have been called (verse 18; cf. 4:4, also Col. 1:5, 27; Heb. 3:1). As elusive as the notion of hope is, this should be especially reassuring to us. Moreover, we are made increasingly aware that ours is a legacy of wealth (verse 18; cf. 3:16; Col. 1:27; Rom. 9:23; 10:12; 11:33; Phil. 4:19).

Besides the gift of spiritual enlightenment that we come to possess in Christ, there is also access to unlimited sources of power and strength (verses 19-20). Nor is this power in the abstract, or even the divine power exhibited in the creation. It is rather the power unleashed by God in raising Christ from the dead—resurrection power. We are assured that it is truly "immeasurable" (verse 19; cf. 3:20; Col. 1:11; 2:12; II Cor. 13:4; I Pet. 1:5; also Isa. 40:26; 52:3).

The extent of God's power is seen in the way Christ's ascension made him supreme over "every Sovereignty, Authority, Power, or Dominion" (verse 21, JB; cf. 2:2; 3:10; 6:12; Rom. 8:38; I Cor. 15:24; Col. 1:13, 16; 2:10, 15; I Pet. 3:22; II Pet. 2:10; Heb. 2:5). Everything has finally been put in subjection under his feet (cf. Ps. 8:6; Matt. 28:18; I Cor. 15:24-25), and he is now the supreme head of the church which literally fills the universe (cf. Col. 1:19). In view here is the cosmic body of Christ that extends throughout the universe (cf. 4:12; Rom. 12:5; Col. 1:18, 24; 2:17).

We can see, then, that Christ's exaltation and ascension has impact on us in at least these two respects: our spiritual wisdom and understanding is sharpened and our sources of strength are deepened. The theological view of Christian existence expressed here is triumphalist to be sure, and taken alone could easily cause us to see ourselves as exalted to the heavens. Unchecked, it might make us Gnostic.

But in this text we are hearing the language of prayer and praise. Every once in a while, perhaps especially in moments of worship, from our view below we should allow ourselves to participate in Christ's ascension. We should sit with him in the heavenly places and view the universe from the vantage point of the One who is over all.

Ascension Day is not as widely observed as a Christian holiday in America as in Europe. But whether or not the day is celebrated, the Ascension is a vital theme in Christian faith, as its statement in the Apostles' Creed made clear quite early. The Ascension provides closure to the ministry of Jesus, declares his enthronement at the right hand of God and proclaims Christ's lordship over the church and over all powers in the created order. The preacher has a choice between two Gospel affirmations of the Ascension. Comments on both are provided below.

Luke 24:46-53

A review of the comments on Luke 24: 13-49 for Easter Evening will set the context for this lection. Luke's resurrection narrative consists of the record of the women at the tomb (24:1-12), the appearance in Emmaus (24:13-35), and the appearance to the eleven and others (24:36-43). Verses 46-53 consist of two parts: instruction, commission, and promise (verses 46-49; blessing, departure, and waiting (verses 50-53).

Verses 46-49 (actually begins at verse 44) confirms three major themes in Luke-Acts. One, all that Jesus said and did as well as his death and resurrection were in accordance with Scripture and fulfilled prophecy. That the gospel is in continuity with what God had been doing and planning through the Jewish Scriptures is repeatedly underscored by Luke. Mary and Joseph did all things according to the law (2:21-40); Jesus based his ministry on Isaiah 61 (4:16-30); he followed the precedents of Elijah and Elisha (4:25-30); he was regular in synagogue worship (4:16); his followers continued temple worship (24:53; Acts 3:1); and the Christian preachers drew their messages from the Old Testament (Acts 2:16-36).

The Christian faith assumes the consistent faithfulness of God rather than a change of mind as strict dispensationalism implies.

A second Lukan them focuses on Jerusalem as the center from which the gospel is to go to the nations (verses 47, 52; Isa. 2:3). Unlike Mark 16:1-8 and Matthew 28 which locate resurrection appearances in Galilee, Luke places them in or near Jerusalem, and describes throughout Acts Jerusalem as the center of Christian activity.

The third theme is the definition of the gospel as the offer of repentance and forgiveness of sins (verse 47; Acts 2:38; 3:19; 5:31; 11:18; 17:30). But all future activity of the disciples must wait on the coming of the Holy Spirit which will empower them to witness (verse 49) in Jerusalem, Judea, Samaria, and to the ends of the earth (Acts 1:4-8).

Verses 50-53 relate briefly the departure of Jesus from the disciples whom he has blessed. The phrase "and was carried up into heaven" (verse 51) is omitted in some manuscripts, the actual description of the Ascension coming later in Acts 1:9-11. The disciples return to Jerusalem in joy, praise (verses 52-53) and constant prayer (Acts 1:14). Easter will soon be completed at Pentecost (Acts 2:1), and the story will continue.

Mark 16:9-16, 19-20

The preacher will want to read sufficiently in the commentaries and check several translations in order to come to clarity and confidence about the question as to whether verses 9-20 belong to Mark's Gospel. The evidence is divided as various translations reflect. The RSV in the 1946 edition ended Mark at verse 8, but restored verses 9-20 with special notation in the 1971 edition. An alternate ending is placed in the footnotes. The NEB puts both endings in the text with notes of explanation. The TEV adds verses 9-20 with a special heading, "An Old Ending to the Gospel." It is important for the preacher to arrive at a conclusion with sufficient confidence to give an informed explanation to the parishioners, whether in the pulpit or in a classroom. All this is not to say there is uncertainty as to the truth contained in these verses. On the contrary, except for verses 17-18 (omitted from this lection), the content is found in the resurrection narratives of Matthew, Luke, and John. It is the writer's opinion that the ending to Mark is, in fact, a summary of the endings of the other Gospels.

Our lection consists of six units: (1) the appearance to Mary Magdalene (verses 9-11), told more fully in John 20: 1-18; this unit also echoes Luke 8:2 and 24:11; (2) the appearance to two walking in the country (verses 12-13), clearly a reference to Luke's Emmaus story (24:13-35); (3) the appearance to the eleven (verse 14; Luke 24:36-43); (4) the commission to the disciples (verses 15-18); like Matthew 28:18-20 the commission enjoins faith and baptism, but unlike all the other Gospels and Jesus' own ministry (Mark 8:12), corroborating signs are promised those who witness; (5) the declaration of Jesus' ascension and enthronement (verse 19); Psalm 110, used often in the New Testament, occurs only here among the resurrection narratives; and (6) a summary of the subsequent work of the disciples (verse 20).

Verse 20 is a conclusion, followed by "Amen." In this regard this account differs from the endings of the other Gospels. Matthew concludes with a commission; Luke leaves the disciples waiting for the power of the Spirit; John, while closing with a kind of signature, ends the story with the words, "Follow me." All these conclusions tend to leave the story open, to invite the reader to enter, and to imply the work goes on. Mark 16:20 *ends* the story without openness, without inviting the reader to participate. In other words, verse 20 makes the gospel history, a finished story. There is a sense in which this is true, and needs to be affirmed. However, there is a sense in which this is not the case, unless one understands the church today as a house of memories and the minister a curator. Other Scripture, history, and our experience agree that is not the case.

Seventh Sunday of Easter

Acts 16:16-34; Psalm 97; Revelation 22:12-14, 16-17, 20; John 17:20-26

The long reading from Acts is the account of the imprisonment of Paul and Silas for driving a spirit out of a slave girl. The account of the conversion of the jailor shows how the faith is spread through the deeds as well as the words of the disciples. Part of the psalm responds to the trouble experienced by Paul and Silas, affirming that God preserves the saints and delivers them from the wicked (verse 10). As a whole, it is a song celebrating the enthronement of the Lord and continues the theme of Ascension Day. The second reading, an anticipation of the return of Jesus, likewise continues the motif of Jesus enthroned on high. The Gospel lection is the last part of the so-called high priestly prayer of Jesus, his petition for all who will come to believe, "that they may all be one" (John 17:21).

Acts 16:16-34

In today's First Lesson, we are presented with two incidents that occurred during Paul's mission in Philippi: an encounter with a demon-possessed girl and the conversion of the Philippian jailor.

At this point in Acts, we have moved into another major phase of the Pauline mission. After the Jerusalem Conference, Paul and Silas launch a fresh mission into western Asia Minor. In response to the Macedonian call (16:9-10), they cross the Hellspont into Greece and come to Philippi as the first major stop. Luke gives a fairly lengthy description of Paul's preaching in Philippi (16:12-40). After leaving Philippi, Paul and his company move on to Thessalonica (17:1-9), and

211

eventually come to Athens (17:16-34). Here Luke uses the occasion to give us an example of Pauline preaching before a sophisticated pagan audience, hence the sermon before the Areopagus court (17:22-31). Then Paul's successful mission in Corinth follows (18:1-18), and this stage of preaching in Greece ends.

Within this overall literary context, there are four significant sections: (1) preaching the gospel in Philippi; (2) opposition to the gospel in Thessalonica; (3) the sermon in Athens; and (4) the successful period in Corinth. With each of these major sections, Luke is portraying a significant feature of the Pauline mission among the Gentiles. With the extensive treatment of Philippi, he depicts for us a typical day in the life of Paul, the missionary to the Gentiles. The events of Thessalonica are recorded to illustrate the type of resistance the gospel typically met in Gentile settings, especially from the Jewish synagogue. Athens provides an occasion for giving us a typical Pauline sermon to Gentiles in a more sophisticated setting. The description of Paul's preaching in Corinth shows us an instance of Paul's successful missionary work when he stayed for a period of time.

Philippi, then, shows us "a day in the life of Paul, the missionary to the Gentiles." Luke chooses to relate three incidents: (1) the conversion of Lydia and her household (verses 13-15); (2) the encounter with the demon-possessed girl (verses 16-24); and (3) the imprisonment of Paul and Silas, the resulting conversion of the Philippian jailor, and Paul's vindication before the civil magistrates (verses 25-40). This careful selection of incidents shows us how the gospel is received by a well-to-do woman inclined towards Judaism. Further, it shows us how the gospel, in conflict with popular pagan religion, wins out. Finally, it moves to the other end of the social spectrum and shows us how the gospel reaches into the house of a jail-keeper to save his life and soul. In the process, it also demonstrates again that the messengers of the gospel live and work under divine protection and that their cause is vindicated before pagan officials.

As we look at the two incidents comprising today's first lection, we notice first how similar Paul's encounter with the pagan girl is to incidents recorded in the Gospels (cf. Matt. 8:28-34 and parallels; Matt. 15:21-28 and parallels; Mark 1:23-38 and parallels). In one sense, the incident merely serves as the set up for the imprisonment scene. It provides an occasion for stating the charges against Paul and Silas that will be cleared up later (verses 20-21). We are not told that the pagan girl is converted, but through the well-known technique of placing a confessional statement on the lips of a pagan, Luke clearly places her on the side of faith (verse 17).

As we move to the imrpisonment scene, we recall similar imprisonments earlier in Acts (4:3; 5:17-26; 12:1-11). As we noted earlier in our remarks on the First Lesson for the Second Sunday of Easter, a recurrent pattern emerges in Luke-Acts. Whenever the gospel meets resistance, such as imprisonment by the authorities, it is vindicated. The more severe the resistance, the more spectacular the vindication. In today's text, even the inner prison and leg stocks are inadequate to hold God's messengers. The divine rescue comes this time in the form of an earthquake (cf. 4:31).

As it turns out, an event that was potentially catastrophic becomes an occasion for experiencing God's salvation. The jailer knows the escape of the prisoners will require his life (verse 30; cf. 12:19; 27:42). Hence, his question operates at two levels. In the context, he is asking what to do to save his skin. But the reader knows that similar questions have been asked earlier (2:37; cf. 22:10; Luke 3:10) and that the real request is for salvation offered by the gospel. It thus becomes an occasion for preaching the word of the Lord (verse 32). What began as an ominous jailing ends as a joyous celebration of faith (verse 34; cf. Matt. 9:22; Mark 16:16).

Luke's imprint is seen throughout this narrative. The theological points that are scored are thoroughly Lukan: the power of the gospel to penetrate every social level, its capacity to attract converts away from Judaism to Christianity, the conquest of pagan superstition, the divine protection of God's messengers, and the vindication of the gospel in Roman eyes.

The story of the jailor's conversion is especially inviting to the homiletician as an instance of Luke's literary artistry. At one level, it is the story of an imprisonment and a miraculous release, or "salvation," of God's messengers. At another level, it is the story of the miraculous release, or "salvation" of a jailor imprisoned in his own prison. The irony is surely there: those who are imprisoned, God's apostles, are really free, while those who are the keepers of the prisoners are really imprisoned. Through role reversal, Paul and Silas become the jailor's deliverers.

Psalm 97

An enthronement psalm, Psalm 97 celebrates the exaltation/ascension of Yahweh and the consequences of this for the world and human existence. This psalm is fundamentally a hymn about Yahweh. The single exception is verse 9 which is prayer or speech addressed to God.

The psalm opens with a central affirmation: "Yahweh has become king." (This appears a better translation than the RSV's "The Lord reigns.") Everything else in the psalm tends to radiate outward from this point. Joy and gladness are the responsive tones that should greet such an affirmation.

Verses 2-8 are a cantata describing the universe's reaction to divine kingship which reaches a crescendo in the assertion that Zion hears and the daughters (cities) of Judah rejoice. The metaphorical descriptions in verses 1-5 borrow from the imagery of thunderstorms—clouds, darkness, fire, lightning—which assaults the earth and devours the divine enemies (see Ps. 29). Tucked away amid this assortment of meteorological metaphors is a calming voice among the thundering sounds—"righteousness and justice are the foundation of his throne." In spite of the violence and apparent irrationality of the characteristics of God, the Divine is consistent, just, and righteous.

God's voice and presence, heard and seen throughout the cosmos (verse 6), are bad news and a destroying presence to those who worship any deity other than Yahweh—even the other gods worshiped bow down (= "worship") to the God of Israel (verse 7).

What others hear in fear and trembling, Zion and Judah, Jerusalem and the Judean towns, hear with rejoicing (verse 8). The two responses of the world (the worshipers of idols) and Zion manifest three reactions to the Divine—being awestruck at the divine might, being humiliated and shamed by discovering the silliness of other worship, and being gladden by the judgments that come as affirmations.

The psalm concludes with what might be called a moral lesson or a theological homily (verses 10-11) and then an altar call (verse 12). If we take the marginal reading of the RSV which provides a literal translation of the Hebrew "You lovers of Yahweh hate evil," the "altar call" begins earlier. Probably the regular reading in the RSV is correct since it merely presupposes that the same Hebrew letter was wrongly repeated. This then gives three affirmations about God, in verse 10, which produces two qualities for humans—light and joy.

Psalm 97 with its assurances of divine rule and of the value of righteousness, even righteous hatred, leaves the reader with a sense of calmness that all is well with the world after all, because Yahweh reigns.

Revelation 22:12-14, 16-17, 20

The vision of the new Jerusalem is now completed (21:1–22:5), and the book of Revelation concludes with a series of miscellaneous oracles, exhortations, blessings, and warnings. Today's epistolary lection represents a selection from this epilogue.

The lection begins and ends with the declaration, "Behold, I am coming soon" (verses 12 and 20). This is a recurrent theme of the book (2:16, 25; 3:11; 22:7). In the context of apocalyptic, this promise serves as a word of reassurance to those who are being oppressed. Within the Johannine Apocalypse, it may be read as an answer to the martyrs crying out, "How long?" (6:10). Certainly those who were suffering persecution under the Roman emperor Domitian (A.D. 81–A.D. 96) would find this a reassuring hope, and this was doubtless the intention of the author.

The final words of the lection are the early Christian prayer, "Come, Lord Jesus" (verse 20). It is preserved in its original Aramaic form by Paul (I Cor. 16:22; cf. 11:26). As it stands here, it should be read as the early Christian prayer of hope uttered in response to the promise of the risen Lord. Thus, the Lord proclaims, "Surely I am coming soon," and the people respond by saying, "Amen. Come, Lord Jesus!" (verse 20).

In today's text, we are assured that the Lord's coming will be a time when we receive judgment according to our works (verse 12). This need not be seen as the harsher side of justice, simply that the Lord will recompense us based on our record. As is typical of apocalyptic, there are only two classes: those who are blessed because of their good deeds (verse 14) and those who are cursed because of their vile deeds (verse 15). The principle of receiving judgment according to what we have done has a long history running from the Old Testament through the various strata of the New Testament (Isa. 40:10; Jer. 17:10; Ps. 28:4; 62:2; Prov. 24:12; Matt. 16:27; Rom. 2:6; II Cor. 11:15; II Tim. 4:14; I Pet. 1:17).

We again meet the familiar refrain that Jesus is "the Alpha and the Omega, the first and the last, the beginning and the end" (verse 13; cf. 1:8; 21:6; also Isa. 44:2, 6; 48:12). In this setting, we are to understand it as a way of underscoring the fact that he stands at the end of history.

The final verse of the first section of the lection is a blessing on the vindicated saints whose robes have been washed in the blood of the Lamb (verse 14; cf. 7:14; also Gen. 49:11; Exod. 19:10, 14; I John 1:7). Omitting the next verse (verse 15) that lists those who are excluded certainly produces a more positive reading, but it breaks the pattern established in the preceding verses: the Lord comes to judge according to our deeds, both the good (verse 14) and evil (verse 15).

The blessed saints have the right to the paradisal tree of life that was lost in the Fall (2:7, 11, 17, 26; 3:5, 12, 21; 21:7; 22:2, 19; also Gen. 2:9, 3:22, 24). Theirs is also the privilege of entry into the gates of the Holy City (verse 14; cf. Ps. 118:19-20). This is one of several makarisms that occur in the book (1:3; 14:13; 16:15; 19:9; 20:6; 22:7, 18). (This in itself might easily form the basis of a sermon as the preacher examines the various grounds for being blessed according to the book of Revelation.)

Verse 16 reaffirms the identity of Jesus as the "root and the offspring of David" (Isa. 11:1, 10; Matt. 1:1; John 7:42; Rom.

1:3; II Tim. 2:8) and the "bright morning star" (cf. 2:28; Num. 24:17).

Verse 17 should be read as an invitation of the Spirit and the Church (the bride) to the reader as it were an invitation to the messianic banquet. The hearers, in turn, respond by saying, "Come." Their response should be understood as addressing Jesus, as is the case in verse 20. It is their way of imploring the risen Christ to come quickly. Finally, the invitation for the thirsty to come and drink the water of life free of charge should be construed as an invitation to the eschatological feast (cf. 7:16-17; 21:6; 22:1; Isa. 55:1; Jer. 2:13; John 7:37).

As today's text unfolds, we are struck by the pervasive eschatological character of these various oracles. This element is not entirely foreign to the Easter Season, especially as we approach Pentecost and remember that the outpouring of the Holy Spirit was originally conceived as the breaking in of the New Age.

John 17:20-26

Luke says that before Pentecost the followers of Jesus devoted themselves to prayer (Acts 1:14). Who could fault that preparation? John says that before Jesus' glorification and the giving of the Spirit, Jesus prayed for his followers. Who could fault that preparation? Our Gospel for today is a portion of that prayer.

The question has been raised as to whether John 17 is really a prayer. This question exists only where address to God and address to the congregation has been sharply divided into prayer and proclamation. However, in the Bible such ditinctions are not always drawn. In many of the Psalms (23, for example), the writer moves easily from words about God to words to God. In Deuteronomy 32–33, Moses' farewell speech addresses both the people and God. Paul often speaks to God in the course of speaking to a church (Rom. 1:25; 9:1-5; 11:33-36). Earlier in the Fourth Gospel one encounters prayers that are also proclamations (11:41-42; 12:27-30). To remember that the audience for both prayer and sermon is God is to become less concerned about the proclamatory nature of Jesus' farewell prayer. The important consideration here is for the reader of John 17 to assume the posture of one being prayed for. It is as though we were in the congregation overhearing Jesus' pastoral prayer for us.

The prayer is that of the historical Jesus (verse 13: "But now I am coming to thee") and also of the glorified Lord of the church (verse 11: "And now I am no more in the world"). One does not distinguish between pre- and post-resurrection materials in John. For example, a post-resurrection statement occurs in the conversation of Jesus with Nicodemus (3:13). The point is, the risen Christ and the historical Jesus are the same.

John 17:1-26 may be divided into three parts: Jesus' return to glory (verses 1-5); Jesus' prayer for his disciples (verses 6-19); and Jesus' prayer for all who believe through the word of the disciples (verses 20-26). This last unit is our lesson for today. Every generation of believers can read verses 20-26 with the assurance that the prayer of Jesus is in their behalf. In fact, all distinctions between first generation and subsequent generations of believers are here erased; there are only believers. This, then, is a prayer of Jesus for us.

The central petition of the prayer is for the unity of all who believe. There is nothing here of unity as political expediency, or as mutual accommodation to error, or as agreement on the level of the lowest common denominator. None of the machinery of unity is mentioned. The unity spoken of here is that which is informed and empowered by the unity of God and Christ (verses 20-23). The line of continuity that authorizes the word by which faith is generated (verse 20) is clear: from God to Christ; from Christ to his apostles; from the apostles to the church. Add to this authorization the gift of the Holy Spirit (20:22) and the church as this Evangelist understood it is both apostolic and charismatic. The unity that prevails when God, Christ, and believers abide each in the other has as its primary purpose the evangelization of the world (verse 21). In unity the witness to the world can be made effectively; without it confusion and division disrupt and erode the witness of the church. If First John is addressed to the same church, perhaps shortly after the Gospel was written, then that letter may reveal some of the tensions, doctrinal disputes, and perhaps personality clashes that disturbed the Johannine church and made this prayer so pressingly important. Present church conditions make it abundantly clear that the prayer is as yet unanswered.

The prayer concludes with the twofold promise already familiar to the reader from 14:1-23. The first is that all who believe may share the glory of Christ and abide with him forever (verse 24; 14:1-3). The second promise is for the church's present just as the first is for the future. Here, as in 14:23, the assurance is that the love that characterizes the relationship between God and Christ will be in all Christ's followers and Christ himself will be within and among them (verses 25-26). The church in every generation, in every place, and in every circumstance which embraces this word in faith will abide in peace, in joy, and in full confidence that the world will finally be drawn to God (16:33; 12:31-32).

Pentecost

Acts 2:1-21 or *Genesis 11:1-9; Psalm 104:24-34; Romans 8:14-17*
or *Acts 2:1-21; John 14:8-17, 25-27*
(If the Old Testament passage is chosen for the first reading, the Acts passage is used as the second reading.)

The focal text is the one which is the basis for the celebration of the Day of Pentecost, the account in Acts 2:1-21 of the outpouring of the Spirit on those gathered for the festival. The alternate first reading, the story of the tower of Babel, provides the backdrop for one aspect of the Acts account, the miracle of understanding foreign languages. The psalm praises the power of God's spirit to create and renew. Both the alternate second reading from Romans and the Gospel lections concern the Spirit of God.

Acts 2:1-21

In the Christian year, Pentecost marks the day on which we celebrate the coming of the Holy Spirit. It marks the conclusion of the fifty days of Easter and the beginning of the period when the church carries forward the ministries it has received from the Spirit.

It is this text from Acts on which the Christian Pentecost is based. Luke has povided this narrative account of the birthday of the church, when the nucleus of the messianic community is formed. The disciples have been instructed by the risen Lord to wait in Jerusalem for the power from on high (Luke 24:47; Acts 1:8). Meanwhile, they have been receiving instructions from the risen Lord concerning the kingdom of God (Acts 1:2). The apostolic circle has been reconstituted with the appointment of Matthias as Judas' replacement (Acts 1:15-26). All is set for the New Age to begin.

The way Luke tells the story shows it to be a programmatic event. The sermon by Peter provides the centerpiece (2:14-36), but it is duly introduced and concluded. Today's First Lesson consists of Luke's narrative introduction to the sermon and the first main section of the sermon. But we should note that the sermon has an appropriate conclusion. The promise of salvation is offered and accepted. Three thousand souls are added on the first day (2:41), and the church immediately becomes the ideal messianic community (2:42-47). Just as Jesus' sermon in Nazareth served to inaugurate his ministry (Luke 4:16-30), so this Pentecost event and sermon serve to inaugurate the newly constituted people of God.

Ever attentive to matters of time and place, Luke dates the beginning of the church on the Jewish Feast of Pentecost and locates its origin in Jerusalem. Also known as the Feast of Weeks, or the Feast of Harvest, this festival was celebrated fifty days after Passover, or the Feast of Unleavened Bread, hence its name Pentecost (based on the Greek word for "fifty"). As a Jewish observance, it marked the end of the wheat harvest. Its importance and significance in Jewish life is well attested (cf. Exod. 23:14-17; 34:18-23; Lev. 23:15-21; Num. 28-29; Deut. 16:1-16). In some traditions, it had become a tme for celebrating the giving of the Law on Sinai, and thus was seen as marking the beginning of a new period in Israel's history. For Luke, this particular celebration of Pentecost clearly marked a new beginning—the arrival o the "last days" (verse 17).

It is also important to note that Jerusalem is the place where the messianic community is reconstituted and begins. For Luke, Jerusalem was more than a geographical place; it was the place where the continuation of God's story had begun (Luke 1) and to which Jesus had been inexorably drawn as God's eschatological prophet (Luke 9:51; 13:33). Here the Christ had been martyred, but here also his cause had been vindicated (Luke 24). It was from here that God's message of repentance and forgiveness of sins would begin to be proclaimed again (Luke 24:47). It was more than the city of Jerusalem—it was Zion, the city of

God, to which all the nations would stream when God eventually reestablished the universal kingdom (Isa. 2:2-4; Mic. 4:1-4). We are not surprised to find a roster of the nations represented at this inaugural event (verses 9-11).

Both the time and place are right for the New Age to begin. And it does begin as the prophets had promised—with the pouring out of the Spirit (verse 4; cf. 2:33; 10:45; Rom. 5:5; Tit. 3:6). This is the first of many such events in the life of the new messianic community (4:8, 31; 9:17; 10:44; 11:15; 13:9, 52). As the story unfolds in the rest of Acts, the church becomes both the witness and bearer of God's Spirit. It is the Spirit who impels the church to mission (8:29; 10:47; 13:2; 16:6) and assists it in resolving its controversies (15:28). Just as Jesus had been the bearer of God's Spirit (Luke 4:18-21), so now his successors, the apostles, teachers, and evangelists bear witness through the Spirit, as the prophets had promised (verses 4 and 17).

From the way in which Luke tells the story, we are not left in doubt that this is an inaugural event. The coming of the Spirit is both audible (sound "of the rush of a mighty wind," verse 2) and visible ("tongues as of fire," verse 3). Perhaps the chief sign is the speaking in other tongues (verses 4 and 11; cf. 10:46; 19:6; also Mark 16:17; I Cor. 14:21). This is only the first of many "signs and wonders" that are to accompany the breaking in of the New Age (cf. verse 19; also 2:22, 43; 4:30; 4:12; 6:8; 7:36; 8:13; 14:3; 15:12). All the confusion of Babel (Gen. 11:1-9) is now resolved as each nation hears the Word of God in its own language, that is, understands it (verse 11).

Today's text closes on a universal note: "And it shall be that whoever calls on the name of the Lord shall be saved" (verse 21; cf. Joel 2:32). As Peter later says, God's promise is now extended to "you and to your children [Jews] and to all that are far off" [Gentiles] every one whom the Lord our God calls" (verse 39). If the celebration of Pentecost means anything, it calls the church to a universal witness, to extend the hope of forgiveness to all the nations, even as it has been extended to us (Luke 24:47). The story begins in Jerusalem but it ends in Rome!

Genesis 11:1-9

It is a complete and self-contained story, this account of the building of the tower of Babel. While it has its place in the primeval history (Gen. 1-11), the pre-patriarchal time, it could easily stand alone. Evidence that it once did is seen in the fact that it contradicts points in the chapter that immediately precedes. While Genesis 11:1 affirms that all people on the earth had "one language," Genesis 10:5, 20, and 31 already accounted for different peoples, "each with his own language." Moreover, Babel had already been mentioned in Genesis 10:10. In spite of these tensions, both the table of nations in Genesis 10 and the story of the tower in Genesis 11:1-9 are, at one level, attempts to account for the same fact, namely, the multiplicity of nations and languages.

In order to be worth telling, any story must have tension, often between protagonists and antagonists. In this case the tension is between human and divine intentions. The account easily divides itself into three parts. The first movement (verses 1-4) concerns the plans and actions of the human race. After setting the scene—the earth had only one language—the narrator reports that the people settled in the plain of Shinar and then set out to build a city and a tower. The only purposes stated are their desire to make a name for themselves and to avoid being scattered all over the earth (verse 4). In the second part of the story (verses 5-8) all attention is given to the Lord's reaction. Coming down to see what the human beings are doing, the Lord is concerned about what they may do next, so he decides to confuse their language and to scatter them abroad. The account concludes (verse 9) with an explanation of the name Babel.

A number of points in the story require some explanation. The "plain in the land of Shinar" (verse 2) certainly is the flat river valley of lower Mesopotamia, known in ancient times first as Sumer and then as Babylon. The narrator seems to be a bit surprised at the building materials, but baked mud brick and bitumen for mortar were typical for monumental buildings in Mesopotamia, where other materials were scarce. The "tower" (verse 4) certainly reflects the common Mesopotamian temple-tower, the ziggurat. Such buildings

223

were artificial sacred mountains, where communication between the divine and human worlds took place.

At one level, the story is an etiological saga, as its conclusion makes explicit. One purpose is to explain the name of the city "Babel" as the place where the Lord confused (balal) human language. But even that etiology bears a note of polemic, for the Babylonians explained the meaning of their city's name as "gate of God." Other etiological purposes concern the origin of diverse languages from a supposed original unity and the dispersion of people all over the earth from the single place of their origin.

On another level the account seems to view urbanization and civilization to be in some way contrary to the will of God. The tension between sedentary, inevitably bureaucratic, and sophisticated culture—including monumental architecture—and nomadic, seminomadic, or rural cultures is well known.

But what is the fundamental point of tension in the story? Why does the Lord disapprove of the plans for the city and the tower? The answer is not at all obvious; there are only hints that the building of the tower is an expression of human pride and arrogance. Certainly in the literary context the plans to build the city and tower are viewed as sinful. The Yahwist, who is responsible for this story, views the history of the race from the first pair in Genesis 2 through this episode, as a history of sin, rebellion against Yahweh. The turning point to a history of salvation will come for him in Genesis 12:1 ff. with the call of Abraham.

Is it ironic that in Genesis 11:1-9 God disperses and confuses the language of the human race and that the Spirit of God reverses that in Acts 2:1-21? In the texts taken together, separation and confusion are viewed as the results of human arrogance—sin—while union and understanding are signs that the kingdom of God is breaking in.

Psalm 104:24-34

The two focuses of this psalm—the world of creation as the work of God and the universal character of God's rule—make it appropriate for inclusion in the lectionary for Pentecost.

A minor but still a significant feature in the psalm, apropos Pentecost, is the associaton of the Spirit of God with the re-creation and renewal of world orders.

The various stanzas in the psalm excluding the summarizing depiction and the conclusion in verses 27-35, focus on the various wonders of creation: the sky (2-4), the earth (5-9), the water (10-13), the vegetation (14-18), the moon and sun (19-23), and the sea (24-26). (It is instructive to compare these with the structure and characterization of the six days of creation in Genesis 1.)

The selection for the lectionary picks up with the depiction of the sixth wonder. Verses 24-34 may be divided into three units: verses 24-26 center on the sea in the world of creation, verses 27-30 offer a reflection on creation's dependence upon God, and verses 31-35 (which are no longer addressed to the Deity) marvel at the grandeur and awesomeness of the Lord of creation.

For the psalmist, the sea (verses 24-26) is God's pond, not some murky, mysterious, monster-laden source of chaos. From the ships and Leviathans (see Ps. 74:14; Job 41:1; Isa. 27:1) that ply its waves to the innumerable creatures small and great that scurry through its waters, they all have been made in the wisdom of God.

Verses 27-30 speak of what might be called "vertical universality." All living things are seen as dependent upon God—for food that fuels and sustains the living and for the breath of life that creates new being. That is, every part of life from top to bottom is the gift of God, not the possessor of that life. When God turns away, the creatures (including humans; note verse 23) become dismayed; when God withdraws his life spirit, the creatures succumb and return to dust. For all the world's greatness, for all its wonder and amazement, for the psalmist, the world is no independent entity. Without divine sustenance it would not survive. Creation is depicted so that, in the words of the Heidelberg Catechism, God "rules in such a way that waves and grass, rain and drought, fruitful and unfruitful years, food and drink, death and sickness, riches and poverty and everything else come to us not by chance, but by his fatherly hand."

The psalm concludes with a confessional statement

addressed to a human audience (verses 31-35). These verses affirm gratitude and praise for the grandeur of the cosmos and its creatures and above all for the God who creates and cares.

Romans 8:14-17

If Acts 2:1-21 speaks of the Spirit as the possession of the church, Romans 8:14-17 speaks of the Spirit as the possession of us as individuals. With this Pauline text, Luke's narrative account becomes personalized.

Who is a Christian? This question is asked and answered in various ways. For some, being Christian is adhering to the creed. It is a test of orthodoxy. We must ask what one believes and confesses before we can determine whether that person is a Christian. For others, being Christian is exhibiting a certain form of behavior. We are Christian if we behave like Christians. It is a test of orthopraxy. We must ask whether one's "praxy," or practice, conforms to Christian standards. Still others locate the answer in liturgy. We can tell if we are Christian by whom we worship and how. And so it goes.

The answer of today's text is simple and straightforward: children of God are those who are led by the Spirit of God (verse 14). In fact, everyone who is so led is a child of God. The term "led" may not be strong enough to convey Paul's meaning. The Jerusalem Bible prefers "moved"—"Everyone moved by the Spirit of God is a son of God" (verse 14). The import of the statement seems to be that if the motivating force, the guiding principle, the central impulse of our life is God's Spirit, then we can claim to be God's children (cf. Gal. 5:18). For Paul, being God's children and having God's Spirit belong together; as God's children, we have received God's Spirit (Gal. 4:6). Just as a child receives the life of the parent, so we receive the life-force of God—God's Spirit.

How can we measure the quality of our "sonship" (or, to be more generic, our "childhood")? By whether ours is a life of enslavement or freedom. If we live in fear, either of ourselves, others, unknown forces, or whatever, we are de facto slaves. It is precisely when children are disoriented from their parents, separated from them, disowned or abused by them that fear sets in; but when the relationship is cemented with love, fear is removed (cf. I John 4:18; also II Tim. 1:7; Matt. 8:26 and parallels; John 14:27). Before we became God's children, we may have been tyrannized by fear, but this is no longer our lot (cf. Gal. 4:8-9).

The metaphor of "slavery" versus "sonship" is made even more precise by Paul's use of "adoption" to explain our changed status. In one sense, God had only one Son—Jesus Christ—but all those in Christ are adopted children, brought into a full filial relationship (Gal. 4:5-6; Eph. 1:5; also, cf. Rom. 8:23).

It may be objected that adoption is not the same as natural childhood. Thus, Paul insists that as children of God, we address God in exactly the same way Jesus did, as "Abba! Father!" (verse 15; cf. Mark 14:36). This Aramaic expression captured so effectively the nature of Jesus' relationship with God that the early church apparently chose to preserve it in its original form. Through extensive study done on the use of this form of address, we now know that if it was not a unique way of addressing God, it was at least distinctive. It became a shorthand way of expressing Jesus' complete obedience, as seen in the Gethsemane experience. As we use this form of address in our prayers, we enter a relationship with God similarly close and intimate.

Our text stresses, however, that it is not just a matter of praying the same prayer as Jesus. It is rather that when we verbally express our relationship this way as God's children, then God's Spirit joins with us in our testimony (cf. I John 5:10; also 3:1). It is as if our inner spirit, along with God's own Spirit, "bear united witness that we are children of God" (verse 16, JB). It becomes a question of reaffirming our own true identity. We are reminded once again of who we really are—children of God in an absolutely unqualified sense.

The implications of this are that we enjoy all the rights and privileges of heirs (verse 17). Having been admitted to a status comparable to that of Christ, we are Christ's fellow heirs (cf. Gal. 3:16, 26, 29; 4:7; Rev. 21:7; also Mark 12:7; Heb. 1:2).

There is one qualification, however—providing we enter with Christ into his suffering. Elsewhere, Paul speaks of this as joining the "fellowship of his suffering" (Phil. 3:10-11; cf. II Cor. 4:10; Rom. 6:8; also II Tim. 2:3, 12; I Pet. 4:13; 5:1; Luke 22:28-30). For Christ, the way to glory was through suffering (cf. Luke 24:26), and this is our lot and privilege as Christ's fellow heirs.

John 14:8-17, 25-27

Easter is completed at Pentecost. Without Pentecost, Easter means the departure of Christ, leaving behind the confused and uncertain disciples who can do no better than return to fishing (21:1-3). With Pentecost, Jesus' promise not to leave his disciples orphaned in the world is kept (14:18).

Pentecost was a Jewish festival celebrating the early harvest but it came in time to be the commemoration of God's giving Israel the law at Sinai. The festival came fifty days after Passover. Luke, who historicizes the events of the Christian faith, says Jesus revealed himself to his disciples for forty days after the resurrection (Acts 1:3). Following Jesus' ascension (Acts 1:9-11), his followers continued in prayer and expectation (Acts 1:12-14). At Pentecost, the promise of power from on high was fulfilled (Acts 2:1-21). This festival, for the Jews a celebration of the giving of the law, became for the Christians a celebration of the giving of the Holy Spirit. Beyond that, the word does not specify a date or season but symbolizes the coming of the Spirit which gathers, constitutes, and empowers the church, whether that story is told by Luke or Paul or John.

It is important for the preacher to keep these three New Testament writers distinct and separate when speaking of the Holy Spirit in the life of the church. Each emphasizes a dimension of the Holy Spirit's presence and work in the church in addressing conditions in different congregations. It would be confusing and unfair to Luke and John, for example, to take Paul's discussion of gifts of the Spirit in I Corinthians 12 as the normative definition of the Spirit's manifestation and then interpret Luke and John so as to make them support and elaborate that text, and vice versa. Our lection for today, then, is not "what the Bible says about the Holy Spirit" but a portion of John's teaching on the subject.

The Holy Spirit is, according to this Gospel, associated with Jesus. Upon Jesus the Spirit came at baptism and Jesus is the one who baptizes with the Holy Spirit (1:33). However, the gift of the Spirit to Jesus' followers had to wait upon Jesus' passion and ascension back to God (7:39; 16:7). Even Jesus' word to Nicodemus about being born of the Spirit assumes the Ascension a precondition for this work of the Spirit (3:13). In other words, the resurrected, glorified Jesus sends the Holy Spirit upon the church.

What has just been said, however, should not be thought of simply as John's "doctrine" of the Holy Spirit. Our lection occurs in the context of Jesus' parting words to the group he is leaving behind. The confused and saddened disciples are asking questions such as, Where are you going? Can we go? Will we ever be together again? (13:36–14:7). Finally, Philip requests, "Lord, show us the Father, and we shall be satisfied" (verse 8). This request lies at the heart of this Gospel in two ways: first, it states a fundamental presupposition of this Evangelist: the basic human hunger is for the God whom no one has seen (1:18), but whom to know is life eternal (17:3). Second, this request looks to Jesus for a revelation of God, which is this Gospel's portrait of Jesus, the revealer of God (1:18). This is the substance of Jesus' response to Philip (verses 9-11).

At this point, Jesus makes a series of promises to his followers which, if believed, should not only relieve some of their pain at his departure, but equip them for a fruitful life after his leaving. In fact, his departure, his ascension, is the precondition of their receiving these blessings (verse 12). In verses 12-17, the promises are three: they will be enabled not only to continue Jesus' work, but even do greater works (verse 12); they will be heard and their prayers answered to meet the needs involved in their life and mission (verses 13-14); they will be accompanied in their life and mission in the world by another Counselor or Helper, the Spirit of truth (verses 16-17). Unlike Jesus, who is now departing, the Spirit will be with them forever.

Verses 16-17 constitute the first of five Holy Spirit promises in the farewell speeches (14:16-17; 14:26; 15:26-27; 16:7-11; 16:13-15). The second of the five is also a part of today's reading. While the first promises the continual abiding presence of the Spirit as Helper and Counselor, the second promises the Spirit as teacher and reminder (14:26). This Evangelist wants no one to misunderstand: if the Spirit in the church is of God (and the spirits must be tested, I John 4:1), it will not lead the church away from the historical Jesus but tie the church by instruction and memory to Jesus. The Christian faith has a memory, and to be a Christian is to be enrolled in a tradition as well as to be set free for the future.

Annunciation, March 25

Isaiah 7:10-14; Psalm 45 or 40:6-10; Hebrews 10:4-10; Luke 1:26-38

In the seasons of the death and resurrection of Jesus this day calls our attention to the announcement of his birth. The Gospel lesson is central here, for the day celebrates the events reported in Luke 1:26-38, the angel Gabriel's announcement to Mary. The tradition represented in Isaiah 7:10-14—the promise of a birth as a sign of God's salvation—stands in the background. Psalm 45 responds to the messianic promise, and Psalm 40:6-10 to Mary's faithfulness. The second reading concerns the purpose for which Christ came into the world.

Isaiah 7:10-14

Since the passage begins with the expression, "again," it is clear that it is part of a larger unit in the Book of Isaiah. It is important to recognize that the unit began in 7:1, and that our reading depends upon and reiterates the point of what preceded in verses 1-9. By the time the Lord speaks "again" to Ahaz, we have been informed of the historical context of the encounter between prophet and king (7:1-3) and heard Isaiah's instructions to meet the king and address him with a message of hope. Isaiah 7:10-14 is the prophet's second attempt to convey the same message.

The historical situation, including the date of the events, is well-known. (See also II Kings 16:5-9.) In 734–733 B.C., the king of Syria, Rezin, and the king of Israel, Pekah, formed an alliance to oppose the advancing Assyrian empire. However, they turned first to the south to attack Judah, probably in an attempt to put someone on the throne who would align himself with them. When Isaiah went to meet the Judean king Ahaz, he had been instructed to assure him that the Lord would deliver him from the threat of these two kings, keeping the promise that a descendant of David would always sit on the throne in Jerusalem (II Samuel 7).

Isaiah 7:10-16 presents that same message in the form of a prophetic symbolic action. The "sign" could be a signal from God that the message already given could be trusted. When Ahaz refuses to "put the Lord to the test" (verse 12), Isaiah produces a sign. But what is the sign here? It is not that a "virgin" shall conceive, for the Hebrew text clearly indicates that "a young woman" is already pregnant. (It is the Greek translation of this verse that read "virgin.") The sign is simply the birth of a child who will be named "Immanuel." The fact that this is the sign is not so remarkable in the context of the Book of Isaiah, for the prophet more than once had given his own children symbolic names: "Shear-jashub" ("a remnant shall return," 7:3), "Maher-shalal-hash-baz" ("speedy spoil, hasty prey," 8:1). Other prophets did similar things, as one sees in Hosea 1.

Since neither the name nor the identity of the young woman is given, various possibilities have been proposed. Some wonder, on the basis of the symbolic names of Isaiah's children, if she was the wife of the prophet. It is more likely, but far from certain, that she was the wife of Ahaz himself, and the child thus quite possibly the next Judean king, Hezekiah.

Far more important than the historical identification of the mother and child is the meaning of the sign, the point of the prophet's message. The message is in the name, "Immanuel," "God is—or will be—with us." It is a message of reassurance and of salvation in a dangerous time. Before the baby "knows how to refuse the evil and choose the good" (7:16) the military threat against the land will be ended. It is a message of stability and security for the nation and for the Davidic dynasty.

The good news of this passage has concrete, historical, and political dimensions. Even those factors still have a place in the vision of God's kingdom expressed in the good news of the announcement of the birth of Jesus, son of David and Immanuel.

Psalm 45

Tradition has long associated this psalm with Christ and the Incarnation. No doubt written by some court composer—a poet laureate at the Jerusalem court—the psalm is addressed to humans, to the reigning king and his bride-to-be. After an opening introduction (verse 1), the king (verses 2-9) and the bride (verses 10-15) are addressed in order before the king is extolled in the concluding words (verses 16-17).

In associating this wedding song with the annunciation to Mary and the Incarnation, the early church took certain liberties with the "original" meaning of the text. Hebrews 1:8-9 connects this psalm with Jesus and uses it to argue that Jesus "the son of God" is superior to angels. That the psalm had been understood to refer to the Messiah in pre-Christian Judaism helps explain its utilization by the early church.

Four features in the psalm can be easily interpreted in commemoration of the annunciation. (1) The theme of the psalm, even if only implied, is the theme of love. The opening heading to the psalm alerts the reader to its theme: "a love song." Divine love for the human condition undergirds the Incarnation. (2) Another theme is that of union, in this psalm, the union of man and woman, groom and bride. In the allegory of Christian theology, the union is between the divine and human, the impregnation of Mary by the Holy Spirit. (3) A third theme is royalty. The king is described as one who rules in righteousness. The Incarnation celebrates the coming of the royal one to whom God has assigned authority and royalty. (4) Finally, the psalm allows the bride to fade into the background and emphasizes instead her offspring. In the offspring, the name of the father lives on and the memory of the mother is held dear (verses 16-17). As a Davidide, Jesus, the offspring, insured forever the line of the son of Jesse from Bethlehem.

Psalm 40:6-10

These verses are portions of a psalm containing both thanksgiving for previous divine favors (verses 1-10) and petitions for further help (verses 11-17). The lection (verses 6-10) is appropriate for the annunciation since it, like Mary's response to the angel Gabriel, is a paradigm of obedience and responsiveness.

In the psalm, verses 6-10 comprise the worshiper's statement of fidelity to God and a rehearsal of what the person (the king? some official?) believes, feels, and does as response to the Divine.

Verse 6 suggests that conventional, habitual religious practices—four different kinds of sacrifices are referred to—are not seen as the only or the necessary components in religion. The writer gives expression to the commitment of one's self in what must have been a popular saying indicating one's hearing of and submission to another—"You have dug ears for me." For the worshiper, what God desires and requires is first of all, a faithful hearing—receptivity.

The hearing response leads to voluntary obedience (verses 7-8). In terms somewhat reminiscent of the prophet Isaiah (see Isa. 6), the person volunteers—"I come" ("Here am I"). The second half of verse 7 with its reference to the book could denote that (1) in the book of his life is written (and preordained) that the psalmist will make the will of God the delight of living, (2) the record of the person's life kept in the divine world demonstrates that the psalmist is one delighting in obedience, or (3) the book of the law, the Torah (the Pentateuch?) was written as if speaking of the psalmist. However one understands the particulars, the affirmation is clear. The psalmist claims a complete submission to and obedience to God. "Thy law is within my inward parts" is an affirmation of the internalization of the law—inward being, the conscience, the heart, the ultimate commitments are devoted to the will of God.

Verses 9-10 affirm the public testimony of the commitment. This affirmation is stated twice positively and three times negatively. "I have told," "I have spoken," "I have not restrained my lips," "I have not hid," and "I have not concealed."

The psalmist thus delineates an action sequence pattern—sincere hearing leads to responsive commitment which leads to public exuberance, the testimony in the congregation.

Hebrews 10:4-10

The phrase from today's epistolary reading that makes it suitable for Annunciation Day occurs in verse 5: "When Christ came into the world." This text occurs as part of a larger argument within the book of Hebrews in which the death of Christ is presented as a sacrifice eminently superior to the forms of animal sacrifice prescribed by the Mosaic law. Thus, our text is introduced with the claim that the blood of bulls and goats is ineffective in taking away sin (cf. 9:12, 19). One of the main arguments the book of Hebrews makes against animal sacrifices is that they had to be made repeatedly—"year after year" (10:1). Rather than taking away sin, these sacrifices merely served as annual reminders of sin.

To buttress this point, the author interprets the incarnation of Christ in terms of doing the will of God. To this end, he quotes Psalm 40:6-8, one of the classic Old Testament texts insisting that obedience is better than sacrifice (cf. I Sam. 15:22-23; Hos. 2:19-20; 6:6; Amos 5:23-24; Mic. 6:6-8; cf. Matt. 9:13; 12:7). The limitations and abuses of a sacrificial system were well recognized within the Jewish tradition. Anyone who knows religious traditions knows the tendency for worship to become a matter of externals—going through the proper motions at the right times in the right way. There is the constant need to remember that service to the Deity is central and fundamental. Without that, all expressions of worship become empty.

The psalmist recognizes that God has not required him to offer burnt offerings and sin offerings merely for the sake of going through with the expressions of worship. In these things per se, God takes no pleasure (verse 6). What matters to God is not the rites themselves but the motivation of the heart that offers the rites, that makes the sacrifices. In a word, doing the will of God—this is what gives meaning to these acts of religious observance.

The author of Hebrews actually places the words of Psalm 40 on the lips of Christ. It is introduced with the words "he [Christ] said" (verse 5). These words are then to be understood as actually providing us with Christ's view of sacrifices and the superiority of doing God's will to offering burnt offerings and sin offerings. The author proceeds to explain the text (verses 8-9). The upshot of his midrashic explanation is that because Christ came to do the will of God, he effectively relegated the system of animal sacrifices to their deserved place of second importance: "He abolishes the first in order to establish the second" (verse 9).

Because of Christ's willingness to do the will of God, his sacrifice counted in a way Levitical sacrifices did not: it made possible genuine sanctification once and for all (verse 10; cf. 10:14, 29; 13:12; also I Thess. 4:3; Eph. 5:2).

As a passage for Annunciation Day, this text provides another perspective for understanding the incarnation of Christ. It might be read with other passages that interpret the purpose of Christ's coming to the earth as doing the will of God (cf. John 4:34; 5:30; 6:38). As one of the well-known texts stressing the superiority of inner motivation over outward religious expressions, it might be explored profitably in this direction. The homilist might choose to examine how Christ himself, in his teachings and actions, sought to get at the essence of true religion rather than concern himself with questions of protocol and prescription.

Luke 1:26-38

Having set December 25 as the day of Christ's birth, the church later set the day nine months earlier, March 25, to observe the angel's annunciation to Mary. This calendarizing of the salvation story is a process not unlike Luke's own way of narrating events: "in the sixth month," "about three months," "at the end of eight days," "for the space of forty days."

There is an advantage to reflecting on Luke 1:26-38 in a season other than Advent at which time the attention on the babe of Bethlehem draws the texts toward Christmas. At this distance the text can be heard in and of itself as a declaration of God's grace and power.

That the text proclaims God's grace is evident in many ways. The story begins as a message from God (verse 26); the message comes to a young woman, a virgin, in an obscure town in Galilee; Mary is not described as deserving or even as a special person who is full of good deeds, faith, or righteousness; the message itself concerns the gift of God's Son whose kingdom will be everlasting; the child's name will be Jesus, that is, "salvation." All of this is pure grace. Of course, we learn in the story the favorable qualities of Mary: she reflects upon the word of God (verse 29); she believes the word and submits to it in full obedience (verse 38). In fact, for Luke, Mary is the ideal Christian. However, none of these qualities are offered as the reason God chooses her for a special task. The reasons here, as in all God's activity, are tucked away in the purposes of a God who expresses favor toward the world.

The text proclaims God's power in the angel's words, "For with God nothing will be impossible" (verse 37). These words are said with direct reference to the pregnancy of Elizabeth, Mary's kinswoman "in her old age" (verse 36). This echoes the story of Sarah and Abraham who were told by messengers of God that they in their old age would have a child (Gen. 18:14). To them the messengers said, "Is anything too hard for the Lord?" a declaration of God's power similar to Luke 1:37. It is most important that the reader of this text see not only the grace of God being extended but also the affirmation of God's power to effect it. Grace and power are inseparable: grace without power whines; power without grace shrieks. The most elaborate interweaving of the two in the New Testament is in Romans 4:16-25. Paul almost reaches the literary heights of Luke when he recites the deeds of the God "who gives life to the dead and calls into existence the things that do not exist" (verse 17). This statement describes the grace and power of the God who creates (verse 17), who gives to Sarah and Abraham (they were as good as dead) a child (verses 18-22), who raises from the dead Jesus Christ (verse 24), who gives life to us, dead in our trespasses and sins (verse 25). The virgin Mary will have a child because God is able; she will have a child for our sakes because God is gracious.

The means by which God's word comes to Mary is a "messenger," the meaning of the transliterated word "angel." Angels, rare in early Judaism, became more common in late Judaism, perhaps in response to the need for mediation between God and human beings. Angels were not the only means of communication. Matthew, telling the birth story from Joseph's perspective, speaks frequently of dreams as the avenue of revelation (1:20; 2:12; 2:13; 2:19), clearly reflecting Joseph the dreamer in the Old Testament. But Luke speaks often of angels as God's means of announcing, instructing, guiding, and protecting (Luke 1:11, 20; 2:8-15; Acts 8:26; 12:7). Not all New Testament writers so understand angels in God's dealing with the world. On the matter some writers are silent while others, such as Paul, do not view angels positively at all (Rom. 8:38-39; Gal. 3:19-20; Col. 2:18-19). But in no instance does faith in God's self-revelation, providence, grace, and power rest upon an opinion about angels. The God who in various ways spoke to our ancestors has now spoken to us in a Son, Jesus Christ (Heb. 1:1-2).

Scripture Reading Index